THE HEART OF CONFLICT

The Heart of
CONFLICT

Brian
Muldoon

G. P. PUTNAM'S SONS
NEW YORK

G. P. Putnam's Sons

Publishers Since 1838
200 Madison Avenue
New York, NY 10016

Library of Congress Cataloging-in-Publication Data
Muldoon, Brian.
    The heart of conflict / by Brian Muldoon.
       p.   cm.
    ISBN 0-399-14180-4
    1. Conflict management.   I. Title.
    HM136.M827   1996   *95-26478 CIP*
    303.6' 9—dc20

Printed in the United States of America
10   9   8   7   6   5   4   3   2   1

This book is printed on acid-free paper. ∞

BOOK DESIGN BY DEBORAH KERNER

Acknowledgments

This book arose out of the everyday heroism of hundreds of clients with whom I have worked over the past two decades. These clients include business owners and insurance adjusters, doctors, lawyers, and advertising executives, couples going through divorce, and communities facing racial, cultural, and environmental challenges. Although many of them are described anonymously in these pages, all of them are very real people to me. They are my true collaborators in this project, and it is to them that I owe the greatest debt of gratitude. Through their struggles, discoveries, and victories, they have patiently taught me the principles I have described in these pages. I am profoundly thankful for the opportunity to stand alongside them as they faced the challenges of adversity with courage, wisdom, and hope.

I am also immensely grateful to a number of colleagues who have worked with me over the past three years to bring this work to completion. First on that list is Barbara Fields Bernstein, who not only inspired and sustained my spirit through the creative ordeal of bringing the book into being but contributed many of her own keen insights as well. I am also indebted to three writers who mentored me throughout the project: Asa Baber, for his early and unwarranted confidence in me as a writer and for his unflagging encouragement and friendship; Mark Gerzon, for getting me started, showing me the ropes, and providing invaluable critiques of the work as it passed through successive stages; and Bill Ury, for his groundbreaking leadership in the field of peacemaking. My thanks also go to David Shannon, who was particularly helpful in clarifying some of the scientific metaphors employed in Chapter Two.

To a first-time writer, there is nothing so assuring as an agent who sees the promise in a book and has the ability to find it a good home. Jill Kneerim of the Palmer & Dodge Agency in Boston not only aided in the book's conception but played a key role in bringing it to term. I was especially fortunate to fall into the hands of John Duff, my editor at Putnam, who has guided me through the process of shaping and reshaping the book with great clarity and kindness. His assistant, Jennifer Kantor, worked miracles in coordinating the myriad complexities of production.

My career in conflict resolution has been blessed by my association with Robert Crowe and David Ferguson, whose friendship I will always treasure. I am also grateful to John Goodson for awakening me to the possibility that lawyers could also be healers. Finally, I acknowledge my original teachers in the field: my father, for teaching me about confrontation, my brother Dennis for teaching me about compassion, my mother for teaching me about containment, and my other siblings for their continuing lessons in collaboration.

This book is dedicated to Barbara, the woman who appeared in my dreams and then became my partner in realizing them, and to my children, Molly, Mickey, and Sean, who bring me such profound pride and joy.

Contents

THE HEART OF CONFLICT

Preface

Dr. Thurston Harper, the head of the department of surgery at St. Francis Xavier Medical Center, has a reputation as one of the finest pediatric surgeons in the country. Medicine seems to be embedded in Harper's genetic code. Both his father and grandfather were physicians, and many of the surgical tools his father developed are still in use today. A dedicated practitioner, Harper lives only a few blocks from the hospital so that he can be available night or day.

But Harper had a problem. Her name was Dr. Rebecca Stone. Dr. Stone is a successful pediatric surgeon with a large private practice located across the street from St. Frank's. She performs virtually all of her surgeries at the hospital, generating a great deal of income for the good sisters who operate the cherished South Side institution. Rebecca is well liked by her patients and is popular with the staff.

But, according to Sister Margaret Mary, the hospital's smiling Irish-born CEO, it seemed that the hospital was witnessing something of a turf battle here, and maybe more. "The whole department is caught in a tug-of-war, and it needs to stop," Sister Margaret Mary explained. "We're not about to start calling in the lawyers unless there's simply no other way to handle it. Whatever we need to learn, it's time to start learning it."

The problems had started as soon as Harper took over as department head. According to Dr. Stone, Harper made it difficult for Stone to get time in the operating room. Harper took the public aid clinic away from Stone just when she had hired an associate to run it. Harper told a doctor who was considering a job with Stone about rumors that Stone had trouble getting board-certified, even though Harper suspected that the rumors were false. Harper made it difficult for Stone to get residents to help out with her cases. And now Harper had changed the department policy so that all consults would come to him even when Stone was on call.

Although he clearly felt exhausted by Dr. Stone's repeated complaints, Harper didn't deny that he had treated her differently from other surgeons in the department. His conduct was entirely out of character when it came to Rebecca Stone. She seemed to push all his buttons. "I can't tell you what made me do it," he said. "When I told that visiting doctor that Rebecca had trouble with the boards, I knew I wasn't telling the truth, but I found myself saying it anyway. I really can't explain it."

"I stopped taking call at the hospital because he made it so unfair for me," Dr. Stone told me as we sat in her lawyer's office. "I had to tie up nights and weekends to be available, but all the billings were going to Harper's service—even if he was out of the country. This has gone on long enough. I'm ready to take the hospital to court for unfair competition, and this time I'm not backing down."

Dr. Stone had a warm smile, but it was clear that she was serious.

"But this isn't about money, even though I've been severely compromised financially. The real problem is this: When I stopped seeing consults, I lost the chance to do the really interesting cases—the trauma cases, the emergencies that push you to the limit. Thurston has made it impossible for me to stay involved in the most challenging surgery by telling the residents to assign all of these cases to him, even if I was on call. I think he just wishes I would pack up and go somewhere else."

Two days later, I visited with Dr. Harper in his office at the hospital. "Well, *why can't* she just move her practice somewhere else? If you asked me what I really want, I guess that would be the answer," he added.

Dr. Harper described how he had worked diligently over the years to build his reputation and his practice. "I'm chairman of this department, and Rebecca has to learn that the position carries a certain level of authority. The simple fact is, she wants everything her way, and that's not how life works," he declared.

Over the next several weeks, I met with Thurston and Rebecca in a small, off-site conference room or at one of the doctor's private offices after hours. In these intimate settings, whenever either doctor's beeper sounded, they chatted amiably about how to manage whatever emergency had disrupted our conversations. However, when we probed into their complaints about each other, the discussion immediately became heated.

Both doctors offered to explain the history of the conflict, which had been going on for more than a decade. It had started a generation earlier. In the early 1980s, Dr. Julius Preston—one of the two leading pediatric surgeons in the country—had become department chair. Preston left his own practice on the West Coast and took the job when the nation's other leading surgeon—Thurston Harper's father—refused the position because he wished to stay independent of the hospital. Now the two leading pediatric surgeons in the country were both practicing in the same department. The two men became immediate adversaries.

Sister Margaret Mary had told me about Preston's arrival. "Oh,

Preston and the Harpers hated each other! The rumor was that both Harpers took Preston aside when he first arrived and told him that he was unwelcome and that they would do everything possible to make his life difficult if he insisted on staying."

Harper confirmed that there had been a lot of tension in the division. "Why did the hospital bring in another *pediatric* surgeon? I never understood that one. It would have been just as easy to get someone with another specialty to run the division, and that way there would have been no need for a turf battle. When my father died, I really worried that Preston would cut me off from consults that came into the hospital."

"So," I asked, "when your father died, did Julius Preston take all the pediatric cases and run you out of business?"

I was surprised when Harper slowly shook his head. "No," he answered slowly. "We were never emotionally close, but he always treated me fairly. He didn't take advantage of his power. He was a complete gentleman. The cases were always assigned equally."

Dr. Rebecca Stone, a young pediatric surgeon, was Preston's protégé and apparent successor. But when the older man became terminally ill, he gave the nod to his adversary's son, Thurston Harper. Dr. Stone promptly left her position as an "in-house" physician to open her own practice.

"I was once a community-based physician, like Rebecca, and I know what it's like to worry about making a payroll. Especially when my father died and while I was still trying to establish my own practice. Julius Preston and I weren't on the best of terms, and he controlled how much work I got. My livelihood was really in his hands. In large part, when he died I took the job so I wouldn't have to worry about being vulnerable to someone else's whim."

But when Thurston Harper took over as department chair, he started to use his position of authority to marginalize the competitive threat posed by Rebecca Stone. He treated her just the way he feared that Preston would treat him—but didn't. In fact, his behavior was precisely what his father had condemned in "those damn administrators." And now, Thurston had become one of them.

"The old man was tough," Sister Margaret Mary had once told me. "Tough especially on his son. Thurston didn't want to come back here to practice. He didn't want to go into medicine at all—got a job in a bank before he finally decided to join the family business. The old man was a hard one. Drove Thurston the opposite way, I suppose."

So perhaps there were two front lines in the turf war at St. Francis. One, a hot conflict between Thurston Harper and Rebecca Stone. The other one, harder to detect, was an internal cold war being waged between Thurston and his father's ghost. Although the old man had railed against the tyranny of medical institutions, it was obvious that he had been a tyrant himself.

Thurston Harper was faced with a choice. Would he continue to try to dominate Rebecca, to run her out of the hospital if he could? Or would he find another way to demonstrate his leadership?

I wanted to know if Preston had really been as hostile to Harper as everyone had remembered him being. Thurston shook his head. "No, not really. In fact, after my dad died, Julius really wanted to become my father, in a sense. He wanted to help me along, coach me. We worked together in the lab, so we were actually together quite often. Ironically, I got the call when Julius was dying. I was with him until the end."

Perhaps it was the memory of Julius Preston that reminded Thurston of a different model of leadership—one that doesn't run away from conflict but doesn't try to impose its will, either. A door opened.

In several intense and sometimes confrontational sessions, Rebecca and Thurston established new rules for handling the "call" schedule. They worked out how they would share the residents. They agreed how to handle complaints about their practices and how to work through any future disputes. Finally, they began to talk about their own relationship. Rebecca acknowledged that she felt like a pariah at the hospital.

"What really brings this home is when Thurston throws his Christmas party every year. They invite all the nurses and the other private practitioners. Everybody in the department comes. They even invite my partner. But I never get an invitation. I'm the enemy. This has been a lonely place to be. Do you have to go that far, Thurston? Am I really that hard to be around?"

Thurston thought about it for a moment. "What do you really want from me, Rebecca? You know I will always help out on difficult cases. I'm trying hard to be fair, even though I don't see why I should have to share the cream of the cases with you. What is it you want?"

Rebecca's answer surprised me. "I want a mentor. I'm not always sure about myself, and I'd like to know that I had a friend I could count on, just someone to talk it over with—someone with more experience, like you."

Thurston was taken aback. It was clear that she couldn't be serious—not after all this. It was one thing to agree on the boundaries of their domains and the rules of combat. But to actually become colleagues? It was asking a lot. "I'll make sure the secretary adds you to the invitation list next year," he said with a sigh.

Two weeks after the written agreement was finished, we agreed to have dinner. At my suggestion, they gave each other gifts. Thurston found an old photograph of Rebecca in surgery with Dr. Preston, and had it framed for her. Rebecca offered a beautiful book of photographs of healing practices throughout the world. We toasted ourselves, ate heartily, and reflected on the remarkable achievement of a new civility.

Even when disputes arose in the future to test the viability of the agreement—and they indeed did—the conflict itself was now under control. We had learned something about the kind of leadership that increasingly is needed to manage conflict—a leadership that has the ability to listen as well as to confront. A kind of leadership that can transform adversarial encounters into productive relationships.

For Thurston, that meant finding a way to create a playing field that was spacious enough both for him and Rebecca. Constantly feeling crowded by Rebecca's complaints, Thurston needed to find a way to expand the container in which they operated so that Rebecca's assertiveness wouldn't leave him feeling cornered. Instead of reacting as her competitor, he learned to assume a more gracious role that included giving Rebecca a fair opportunity to develop professionally. Only by so doing could he rightly claim the mantle of Dr. Julius Preston, who had understood the ethics of authority.

For her part, Rebecca also demonstrated an essential aspect of leadership—the capacity to directly engage an adversary without seeking to defeat him. She was interested only in leveling the field of play, not in embarrassing Thurston or recovering monetary damages. When Thurston confronted her with a file of rumors and complaints dating back to her residency many years before, Rebecca calmly addressed each case in the spirit of accepting responsibility for any genuine error. She struggled to understand Thurston's expectations and worked diligently with him to set some objective standards with which they both could live.

Even in the midst of their conflict, both Thurston and Rebecca were able to accept the fact that they needed to learn to live with each other—and with their differences. The existence of conflict didn't preclude their collaboration.

As we move into the twenty-first century, it is apparent that we can no longer afford to sustain leadership based on the imposition of authority by those in power. The hierarchical model of social organization is rapidly being replaced by what I call "panarchy"— governance by the *whole*, rather than by the few or even the majority. Leadership in an age of panarchy requires not only singular vision and courage but the ability to bring diverse and even adverse visions together.

The ability to reconcile passionately held differences is premised on understanding conflict as a *system*, rather than as an event. To borrow a medical analogy, conflict behaves like a virus or an infection— or, better yet, like a parasite. When conditions are favorable, conflict invades human relationships, takes up residence, and starts consuming energy and attention. It feeds on the fear, mistrust, and animosity that are generated when adversaries turn on one another.

Conflict becomes difficult to manage when parties direct all their attention at one another—as if "the other side" was the problem—rather than on the insidious dynamic that holds them hostage to their hostility. By shifting the focus to finding an effective treatment for the disease of conflict, rather than blaming or attacking those who have been infected, disputing parties can be liberated from the strong emotions that keep us captive in our own trenches.

From a systemic point of view, conflict consists of three elements: (1) the dynamics of the conflict; (2) the attitudes and aptitudes of the parties; and (3) the issues about which they disagree. Most of our resources are devoted to the factor that has the smallest role to play in conflict resolution—the merits of our position—and the least amount of thought is given to understanding and managing the dynamics of the conflict, which largely determine when and how it will be resolved.

Conflict is a subject worthy of careful study, for our lives are rich with adversity. It may portend a tragedy or follow a painful loss. Conflict threatens our very survival as a species, but, paradoxically, it is also indispensable in making the human experience bearable. The process of confronting and resolving conflict can help us organize our lives in a way that gives it meaning.

We awaken each day to a world suffering from its inability to face and resolve conflict. The end of the Cold War has spawned a multitude of smaller but hotter wars as repressed hatreds have blasted their way through the streets of Sarajevo and a hundred other villages and cities throughout the world.

For thousands of years, we have used the power of repression and domination to hold conflict in check. But the energy released by the global process of democratization is also fuel for the buried ambitions of darker forces. Conflict cannot be outlawed or exterminated or exiled. Conflict is infinitely patient. Conflict knows that its time will come.

These are dangerous times. We can no longer afford to leave the business of conflict resolution to the Pentagon or the police department or to uniformed peacekeepers. We have neither the resources nor the right to bring force to bear in every case of domestic violence or tribal warfare. Our court systems have reached the limit of their ability to process our grievances, and other institutions will continue to come apart as the rate of change becomes exponential. All of us must take direct responsibility for managing the conflict in our own lives. We simply can no longer expect someone else to take care of it.

Conflict itself is not the problem. Conflict is woven into the fundamental fabric of nature. The sea and the land meet in violent conflict and make waves together. The plow turns the meadow and wheat springs forth. Conflict is liable to be present wherever we go. It shows up at family reunions, departmental meetings, sales calls, budget sessions, crowded parking lots, PTA meetings, checkout lines, counseling sessions, church meetings, football games, funerals, and motel rooms. Conflict is evidence that human beings are engaged in something interesting.

Conflict is the spice that seasons our most intimate relationships. Two six-year-olds get into a brief and bloody fight and become lifelong friends. Two lawyers battle one another in court and decide to become partners. A man falls in love with a woman who is his opposite in every way and a family is created in the ensuing hailstorm.

In a variety of cases and circumstances to be discussed in some detail in the coming chapters, it will become apparent that conflict plays a key role in the growth of character and the development of stable relationships. Conflict makes us into who we really are.

The thunder bolt of conflict carries the power of both destruction and creation. Conflict is the spark of life itself. Conflict demands that we respond. Instinct gives a choice between fight or flight, but the wisdom of our soul counsels that something more is possible. Will our reaction be impulsive and self-defeating, or is it possible to discover a new route through the jungle of emotions? Whether it occurs at home, in our business relationships, or in our political interactions, conflict runs the same course. Conflict always engages our emotions, whether provoked by a broken contract or a broken heart. Conflict is predictable. Its ways are known.

The first part of the book describes the origins of conflict and four "meta-strategies" for managing it successfully. The term *meta* means "change." Each strategy is a powerful tool for fundamentally altering the contours of conflict so that it might be more easily resolved. *Meta* also means "comprehensive." While each conflict demands its own particular strategic response, there are four overarching patterns of conflict resolution. These fundamental meta-strategies are containment, confrontation, compassion, and collaboration.

The first strategy helps us get a handle on conflict. Especially when conflict has become chaotic, overheated or gotten out of hand, containment provides a way to bring order to the situation. We can do this either through a static approach, in which we help the fire to burn itself out, or through a dynamic model, in which we resolve the matter through a step-by-step process of reaching an agreement.

The second strategy is confrontation. Many conflicts persist because no one wants to face them head-on. These conflicts lurk in the shadows or just beneath the surface of the water, like an iceberg. Depending on the circumstances of the conflict and the nature of our opponent, we can follow either the *high road* or the *low road* of confrontation. Ideally, our adversary will rise to the occasion, but we may have to play to win if she initiates coercive or deceptive measures.

Many times our opponent is prisoner to his own suffering, and is unable to see past the pain. It may not be possible to persuade a wounded adversary to come to terms or even to negotiate until his emotions have been expressed and acknowledged. Mastery of conflict resolution may then require compassion. The principal way that we show compassion to an adversary is by *actively listening* to his story without attempting to interpret or respond to it. Without *doing* anything, the conflict begins to resolve itself.

Collaboration is a strategy for moving the parties beyond conflict by engaging them in a creative partnership. Rather than focusing on past grievances, they redirect their attention to forging a relationship that makes the future more productive for them both. In the framework of that relationship, the conflict ceases to be a controlling factor in their lives.

One of the most useful ways to employ these meta-strategies is in the context of mediation, which employs all four approaches in succession. Mediation also is itself a strategy, and is used most commonly when parties have reached an impasse. Bringing the force of a third person into the arena dramatically shifts the dynamics so that progress can continue.

The second part of the book takes us into the inner dimensions of conflict, which influence the behavior both of individuals and groups. Groups are able to make productive use of the energy of conflict through the experience of confluence. Confluence is the force by which contending elements of the whole are synergistically drawn together and move forward as one. Rather than jostling for superiority over one another, they are able to work—and think—on behalf of the whole system of which each is a part. In this way, each player can grow beyond her limitations as the group itself evolves.

Recognizing that not all conflict can or even should be resolved, we examine the role of natural boundaries. When conflict arises from a perceived threat to our essential identity—whether ethnic, religious, or even corporate—we must find ways either to go around or to collide with the rock that sits so solidly in the midst of life's moving currents. How we respond may have more to do with who we are than what we can accomplish.

Grappling with these irresolvable challenges brings us to the heart of conflict, where we encounter life's paradoxical wisdom. We discover a rare gift in our struggle with relentless opposition— our own "genius." Conflict is seen at last to be life's harsh but unerring guide in the soul's quest for meaning.

The purpose of this book is to provide simple and straightforward strategies to deal effectively with conflict. The principles of conflict resolution described in this book have been applied to thousands of disputes of every conceivable kind and magnitude. These strategies have worked for me in my mediation practice and they will work for you.

In 1985, I was a founding partner of Chicago's first firm of full-time professional mediators. Mediation is a nonadversarial process for resolving disputes voluntarily out of court. My partners and I have traveled across the country and have helped resolve disputes of all kinds over the years. We have worked with lawyers, business-people, insurance companies, schools, nonprofit organizations, politicians, community leaders, government officials, divorcing couples, religious leaders, and therapists. Time after time, we have had the privilege of witnessing the power of the human spirit to renew itself in the midst of disputes that originally seemed intractable.

This book is written in appreciation to all those clients who have been willing to teach me with their courage and imagination. It is dedicated to those who have found their own genius on the harrowing journey to the heart of conflict.

Brian Muldoon
February 1996

PARADISE LOST

Midway upon the journey of our life I found myself in a dark wood, where the right way was lost.

Dante, *The Divine Comedy*

THE FALL FROM GRACE

When I first started in law, I was with a firm that represented corporate clients in major lawsuits. The stakes were high, and the issues generally were impersonal, even if they carried a lot of emotion. Our clients were well-versed in the use of the courts to protect or obtain advantages over their competitors. They tried to keep their own feelings out of the way. As the Mafia hit-man always says in the movies, "This is just about business. Nothin' personal."

Eventually, I joined with some other ambitious young turks and we started our own small firm, gladly accepting any cases we could find. We represented individuals and small business owners, handling their divorces, landlord-tenant disputes, and the routine legal matters of everyday life. Instead of dealing with faceless corporations with sophisticated in-house lawyers, our clients were "real people." They were deeply and emotionally involved in every aspect of their cases. From the lawyer's intimate perspective, I began to learn about the high price that people pay when their lives are dominated by the passions of conflict. I remember one case especially well.

Maggie and Dick had been married for eight years. Dick was crazy about Maggie from the first instant they had met. Maggie was a beautiful, extroverted blond. She loved to socialize, but it was also obvious that she adored Dick's children from his first, tragic marriage.

Dick and the kids had watched in shock as the fire department paramedics pulled up the pale corpse of Dick's first wife from the bottom of the swimming pool. They would never know if it was suicide or if she had fallen in a drunken stupor. Maggie had rescued Dick from his depression, and she seemed like a godsend—or a goddess—to him. Maggie knew his thoughts, anticipated his needs, helped him make a success of his struggling business. Maggie brought life back into the family. Dick had forgotten how good it felt to be in love.

True, she seemed to lose her temper at the smallest things, but Maggie gave her all to the family and treated Dick's kids as her own. Five years into the marriage, however, things began to change. Maggie started to explode in fits of rage, and their once-intoxicating sex life had become almost entirely dormant. Dick soon found himself in the consoling arms of the dark-haired sales manager at one of his key accounts.

Maggie started asking questions. Slipping into a chronic depression and inexplicably moody, she accused Dick of favoring his own children over Maggie's daughter from her previous marriage. Her threats became increasingly irrational and hostile. One day Dick came home from work and saw that Maggie had taken down all the family photographs from the walls. "We aren't a family!" she screamed. "This is a fraud! You're a cheat and a phony, and one day everyone will know the truth about you!"

Dick tried to hold his tongue, but she just kept pushing him. They often entertained clients at their home in the desert foothills outside Phoenix, and Maggie was beginning to embarrass him in front of some of his best accounts. She intimated that there were secrets that, if revealed, would forever destroy Dick's reputation. After one especially disastrous dinner party, Dick moved out of the house and filed for divorce.

When Dick came to my law office, it wasn't divorce advice that he was seeking. "I've got a loaded pistol in the glove box of my car," he blurted out after we were introduced. "Either you take care of her— or I will." I had never seen anyone so distressed. His face looked like it was about to explode. He was a large, athletic man, but the only strength he seemed to possess came from the energy of his hatred.

Dick handed me a document about twenty pages in length. "Take a look at this. Read it over. I want to sue that bitch for libel. Whatever she gets from me in the divorce, I want it back in a libel judgment. She's ruined my business. Nobody will talk to me. The banks won't give me credit. I'm finished. It took me twenty years to build that business, and now it's gone. I was making over a million dollars a year. I'll be lucky to make my mortgage now."

The document Dick had handed me was a lengthy, single-spaced letter that Maggie had written and sent to a hundred of Dick's clients, friends, bankers, and family members. In great detail, she laid open the most private wounds, misdeeds, and humiliations of Dick's life. She accused him of causing his first wife to commit suicide—or worse. She revealed that Dick's son was actually fathered by Dick's former boss, who had had an affair with Dick's first wife. This was stunning news to Dick's son, now twenty years old, and to the rest of the shattered family. Maggie described questionable business practices, potential tax problems, and sensitive competitive information. She painted a lurid picture of Dick's affair and claimed that all his salesmen were implicated in a night of debauchery, identifying them by name.

Maggie's letter seemed to include virtually every form of libel known to the law. There were false statements, assaults on Dick's character and reputation, and invasions of his privacy. My partners and I got Dick into therapy and asked him to get rid of the gun. Then we started preparing the case for eventual trial.

My basic strategy was to get Maggie to admit that each of about twenty-five statements in the letter was libelous. In nine days of examining her under oath in a pretrial deposition, she admitted that her campaign of destruction was quite intentional. Her only defense seemed to the depth of her own suffering in the marriage. She held nothing back, even when her lawyer objected. She wanted me to know how much she hurt, and why it was so necessary to hurt Dick.

Maggie was giving us a strong case for punitive damages. The case got even stronger when, at Dick's suggestion, I started to explore Maggie's relationship with her deceased stepmother.

Maggie's mother died when Maggie was quite young and her father remarried several years later. She hated her stepmother almost from the beginning. Her own mother was an angel, but this woman who stood between Maggie and her father was evil. After her father's death, Maggie occasionally returned to the small Oklahoma town where her stepmother still lived. They fought constantly. One day, Maggie sent a letter to her stepmother's pastor and some of the family members, describing how her stepmother had beat her as a child and how she had come between Maggie and her father. She was especially furious that her stepmother would never let Maggie hang up pictures of her mother—even taking down pictures of Maggie's mother in Maggie's own home when she came to Phoenix for holiday visits.

In a small town, word spreads fast. Three days after Maggie's letter arrived, her distraught stepmother went into the backyard with a shotgun. Maggie returned to Oklahoma for the funeral of the woman who had raised her. One uncle wrote Maggie a letter attacking her for destroying her stepmother's reputation in town. The rest were too scared to say anything to her.

In her deposition, Maggie cried when she spoke about her stepmother. She missed her. She had had her faults, but she had been a good mother. Maggie had never allowed herself to see that there might be a connection between her damning letter and her stepmother's bloody suicide.

A second legal strategy emerged. Perhaps we could get Maggie to admit that she had intended to drive her stepmother to extremes. That would make it possible to introduce evidence of this previous event, which surely would strengthen Dick's claim for punitive damages. If Maggie wouldn't admit her motives, maybe we could at least batter down the wall of self-justification.

Dick gave me something that he was confident would push Maggie's button. Her only memento of her stepmother was an afghan she had knitted many years before her death. The mere sight of it would have a big impact on Maggie. Maybe she would fall apart, admit her malice, and see the harm she inflicted on others. I kept it for weeks in my desk drawer, planning to bring it out in the course of the deposition—and wondering if we were going too far. I couldn't bring myself to schedule the final round of Maggie's testimony. Every time I opened my desk drawer, it was like touching a loaded gun, ready to go off.

I had become infected with Maggie's hatred and Dick's thirst for revenge. I knew that by pulling out that afghan at just the right moment in the cross-examination I had scripted, something inside Maggie would probably break, perhaps forever. Something evil was afoot, and we were all playing into it. Both Maggie and Dick were now carrying loaded guns. Maggie had recently gotten a restraining order against Dick when he broke down the door to their wine cellar with an ax after she refused him entry into the house. Anything could happen. Death was waiting in the wings, watching each step of the drama unfold.

With this sobering realization, it became clear to me that winning a libel case wasn't going to do anyone any good. It would be far better if we put our energies into getting Maggie into therapy and rebuilding the relationships she had damaged. I called Cary, Dick's adult son, who officially was our client (since Dick could not sue Maggie directly while the divorce was pending). Would he rather have money from a court victory or find some way to reconcile with Maggie? Maggie had been a mother to Cary and his sister. He stood behind his father, but he wanted to find a way to help Maggie, if that was possible. Nobody would really benefit by driving her over the edge.

But Dick was adamant. He wanted blood. There would be no letup in the case. I withdrew and was replaced by one of my partners who concurred with Dick's objectives. Shortly after that, I left the practice of law and began my search for ways to deal with conflict that were less destructive.

A year later, I learned that Maggie had agreed to pay Dick a substantial settlement just before trial. By that time, Dick had lost his business and the house in the foothills. Maggie never paid the court settlement, and Dick finally dropped his subsequent lawsuit to enforce the agreement because he was unable to pay the legal fees. The collapse of Dick and Maggie's marriage produced a shock wave that sent their lives into chaos. It didn't have to end that way. But their fall from grace was every bit as passionate as the love that had brought them together.

CONFLICT AND PASSION

What sustains conflict, at its base, is *passion*. Without passion, conflict quickly blows over, like a hot gust of wind on a summer day.

The word "passion" grows out of a root that means "to suffer or endure, to submit to an external influence." When we are in the grip of passion, our strongest feelings come to the surface of the emotional pond: rage, fury, lust, desire, unquenchable love, burning hatred. Passion is the raw fuel of human existence. It overthrows the rule of reason and cool self-control. Passion is urgent, primal, powerful. We yearn for passion from the marrow of our bones and yet resist it with all the strength of our will.

Paradoxically, passion is the opposite of action. Passion renders us passive—it is the state of being *acted upon*. In the grip of passion, we all are victims. Eros arbitrarily shoots us with the arrow of love, and we are lost. Or we are betrayed by a spouse or a trusted employee. A child is molested in an abandoned building or caught in the cross fire of a gang war. A religious shrine is defaced or a border violated under the cover of night and broken promises.

These events simply happen, without warning, careering like a drunken driver into our ordered lives.

Finding ourselves in the wreckage of the familiar, we seem to become someone we never knew. When we are visited by passion, everything we believed about ourselves is thrown into question. Under the spell of passion, quiet neighbors become violent enemies. Passion transforms a marriage into profound bliss or a soap opera. Passion moves corporations to bankruptcy and nations to war. Most murders are crimes of passion. Most revolutions are ignited by the unlikeliest candidates—lawyers, doctors, aristocrats—suddenly possessed by overwhelming passion.

The feelings of helplessness that accompany passion trouble the deepest waters of the soul. From these roiling waters emerge love songs (especially those that speak of despair and pain), poetry, art— and conflict. The lover knows passion. The warrior knows passion. Passion is a matter of life and death to the mystic and the martyr. Passion has the power to make everyday experiences meaningless or magical. It carries us to the farthest shores of human experience. Without tasting passion, we remain forever unfed.

THE SPRINGS OF PASSION

Passion means suffering. Suffering is at the root of conflict. Anyone engaged in true conflict knows the experience of fear and pain and anxiety. Where does it come from? What gives rise to this passionate suffering?

The hot springs of passion run deep within us, beneath our cool exterior and carefully constructed social persona. Like Old Faithful geyser in Yellowstone National Park, the pressure builds up over time and must find its release. The rising water and steam search out the weaknesses in the surface and blast through the fault line.

Like the planet, we all have our personal fault lines: loss, fear, shame, greed, rage, arrogance, poverty, boredom, desire. It is through these cracks that conflict, like the dark spirits in Pandora's box, escapes into the world.

The most universal cause of passion is *loss*, whether the loss is on the horizon or in the past. The passion of lovers comes from what they stand to lose in order to have their love—the greater the loss, the shorter their time together, the more intense the passion. The passion of enemies is not so different.

Loss can also lead to conflict when we condemn ourselves. In fact, the more strongly we feel our failure and moral culpability, the more we tend to project that blame onto others. The death of a child, no matter how unavoidable, almost invariably leaves the parents with a terrible legacy of guilt. Survivors of war and violence often suffer from the irrational wish that they, too, had died. The need to resolve these inexplicable feelings of guilt or self-hatred can quickly lead to an attack on others. Guilt drives us to attack either to allow us to shift responsibility to others or to stimulate a counter-attack against ourselves. When others attack us, it at least allows us to imagine that there is a logical explanation for our suffering.

Grief is the most natural and healthy response we can make to loss. But sometimes grief seems to be an impossible luxury when the loss is deep and has no explanation apart from the evil we see in others. Grieving only confirms our vulnerability. Better to fight than to cry. A friend is shot, so a posse forms. A marriage fails, and lawyers prosper.

Fear and anxiety arise in anticipation of loss. These emotions are a kind of defense mechanism through which we protect ourselves from our innate tendency to be trusting and vulnerable. It counsels us that the best defense is a good offense.

All of us can think of instances in which fear has engendered conflict. Show fear to a guard dog and he will attack. Teach a child to be afraid and condemn him to a life of rebellion. Our survival instincts tell us to attack or avoid those we fear. When fear enters a relationship, conflict is always nearby.

We are capable of responding differently to fear, of course. An ancient guide to samurai warriors advises to "keep fear on the tip of your sword." Don't let fear paralyze your sword hand—keep the fear in front of you, on the edge, where its energy can be used to focus your attention.

The problem with fear is that it can turn an eagle into a snake. We protectively retreat into the darkness and strike out only when the crushing heel has passed by. Or we abandon any pretense of control and simply surrender to rage.

Rage is pervasive, it seems. The post-modern era in which we now live is characterized by a widespread feeling of depression, reflecting our powerlessness in the face of profound and rapid change. Every moment we grow more acutely aware of the impermanence of our world, and are increasingly burdened by the consciousness of what we are losing with each rotation of the planet— plant and animal species, political structures, nations, empires, natural resources, relationships, careers, industries. Often, in a desperate attempt to recover our feelings of potency and significance, we make a pact with the devil. When circumstances have shattered self-esteem, when we have lost the threads that held us together, we seek to force ourselves into existence by unleashing our rage on others. "I rage, therefore I am."

Rage has become the ultimate explanation for this outburst of unrestrained passion. Rage by women against discrimination, repression, harassment, rape, violence, betrayal, abandonment, disempowerment. Rage by men against joblessness, preferential treatment, the privileges of the elite, imprisonment, discrimination against fathers, conscription, and the regimented oppression of work itself. Rage by the underclass against deprivation and marginalization. Rage by religious fanatics against a world that does not bend its knee to their gods. Rage by militant misfits against order itself.

So pervasive is rage that it is increasingly viewed as normal and even useful. In *Female Rage: Unlocking Its Secrets, Claiming Its Power*, authors Mary Valentis and Anne Devane attempt to sanction rage, even as they recount its destructive force:

Rage is the gateway to self-assertion, deeper psychological development, and emotional well-being. . . . Rage is a primal and raw emotion from which civilized people *try to dissociate; we want to believe that we have progressed far beyond our primitive beginnings and that we act on reason rather than instinct. But* rage is normal; *it is human; it is real.* [Emphasis added.]

We expect rage to fuse the self back together in an act of unambiguous aggression that eases the anxiety created by our vulnerability. Rage is the ego's "big gun" by which it tries to restore its feeling of control over others.

The power of rage was personified by the legendary Celtic "berserkrs," so named after the unarmored bear coats they defiantly wore into combat. Berserkrs terrified their adversaries and inspired awe from their comrades. Before battle, they induced a state of rage in themselves, either through drugs or psychosis, which provided boundless strength and the ferocity of a wounded animal. They threw themselves into battle without armor or a thought for their own safety. Oblivious to their own injuries, they literally would tear their opponents to pieces.

Modern military scientists continue to look for ways to harness the power of rage. In the fictional movie *Jacob's Ladder*, dark forces in the American military in Vietnam experiment with a powerful drug intended to transform ordinary soldiers into berserk killing machines. The experiment goes awry, and in a murderous frenzy, the soldiers savagely turn on themselves.

This sense of power, especially if it can be accessed when we feel powerless, can be addictive. The term "rageaholic" is often used to describe people who fall into a fit of rage whenever they need to bolster their sagging egos.

The essence of rage is its murderous impulse to obliterate *the other*. This is possible only when we are convinced that we and the other are completely separate and distinct. Conflict dramatizes our sense of separation, and so gives a kind of legitimacy to the free expression of rage. "All's fair in love and war," the saying goes.

As we saw, Maggie's world had come apart. As her family began to split, so did her psyche. She was afraid, so she became aggressive. She believed that she could protect herself from further pain at Dick's hands by hurting him first. Aggression usually comes from fear, and it is rare that it is not met by counteraggression.

Shame is almost as powerful a stimulant for conflict as rage and fear. Shame is a form of loss of self. Those who feel worthless must press against the outer world in order to experience themselves as real. Like a child who "acts out," even negative attention is a relief to the soul famished by shame. The loss of self-esteem can be so damaging that any attempt to restore it can seem justifiable, regardless of the cost to myself or others.

Maggie felt shamed by Dick's infidelity to her. It wounded her where she had the greatest pride and least confidence—her femininity. It made her feel that she was without value. So she responded in kind, by shaming Dick. She exposed the humiliating secret that his son had been fathered by another man—Dick's boss, at that.

Shame begets a potent chain reaction. Insult a national leader and prepare for war. "Dis" a gangbanger on the street corner and lose your life. Verbally abuse your mate and lose your bed. The shame of sexual abuse can create a cycle that lasts for generations.

Desire is another response to loss. When we don't have what we need, or believe we need, the heart becomes restless. It hungrily scans the horizon or quietly waits in the darkness. When desire is starved too long, it becomes resentful, sullen, dangerous.

Dick lived in a state of desire. He longed for material possessions, a beautiful wife, social status, acceptance by friends. Nothing quite satisfied him, and his heart was always restless. He had lost his first wife to death, and his second to her own demons. There was an open door to the room of Dick's life. The right woman could walk in anytime she wanted. The saga of his divorce followed the simple logic of his losses—and his desire.

MORALIZING DIFFERENCES

Loss is a tremendously lonely experience. It sets us apart from the rest of the world. We are defined, in great measure, not by what we have but by what we have lost. We are not unique in losing a parent or a friend or a business, of course. The loss of *this* parent, *this* friend, *this* dream of success does, however, make us different.

We all react differently to the experience of being different. Differences do not, of themselves, cause conflict. It is not the fact of skin color or the disparity of religious views or the contrast of personality traits that causes conflict. The real cause of conflict is *moralism:* the habit of dividing the world into those who are right and those who are wrong. Moralism is dualism with an attitude.

Moralism should be distinguished from *morality.* The proper function of morality is to help us attain integrity and quality in our lives by revealing the value of our conduct and choices. Morality is integrative because it brings resolution to the difficult decisions we must make. Morality counsels us to be the best we can be, to embody the finest qualities of character we possess. Morality is nonjudgmental. Morality is about choices, not persons. Morality becomes moralism when we start to project our standards and principles onto others. Morality asks: What is right? Moralism declares: You are wrong.

As morally free beings, we bear responsibility for our own survival and happiness, neither of which is guaranteed. When we feel threatened at either level, it engages a whole complex of survival mechanisms. Whether the threat is physical or metaphysical, the animal in us reacts instinctively. But once the immediate danger has passed, the instincts fade. They are of limited value in assessing dangers that are distant or gradual. Getting beyond the immediate reaction of instinct requires us to draw on our clever mind, which has the additional ability to fabricate complex strategies of domination. Because these strategies may require a sustained effort, we require powerful and long-lasting emotions that will keep us motivated.

Perhaps the intellect created moralism to meet this need. "Being right," as it turns out, is the ideal accelerant for the fires of conflict. When a grievance or threat becomes a matter of principle, it can sustain itself indefinitely. Moralism is the means by which the intellect becomes the servant of the survival instinct.

With the thrust of its moral booster rockets, the intellect is able to exceed the range of mere animal instinct. Moralism makes it possible to perceive the existence of a threat that no longer registers on our instinctual radar. Moralism allows hatred and resentment to linger for a lifetime, even generations. Moralism gives meaning to revenge. Moralism justifies our principled attack of others, even when it costs us our job or bankrupts the company. Moralism is the shadow of society and the cause of most wars and lawsuits. In short, moralism is the engine that drives almost all conflict. Without moralism, human conflict would consist of brief, largely ritualistic skirmishes.

The combination of passion and moralism can be lethal. When we feel both threatened and in "the right," almost any behavior can be justified. The habitual combination of fear and moralistic thinking produces a state in which the mere fact of being right automatically triggers conflict, even when no threat exists. If we are in the "right," the other side must pay the price.

Dick and Maggie, as we saw earlier, had fallen under the spell of passion in every sense—desire, loss, fear, and shame. It might have passed with minor casualties—anger, grief, loneliness, sadness, acceptance. But their suffering became a battle to the death when Maggie came to the conclusion that Dick had "wronged" her. In her moralism, there was no limit to the kind of response to which she was entitled.

WHAT'S WRONG WITH CONFLICT?

The problem with conflict is our difficulty in responding effectively to it. We all complain about the hardship, but once the smoke has cleared, we are often able to notice the ways in which we have been deepened and strengthened by conflict. We remember not only the difficulty of the challenge but also the moments of extraordinary performance or stubborn perseverance. These are called "war stories." We tell them with pride.

In the same way that passion is a defining characteristic of human nature, conflict is an essential ingredient in the evolution of every individual and nation. Our very being is a complex mosaic of struggles with inner and external adversaries. To be human is to encounter conflict.

There are those who try to avoid conflict on religious grounds. But conflict, at least in the Western world, is an essential dynamic in spiritual growth. Even Jesus agonized in profound conflict in his final hours in the Garden of Gethsemane. He was engaged in a fierce struggle with the religious leadership of his time for the soul of the Jewish people, and had no intention of walking away from the battle:

> *I have come to light a fire on the earth. How I wish the blaze were ignited! I have a baptism to receive. What anguish I feel until it is over! Do you think I have come to establish peace on the earth? I assure you, the contrary is true; I have come for division.*

The image of fire appears throughout sacred literature. In Greek mythology, we are told that the work of creating mankind was left in the hands of Prometheus. Seeing that all the really wonderful forms of self-defense, such as claws, fur, and teeth, had been given to the animals, Prometheus stole the fire of the gods from Zeus himself and brought it earthward in the stem of a flower. With fire, mankind could learn to make tools and weapons both. Without it, he was weak and helpless.

For this act of defiance, Zeus chained Prometheus to a distant crag and condemned mankind to everlasting conflict. In the myth, only men existed at this time of golden harmony. Woman, or "the other," did not. So Zeus created the first woman—beautiful Pandora with her dowry of shadow forces. Zeus knew that men and women—and all opposites—are drawn together by natural attraction. Thus Pandora was "an evil over which everyone may rejoice in his heart, but [in embracing her] he will lovingly embrace his own destruction at the same time."

So Zeus took part in completing the creation of mankind by elevating the tool-making fire that Prometheus had stolen into the transformative fire of conflict, the divine agent of consciousness. In the fiery crucible of conflict, we win our full humanity. As in the story of the Garden of Eden, to which we will come later, character is forged as a direct consequence of our rebellion against the established order.

Conflict itself is neither good nor bad. Conflict is morally neutral. Like the weather and falling in love, it simply happens. Conflict is a storm brewing in the middle of the Atlantic—a chaotic natural system that acquires meaning only when it crashes into the lives of moral human actors.

What matters about conflict, in the end, is how we respond to it. When the hurricane hits the shoreline, we can either loot the unguarded stores or provide shelter to a stranger. When drawn into a lawsuit, we can decide to pound the other side into submission or to pursue a fair outcome. It is only at the point of responding to conflict that we can say whether the experience has been useful or destructive.

If conflict is part of our nature, it also presents one of our greatest challenges. Conflict has the power to transform, but it may well also destroy us.

BROTHER CAIN

We live in a world where brother is set against brother. The family is the seat of violence: each year, two to four million women are the victims of domestic violence. The majority of all homicides are committed by those who are known to the victims, either friends or family members. Gangs prey on neighboring youth, separated territorially perhaps by only a few yards.

There is something primal in this. An ancient story tells us that our first parents—our essence—were banished by their Creator from a place of preconscious bliss. Having fallen into a humbled humanity, they produce two sons. Tragedy soon strikes. Cain, in the story, has killed his brother because God prefers, for no apparent reason, Abel's offering of the blood of a lamb to Cain's harvest of grain.

The basic theme of the foundational story of fratricide is "differentiation"—God has regarded Cain and Abel differently without explanation. It is precisely because they are brothers that this divine arbitrariness is so painful. Close, but not good enough. Suffering from divine disrespect, Cain has lost God's good will. It is against God that Cain strikes out, although his brother receives the blow.

God's preference for Abel isolates Cain, thrusting upon him the first appearance of the you-versus-me duality that was implied by his parents' loss of Eden's primal unity. Cain goes through the full ordeal—he has lost favor with the divine, fears for his soul, desires redemption and envies Abel's unaccountably good fortune. Murder follows.

Cain, in fact, although traditionally regarded as irredeemably monstrous and evil, has been portrayed in much of modern Western literature as a positive agent of change and evolution. Abel represents a kind of naive spirituality that cannot comprehend the fact that "it's a dog-eat-dog world out there." Cain, through bitter experience, has become a realist. Envy and violence rise up in Cain as he strikes out against Abel's simple-minded adherence to the illusion of harmony.

Cain recognizes that the world is a place of violence where whole species face extinction and genocide awaits the weak. Marked by divine immunity, Cain wanders forever with us, shocking us with the force of our differences, anticipating the arrival of a higher level of integration. Cain grabs us by the collar and pushes our face into the mirror so that we must confront our racism, violence, child abuse, betrayal, hatred, greed. While he himself cannot bring atonement or reunification, Cain knows from bitter experience how desperately mankind needs reconciliation because his own soul is split asunder. Cain is the force of change. Denied or abandoned, he will wreak havoc. The challenge is to incorporate and acknowledge the dark brother who lives in each of us.

The story of Cain and Abel teaches us that human consciousness is fundamentally split between the beloved and the damned. As Robert Pirsig explains in his philosophical novel *Lila*, our existence is a constant dance between the static and the dynamic principles. Part of us defends the status quo, but part of us is a revolutionary. Life is the process of reconciling the two, with morality hanging in the balance. Abel is that within us that glorifies things as they are; Cain demands change, whatever the price.

So it was that Dick and Maggie came to know the force of Cain in their marriage. Dick invited Cain into his life when he started to question his feelings for Maggie and had an affair. He rejected Maggie, as God rejected Cain, for reasons that could never be articulated or understood. Maggie, already unstable, became possessed by shame and hatred.

When shame is born of rejection, it unlocks the door to an unremitting and skulking neediness. We are devastated by the shriveling of our own heart. Only revenge—the destruction of the other—can satisfy envy's limitless thirst and restore the wounded self to life. Everything about Dick that had value to him, everything that was good, became Maggie's target. And Dick, stunned by the ferocity of Maggie's reaction, vowed to repay her in kind.

And so it is with Cain, for violence breeds a response in its own likeness. Until we graduate to a higher sense of morality, murder cannot be healed, because our flawed nature demands revenge. Gang wars, and all wars, are nearly impossible to stop in their early stages because blood cries out for blood.

MASTERING CONFLICT

It is our nature both to be drawn to conflict and to resist it with all our might. Conflict deprives us of the illusion of control over our lives. Conflict brings loss, separation, and unwanted independence.

It requires us to develop talents and draw on resources that we didn't think we had. Conflict forces us beyond our limits. It disturbs our sleep, rattles our cage, pushes us out of the nest, deprives us of comfort, makes us stand on our own two feet.

So we avoid it, deny it, repress it, hang up on it, transfer it to the next department, refuse to answer its letters, pretend not to see it, get confused by it, and try to sleep through it. We just want it to go away. But conflict doesn't go away. Generally, conflict gets worse until it gets noticed. Being the most subtle of the beasts, conflict knows well how to disguise itself and often hides in the shadows. It plays on our fears as well as our grandiosity. It distracts us with all the tricks of the human subconscious. Conflict is impossible to avoid but difficult to catch. But, like the mythical Rumpelstiltskin, once we know its name, we have power over it and are no longer controlled by its dark urges.

Conflict resolution is essentially a process of bringing a submerged issue out of the darkened waters and up to the surface where it can be seen. Once exposed to the light, conflict can be a powerful teacher. It tells us what we don't want to hear but need to know.

Conflict is not resolved through pretense or wishful thinking. Cain's lesson is that our differences are real and the cost of reconciliation may be high. We must accept the full challenge of our humanity if the peace we seek is to be a real and lasting integration of parts once divided.

CHAOS TO ORDER:
Containing the Fires of Conflict

God is a circle whose center is everywhere and whose circumference is nowhere.

Nicholas of Cusa, 15th century

CHAOS IN THE SCHOOLS

A school we will call Luis Muñoz Marin Community Academy is an eight-story glass-and-steel cube on the West Side of a large metropolitan area. Named for the charismatic political leader and social visionary from Puerto Rico, Marin Academy is responsible for the education of nearly 2,500 energetic high-school students. Almost 70 percent of the students are Puerto Rican, another 15 percent are Mexican-American, 10 percent are African-American, and the remainder are Vietnamese or Asian. The dropout rate approaches 80 percent and test scores have steadily slipped over the past decade.

Before Marin Academy was built in 1974, its students attended Brookside High School, a traditional public school through which generations of various ethnic groups had passed. Over time, the West Side served by Brookside had become home to increasing numbers of Puerto Ricans. While the Brookside student body was changing, the faculty remained overwhelmingly Anglo. Little attention was given in the curriculum to the culture or aspirations of the Puerto Rican community growing alongside the self-contained Polish and Ukrainian neighborhoods that skirted Brookside.

In 1973, several hundred Puerto Rican students, under the leadership of one of the school's *independentista* faculty members, took to the streets in protest of the policies of Brookside's principal. The protest was loud and threatening, and there were dozens of arrests in what the local press dubbed "the Brookside riots." The Board of Education, which already was considering building a new school to replace Brookside, decided that it was time to move ahead with its plans. The resulting institution was christened Luis Muñoz Marin Community Academy, and it eventually developed a distinctively Puerto Rican character.

THE STRUGGLE FOR SELF-GOVERNANCE

In 1992, the state legislature embraced the principle of local school governance as a way to reform the huge, unwieldy, and ineffective bureaucracy of the public school system. Among other measures, the reform legislation gave each community the power to elect its own local school council (LSC). The LSC, consisting of parents, community leaders, a student representative, teacher representatives, and the school administrator, now had the power to hire and fire the principal and to allocate the expenditure of substantial sums of money for each school's programs.

The newly elected LSC wasted no time in undertaking the process of reform. The curriculum was to be changed to reflect a student-centered, multicultural perspective, and the community was invited to become involved in the daily operation of the school. Practices deemed politically unacceptable were ended, and the American flag was taken down. All students were required to study Spanish, and murals depicting Puerto Rican and other Latin American freedom fighters were painted in the hallway. The teacher who led the "Brookside riots"—now in federal prison for her part in a plan to bomb a government facility—was one of those honored as a hero for her part in the struggle.

Many of the teachers have been at Marin, and Brookside before that, for twenty or even thirty years. While supportive of the cause of Puerto Rican independence, most teachers have resisted what they regard as the politicization of the school. Feeling intimidated by the local school council, many teachers have stopped voicing their opinions out of fear of being labeled as "racists."

They have also largely resisted many of the changes in Marin's academic curriculum. Distracted by the daily skirmishes, the administration neglected to take any meaningful steps to implement reform. In the confusion, even those who ran "favored" programs have been left behind. All decisions seemed to be based on whether a given option strengthened or weakened those in control. The resulting power struggle badly fractured the school. Twenty years after the Brookside riots, Marin was an institution in turmoil.

Marin Academy is a study in the chaos that comes from exclusionary practices and nonparticipatory decision-making. As one LSC member told me, "Why should we have to work with the teachers—they work for us! Why should we cooperate? They're the enemy. They want to stop eveything we're trying to accomplish." The adversarial struggle has resulted in an atmosphere of rigidity and repression. "Marin is a closed system," one of the school's counselors said to me. "It's run like a dictatorship."

Marin's internal battles spilled out onto the streets. When a white teacher unwisely expressed her personal views to a local newspaper about the students and their home environment, she stunned even some of her best friends and was used as a symbol of institutionalized racism to many in the community. The fact that she won a court case for libel against her detractors, along with a monetary settlement and injunction, did not ease the hostility.

Marin is most widely known not for its internal power struggle but for its reputation as a tough environment for students. Marin students are active in eight different gangs, and fights are common. With the departure of paid teacher aides working as security guards, students and teachers had to fend for themselves. If there was a shooting over the weekend, its effects were felt immediately throughout the student body. As many as a hundred students at a time would engage in melees in the open spaces near the school's escalators. Hallways had become impossible to manage between classes, fires were often set in the lockers, and students of both sexes routinely pushed and kicked one another throughout the day. In the face of these threats, many teachers simply closed their doors and tried to carry on as if nothing were happening. There was no uniformly enforced disciplinary standard. It was into this divided community that I naively came in 1992 to develop a program of peer mediation to help students manage the disruption caused by daily incidents of violence and intimidation.

Working with two of the school's most progressive faculty members, Les Bataglia and Maria Gardenas, we developed a two-tiered approach to bringing some order back to Marin. First we would work with the faculty and the administration, then with the students. Maria was adamant that the adults become models of collaboration. "The students must see that the adults are practicing what we're preaching. They know that there's hostility between the various camps. If they don't see us handling our own conflicts, they'll never buy the idea that they should, either."

For the next year, I worked with the teachers and administrators at Marin to resolve old grievances, find a common purpose, and move beyond the political hostility and exclusionary management practices that had brought school reform to a complete standstill. Without that reconciliation, the new curriculum would never make it into the classroom. Every program change advanced by either side seemed to be stalled in its implementation by the other. New curricula were put away in the desk. Requests for new equipment were routinely rejected. The teachers and the school council had reached an impasse.

FIRE AND ICE: HOT AND COLD CONFLICT

Marin Academy is an excellent example of what we might call "hot" conflict. Conflict generally is either submerged or "cold," or incendiary, like a fire burning out of control. While cold conflict needs to be brought up from the chilly depths so that it can be seen and addressed, hot conflict must be contained first so that it doesn't consume everything in its path before reaching a productive resolution. Cold conflict, and strategies for warming it up, is discussed in Chapter Three. Here we are concerned with ways to manage conflict once the fire breaks out.

Wars, riots, custody battles, violent strikes, corporate takeovers, revolutions, lawsuits, and other overt power struggles typically break out into hot conflict. Its dynamic is volatile, destructive, and chaotic. Once ignited, it is impossible to predict the course of hot conflict. It spreads like a grass fire into a dry forest or steals silently through the corridors and vents of a high-rise office building.

Hot conflict often provokes aggressive behavior. When threatened, we find it easy to justify an assault on the grounds that "the best defense is a good offense." We like to believe that we can foresee the consequences of our aggression. Assassinate an enemy leader, we tell ourselves, and his opponents will become our allies. Bring a lawsuit for libel and demoralize our antagonist. Claim child abuse or mental illness in a custody dispute and seize the upper hand. Hot conflict begins with the promise of quick victory but generally ends in confused exhaustion. Nineteenth-century social critic Ambrose Bierce fittingly defined a lawsuit as "a machine which you go into as a pig and come out as a sausage."

Hot conflict usually cannot be resolved through direct confrontation because reactive countermeasures simply prolong the cycle of reaction. Or, as Gandhi put it so well: "Follow the philosophy of an eye for an eye long enough and we'll all be blind."

It is easy to fall into the "eye for an eye" syndrome if you assume that the course of hot conflict is predictable. Just hit back hard enough and the outcome is assured. But hot conflict is not predictable—it is *chaotic*. The forest may be in ashes by the time we have figured out which way the winds of chaos are blowing. Chaos, which is a phenomenon of the physical world, provides a powerful metaphor for understanding human conflict. Strategies that are effective in a logical, predictable universe simply collapse in the world of hot conflict, where chaos is king.

TURBULENCE AND CONFLICT

In 1987, James Gleick published *Chaos*, a hugely popular account of the science of "nonlinear systems"—turbulent natural events and processes whose outcomes largely cannot be predicted. Historically, science had treated all natural phenomena as comprehensible, within a small margin of error, in accordance with the mechanistic model of physics developed by Isaac Newton. Our knowledge of the future was thought to be limited only by the natural barriers to the collection of data and the accuracy of the calculations with which we analyzed it. Assemble enough data, it was thought, and one could predict the outcome of all natural events as easily as one could chart the orbits of the planets.

Unfortunately—or perhaps fortunately—our clear view of the future is blinded by the kaleidoscope of chaos. What at first appeared simple—say, calculating the rules for predicting weather—is rendered incomprehensible by the presence of chaos. No matter how much data you collect about cloud formation, low pressure fronts, and ocean currents, it will never be possible to predict weather more than a few days in advance. The tiniest fluctuation in any one of a thousand influences will dramatically alter its course in ways that not even the most advanced computer could anticipate. Weather is a chaotic system.

Chaos is not confined to the realm of the bizarre or arcane. Economics is largely chaotic, as is the rise and fall of animal populations and the crystallization of snowflakes. Artistic and cultural trends, political movements, the stock market, urban migrations, patterns of crime and drug abuse, and human relationships in general are chaotic. In fact, as it turns out, there is an element of chaos in virtually everything that is interesting and complex.

Chaotic systems are extremely sensitive to small changes. That means that the whole system suddenly can veer off in a totally unexpected direction if we make even the most seemingly inconsequential alteration in the conditions. The classic example of sensitive dependence is what is known as the Butterfly Effect. It is said that a butterfly flapping its wings in Beijing can initiate a series of cascading disturbances that eventually cause a snowstorm in Central Park. In a chaotic system, there are an infinite number of potential butterflies. It is for this reason that prediction is not feasible when dealing with chaotic processes.

Hot conflict, which is by its nature turbulent, is a chaotic phenomenon. Its behavior mirrors the tornado-like funnel of a sirocco, rising in a fever of overheated air from the desert floor. It blindly lurches across the landscape, filling itself with dust and skeletons of sagebrush. We know something about the swirl of such cyclones and how they look, but we can't anticipate where they'll wander or what will turn them. The same applies to conflict.

Marin is an example of a chaotic system. Each decision made by one faction was quickly undone by the other. There was no observable sense of direction or purpose, and the students generally reported feeling abandoned by most of the adults in the institution. Every policy decision was immediately interpreted as a personal attack against a group or individual. Minor slights became major causes. Not only did the factions undercut one another but they undercut themselves as well. Programs favored by the local school council were as likely to be forgotten as those programs they opposed. Without a sense of direction, the players tended to define themselves simply by their relentless opposition to everyone else.

TAKING CONTROL

How does one respond to hostility that is unpredictable, irrational, and extremely sensitive to the slightest disturbance? First, an important distinction must be made between *taking control* and *establishing order*. The opposite of chaos is not control, but order. Tyrants take control; kings bring order. Hot conflict, particularly when it is directed our way, tempts us to react, to strike back, to assert our dominance. In the face of our own vulnerability, control promises to make us feel strong. It appeals to the tyrant in all of us—there's nothing like an unprovoked attack from an unexpected quarter to bring that dark force to life.

When it comes to the chaos of hot conflict, however, attempts to take control generally backfire. We only have to think of the tragedy in Waco, Texas, when federal agents lost patience with the pathetically messianic David Koresh and his followers and launched an assault against the compound. A hundred lives were lost because the agents assumed they were facing a rational, linear condition and could establish control of the situation by an overwhelming show of force.

History is filled with dramatic stories of the failure of linear, action-oriented thinking to resolve hot conflict. In our lifetime, the most telling example is Vietnam. American military strategists employed a linear analysis and vastly underestimated the determination of the Vietcong to undergo whatever suffering we imposed upon them. The more aggressive we became, the more committed they became. The weaker our will to prevail, the stronger became their will to overcome. Nothing we did seemed to work. We were focused on action, on force, on taking control. The North Vietnamese held to the big picture, the long-term vision, and deftly reacted to the slightest fluctuation in circumstance.

We are always surprised when, as the greatest military power on earth, we are unable to engage successfully in straightforward interventions in myriad hot conflicts. We entered Somalia on a mission of peace and were unable to defeat—or even locate—a Third World warlord, who taunted us on our own media. Although we crushed the Iraqi military in Desert Storm, the long-term political effects of our engagement are not clear. We do know that the destruction of the Kuwaiti oilfields by Saddam Hussein has permanently damaged the ecological balance of the Gulf and that the Iranians are exploiting Iraq's temporary vulnerability to expand the cause of Shiite fundamentalism. And Saddam continues to threaten when it suits his ambitions.

The deeper one goes into the study of chaos, the more miraculous it seems that order should ever appear at all. The Second Law of Thermodynamics suggests, at the molecular level, that entropy eventually overtakes us all. Without the introduction of external sources of energy, all organized systems fall into a state of winding down, decaying, dying. The Norse god of chaos, Loki, was believed by the Vikings to be the eventual victor in the war between the forces of light and darkness, because entropy seems inevitable.

Following the metaphor of entropy, what is it that creates order in the midst of chaos and disintegration?

CONTAINING CONFLICT

Although we often speak in terms of "establishing" order or "restoring" order, chaoticians teach us that order *emerges* from chaotic systems. Under the right circumstances, order literally catalyzes its own manifestation. To do so requires that limits be placed on the chaos. The process of setting these parameters so that order is able to arise out of the chaos of conflict is called "containment."

To *contain* is to hold something, to keep it together, to give it definition. A pot contains water so that it is useful when it reaches the boiling point; simply thrown on the fire, water evaporates. A poem contains feeling and insight and beauty. A symphony contains complexity and passion. A body contains life. A library contains books. Religions contain meaning. Governments contain power. A dance contains freedom. Marriage contains partnership. A corporation contains enterprise.

What we would protect and bring into order must be contained. What is not contained is inchoate, or partly formed, chaotic. Just as the tyrant is motivated by the need to take control, it is the nature of the king or queen—an archetypal pattern embedded in the human psyche—to create order. Without order, the entire realm suffers, the fields languish, and game disappears. The function of justice is not retribution but the restoration of harmony. The monarch is not concerned with "getting back" but with moving forward.

Internal containment allows us to absorb intense emotional encounters without exhibiting an obvious reaction to them. This requires maturity and discipline. The point isn't to deny the emotions or repress them but to hold them without yielding to impulsive and possibly counterproductive urges. This allows one to choose the response that best advances the process. A person who has not developed the capacity to contain himself is likely to act out his emotions in a highly reactive way. Adolescence might be understood as a struggle to learn containment. Much of the world's conflict is created by those who can't contain their experiences and must rely on the opposition of others to achieve a sense of order.

External containment also requires self-restraint. Containing another is not the same as dominating. The tendency to control the other person must be resisted. Rather, one must objectively determine which framework will bring matters to a satisfactory conclusion, without being sidetracked by the transitory need to come out "on top."

Containment can take two forms—*static* and *dynamic.* The purpose of static containment is to cause the chaos to burn itself out without destroying everything in its path. Static containment is a defensive strategy that restores order by allowing the chaos to consume itself. In other words, it preserves order by surviving chaos. Dynamic containment, on the other hand, has higher ambitions. It transforms chaos into order through a step-by-step process that changes the chaos into a manageable dispute that can be negotiated to a rational conclusion.

The choice whether to employ static or dynamic containment

depends largely on the temperature of the chaos. If the fire is raging out of control, any attempt to extinguish it will simply be a waste of water. Such cases call for a response of non-reaction, or static containment.

HOLDING THE STILL POINT: STATIC CONTAINMENT

The purpose of static containment is to cause conflict to wear itself down before it wears us out. It is static because it appears to do nothing. When a hurricane, which feeds on the energy created by the evaporative cooling of warm oceanic waters, runs aground, it cannot sustain its destructive course and peters out when it gets past the coastal towns. The land defeats the storm and the winds *just by being there*.

Static containment is the strategy of firefighters who confront blazing forests in the midst of the summer. They understand that it would be impractical to attempt to extinguish the inferno, so they work to ensure that it doesn't reach the nearby village or jump the river that lies between the flames and the next ridge. They dig trenches, clear a buffer zone, and pray for rain. Foresters know that fires can restore the landscape, but they also understand the need for limits. Static containment produces no resistance but causes the conflict to extinguish itself from the lack of fuel by turning inward. When it is no longer fed by external resistance, the conflict literally becomes nothing.

People who are in the grip of hot conflict are blind. They have lost the awareness of the connection between cause and effect, and often engage in activities that are either pointless or self-destructive. We interpret their actions as ruthless, calculating, and vengeful, when the simple truth is that they may be blinded by some overwhelming fear or sense of desperation. In a sense, they have lost their minds.

It does no good to react. If we allow ourselves to become players in the drama of their chaos, we lose the capacity to contain it. To contain such chaos means to observe it, to reflect it, to witness it without reacting to it. As the Buddhists say, we must become empty. We must make no noise so that the madman can eventually hear the echo of his own rantings.

Society is filled with various forms of static containment. A prison is the classic form of passive containment; in theory, it rehabilitates by forcing the inmate to confront himself and what he has done. A chaperone is an externalized conscience whose silent presence is a reminder of the rules of social etiquette. Psychiatric wards and mental institutions hold those who cannot hold themselves together. Elections are closely monitored by observors who watch for signs of corruption. Aleksandr Solzhenitsyn's *Gulag Archipelago* was essentially a listing, an account, of the thousands of innocent prisoners stranded on the islands of Soviet repression. Block-watch neighborhoods keep an eye on suspicious strangers. Television cameras peer into our courtrooms and our council chambers, where they are joined by "court watchers" in tracking the work of the judiciary.

Electronic media are powerful witnesses. Hand-held video cameras can be very effective in setting limits, as the Rodney King assault demonstrated. The video camera can be an excellent tool for allowing bitter enemies to engage in dialogue without ever entering the same room. The camera not only allows us safely to observe the adversary but to see *ourselves* in action. It is a sobering experience. Most marriages would benefit from the presence of a camera, whose product nightly should be monitored in the place of other people's news.

A friend of mine was involved in a bitter divorce and began using a tape recorder every time his wife called him. She was hysterical and vindictive, and he always found himself shouting back in frustration. But once he started recording the conversation, my friend naturally tended to modify his own remarks so as not to seem provocative. After a week of taping, to his amazement, the man discovered that his wife's harangues ceased to bother him. He was consistently polite and disengaged, and no longer reacted to anything she said. The tape recorder provided the containment he needed—not because it contained *her* but because it passively limited his own responses. The machine became a model for him—its emotional indifference provided the buffer he needed to recognize and change his own behavior.

A lawyer friend named John told me a story about how he developed a lifelong friendship with the school bully. In high school, John's locker was next to this fellow's locker, and every day the kid would slam John's locker shut and taunt him with invective. John always smiled, and said, "Good Morning!" in the most cheerful voice he could muster. Finally, after several weeks of this, the bully was exasperated.

"Why are you always so nice to me? Don't you know that I hate your guts?" the bully said.

John smiled. "I treat you this way because I realized the first time I saw you that we were going to be best friends. I've just been waiting for you to find that out yourself." Forty years later, they are still best friends.

There is a still point even in the midst of the most violent hurricane. To find it requires patience, self-control, and the ability to hold the center while great winds blow on all sides.

DYNAMIC CONTAINMENT: CHANGING THE GAME

There are times when a more active form of intervention is possible. To continue the metaphor, dynamic containment is indicated when the fires have subsided to a point that it makes sense to bring out the hose. The risk of being consumed by the blaze has now passed, and it is time to take action.

The goal of *dynamic* containment is to change hot conflict into a cooler, more manageable substance. We do this by changing the nature of the interaction, or game, in which we are engaged. Hot conflict, as a chaotic system, has no purpose and, as a result, cannot be brought to fruition. It just keeps going, but never gets there. There's nothing it wants, so it is never satisfied. Hot conflict is a game that has no winners because it systematically destroys all the players. It feeds on their energy but never produces anything in return. Hot conflict is a game that can't be won or even ended.

Nevertheless, hot conflict can be "stepped down" into a rational exchange susceptible to resolution. The basic process is one of reframing the conflict into a *dispute* and then reframing the dispute into a *deal.*

THE FOUR STEPS OF DYNAMIC CONTAINMENT

Before one can start transforming conflict, it must be stabilized. If the chaos of conflict has disabled the rudder of life's ship, the wisest move is to drop anchor. But because the seas of conflict are deep and swirling, we must throw our anchor far from the ship, into the future, toward the horizon. We anchor ourselves not where we are but where we want to go. The first step in restoring order, then, is to start at our final destination.

1. START AT THE END. The possibility of an ending changes the basic dynamics of hot conflict. Without a sense of direction, conflict wanders aimlessly, bumping into the external world like a drunk on the dance floor. The first step in managing hot conflict, then, is giving it a destination, no matter how distant or unimaginable. Once there is a recognition that light might be found at the end of the tunnel, the tunnel changes from a prison into a passageway. By giving an ending to the story, dynamic containment makes the story make sense.

The notion of an "ending" is a powerful organizing principle. That which ends must have some direction, some purpose. It goes somewhere and there comes to rest. From the point of view of its conclusion, conflict can have meaning. Without an end, however, conflict is meaningless and chaotic.

But it is not so easy to plant the seeds of ending in the burning fields of hot conflict. Making peace can be a kind of death. Better to keep fighting than to give up the engagement. Combatants often have compelling reasons for resisting the end of their conflict. What will I do once the divorce is final? How will I handle the grief of loss once the lawsuit is over? What will happen to me after the corporate acquisition is completed? How can I survive the obscurity of retirement? Who will care for my ravaged troops if we sign a peace treaty?

Paradoxically, conflict creates a kind of relationship that may otherwise be lacking in our lives. Some married couples find intimacy only when they fight. Conflict is mesmerizing precisely because it is based on a confusing blend of love and hate. Most violent crimes are acts of passion, perpetrated against family or close friends. Even in commercial disputes, combatants are much more aggressive with those with whom they have been affiliated than with strangers. Conflict sometimes lingers because we are so frightened of what might happen if we let go.

The resistance to working toward a conclusion must be met by calm persistence. One of the best questions a lawyer, mediator, or therapist can ask a client caught up in conflict is, "How do you want your life to look when this is all over?" It is also a question we might routinely ask ourselves at every stage of life, in the face of every encounter. An awareness of endings gives life purpose because it establishes a direction.

In my work at Marin Academy, we found our anchor by creating a mission statement for the school. Representatives of all factions were invited to participate in a three-day "Conflict Summit" facilitated by a multiracial team of mediators and diversity specialists. We acknowledged, but did not emphasize, Marin's historical tensions. Instead, we struggled to articulate a vision of the school as we wanted it to become—a safe, loving, learning environment dedicated to the highest standards of excellence.

For the first time, there was agreement on Marin's direction. This gave the group a context for seeing its conflicts. It became obvious that some disputes were pointless and others needed our full attention if the school's mission was to be realized. For the first time in over a year, I saw real hope and possibility emerge.

Once the possibility of a destination is established, dynamic containment becomes a matter of engineering. The next step is to build the containers into which the passions might flow more productively.

2. CHANGE THE CONFLICT INTO A DISPUTE. Although the words "conflict" and "dispute" are often used interchangeably, they have quite different meanings. A dispute is amenable to an orderly disposition. Whether the disagreement is about facts or the law or the nature of reality, a dispute simply concerns the existence of two seemingly irreconcilable positions. One or the other position is correct, or more nearly correct, even if we can't decide which. Or perhaps they can be reconciled in some way. But the very fact that positions are taken and advocated demonstrates that order is involved. A dispute may conceal a conflict, but it is not itself chaotic. A dispute, by its nature, anticipates its own conclusion.

Not so with conflict. Because conflict inherently is chaotic, the parties are often unable to articulate an argument to support their positions or even describe what they are fighting about. Conflict is the struggle to dominate. Conflict doesn't care about the issues or the equities. When we are in conflict, we are in chaos, and the only way out of it is to defeat the enemy. We just want to *win*.

Disputes are often symptoms of an underlying conflict. If I just can't get along with my neighbor, chances are that we'll argue about politics, the fence line, and the weather. Resolving the individual disputes won't necessarily end the conflict. We'll just find something else to fight about. An argument with a child about whether to watch a television program, for example, may be the result of an unresolved conflict about authority—or arise out of marital or even workplace stresses.

If conflict is like the funnel cloud of a tornado, disputes are often thrown off by the velocity of the winds. When these projectiles land on us, they can cause damage. It doesn't take much analysis to see, however, that the original cause of our distress was the tornado, not the tree limb.

Fortunately, however, a dispute can be useful as a vehicle by which the underlying conflict is resolved. Just as warring armies once decided a battle by pitting one soldier from each side against the other, so too can an individual dispute be "loaded" with a conflict so that the resolution of one is the termination of the other. In short, a dispute can be used to *contain* a conflict.

At its best, a lawsuit is a form in which a conflict is contained as a dispute. For example, a conflict may arise in a corporation in the form of a power struggle between major shareholders. Meeting after meeting may be consumed with arguments about acquisitions, financing, and distribution of profits. Finally, an alliance of shareholders reorganizes the board as a way to marginalize the voting rights of the "dissidents." All hell breaks loose. A lawsuit is filed.

The parties now focus their energy on the litigation. All decisions are scrutinized carefully in light of their possible impact on the case. "Don't talk," the lawyers advise their clients. And the power struggle gets resolved not on the basis of pure power but through a surrogate issue that determines the outcome of the lawsuit. Perhaps it has something to do with whether the majority shareholders gave proper notice of a meeting or proved that their decision satisfied a legal standard having nothing to do with the true reason for the transaction. But the lawsuit is settled or decided and the power struggle is resolved, one way or the other.

The courts can be very helpful in rechanneling the destructive force of a bitter divorce. Perhaps the father has moved out and the mother has hidden the children with a neighbor as a way to force the father to pay the mortgage. When he comes to pick up the children, and finds a note describing the terms under which he will get to see them again, violence becomes a real possibility. The conflict becomes extremely hot, chaotic. Normal parenting responsibilities resume only after a temporary court order is entered that defines his support obligations and the parties' visitation rights.

Many times, however, the conclusion of a lawsuit does not resolve the underlying conflict in any real way. Most judicial institutions are designed to resolve disputes, not conflicts. A court can decide "technicalities," like whether the plaintiff gave proper notice of his intention to evict the defendant, or whether the police officer needed a search warrant before entering a house where a hostage was being held, but a lawsuit rarely confronts the real issues that brought the parties to court. The legal process is structurally unable to deal with fundamental issues of hatred, intolerance, vengeance, exploitation, or abuse.

Dispute resolution requires the consent of those engaged by the conflict to "carry" a conflict. At some level, the parties must agree that the disposition of the dispute will resolve the conflict as well. Perhaps they have indicated their consent by the mere fact of their participation, by hiring lawyers, by responding to a letter or formal allegations. But the more explicit their consent, the more profound will be the resolution of the underlying conflict. Once the relationship between the dispute and the conflict is made explicit, it renders the conflict *contingent*, rather than having a life of its own.

The process of transforming a conflict into a dispute is remarkably easy. One simply creates a setting in which each party is asked to tell the story of the conflict, or to explain her "side" of the story, or to describe his "position" in the matter. "Stories" may very well be the basic organizing structure of human experience. Once we arrange our thoughts and reactions and opinions into a narrative, the chaos is given containment. It starts to become linear, to make sense. We begin to relax.

Moreover, most stories, from Aesop's fables to neighborhood gossip to novels and Hollywood movies, are based on the distinction between the "good guys" and the "bad guys." Particularly when we tell our own story, we take a position. We reveal the inherent polarity between ourselves and our adversary. Telling our story crystallizes the conflict in a zero-sum, or win-lose, framework. What once was a rudderless, free-form conflict has now become a bipolar dispute.

As simple as this seems, consider how easy it is to become lost in the endless details that characterize most conflicts. There may be years of grievances to describe, countless instances of wrongdoing and betrayal. But when forced to tell a fifteen-minute summary of the conflict, most of us can organize the details into a pretty convincing—and one-sided—story of our own rectitude. Essentially, this is what lawyers do—organize a messy hodge-podge of facts into a coherent story that makes the other side wrong.

This transformation takes on even greater significance when we—or a skillful third party—are able to sort through the facts presented in both stories and identify a *single pivotal issue*, the resolution of which would conclude the matter. The essence of dispute resolution is winnowing through various issues, facts, theories, and opinions until the parties encounter the one question that separates them.

Most disputants resist this kind of simplification, of course. We tend to camouflage what lies at the heart of our conflicts with a confusing array of gestures and objections, but still are drawn by the elegance of the idea that, ultimately, the resolution of the matter will depend on the determination of a single question. The art of dispute resolution is in framing this question in such a way that all participants will invest it with the power to conclude the entire matter.

In the case of Marin, its long history of conflict seemed to show up every time anyone discussed the future of the conflict resolution program itself. Making peace, it seemed, had become very controversial. The very process of identifying areas of conflict had opened old wounds and increased the sense of anxiety and mistrust. Some members of the local school council wanted to end the program because it had given the teachers a platform for airing their complaints; many of the teachers refused to participate because they didn't want to be let down again. The same dynamic of mutual disempowerment had turned the conflict resolution program into a political football.

Several weeks after our summit, we called a meeting of the participants, and invited a number of students and parents to attend. The old questions of power and control immediately surfaced. Administrators wanted to know why more teachers hadn't come to the meeting, and teachers started blaming the LSC for undercutting the program.

After listening to the teachers and administrators joust and jab, one of the students spoke up: "I can't believe that we are being asked to work out our problems when the adults can't even treat each other with respect. I had no idea that you people had such a hard time dealing with your power trips. Did you somehow forget about why you're here—to teach the students how to deal with life?"

Silence fell over the room. Finally, one of the teachers said, "Shouldn't we make a decision about whether we want to take the next step? Weren't we going to start a peer mediation program for the students?"

A critical shift had taken place. Out of the chaos of generalized blame and finger-pointing, a single disputed issue had surfaced that would determine whether the teachers and administration would work with or against each other. One of the *independentistas* spoke up. "We don't agree about much, and I think it's useless to try to resolve our basic differences. But I think we should make a decision about working on this conflict stuff with the students. If we can't come to some agreement about that, then we don't deserve to be here at all." You could hear the whole room breathe a sigh of relief. Now, at least, there was something very specific to address. The conflict had been contained.

The same process works in most conflicts. The same couple that can't work out their power struggles in therapy, which is open-ended and deals with the relationship as a whole, often is able to resolve particular disputes in the course of mediating a divorce. As a result, there is less conflict between them in general. Two partners who strongly disagree about the firm's management philosophy are still able to come to terms with specific hiring decisions.

The second step, then, transforms a general conflict into a specific dispute. Once the playing field has been narrowed, a further change in the rules of the game takes place.

3. TURN THE DISPUTE INTO A DEAL. A dispute is a bipolar process. It pushes the parties into extreme and generally incompatible positions. One person is right, and the other person is wrong.

The dispute may be about such matters as *facts* (the distance from the earth to the moon), about *quality* (whether a peer mediation program is helpful or not), about *morality* (whether abortion should be legal or not), the *future* (whether the loss of a key employee will hurt sales next year), or about *logic* (whether free enterprise and welfare are compatible).

It can be extremely important to pursue these disputes to their conclusion. Debate is an essential form of civilized discourse. It forces the parties to penetrate a problem more deeply than is possible in casual conversation, and can generate clear and useful distinctions. Disputation is at the heart of the scientific method ("Prove it!") and is our hedge against superficial thinking and unexamined prejudice.

Argumentation can be a high art as practiced by Buddhist monks, advanced scholars, experienced lawyers, trained theologians, and even local politicians. Unfortunately, we are in a time when disputation is not esteemed, which is a reflection of both the complexity of our social problems and our weariness with the high-volume aggression that is promoted as "debate" on television and radio. Our faith in the very notion of truth has been shaken by the post-modern proliferation of many truths. In response, we have tended to be pragmatic when wisdom may be required.

One of the basic consequences of most argumentation, however, is impasse. No matter how carefully we articulate and support our position, it is rare that the other side will concede its superiority. Disputation requires the intervention of an outside agency—a judge, jury, encyclopedia, or CEO—to settle the matter. Such agencies are often unavailable or costly or unpredictable. Having clarified the details of a dispute and having explored its implications, it may become necessary to shift into a different problem-solving mode to bring things to conclusion. That problem-solving process is called *negotiation*.

The word *negotiation* in Romance languages means "to do business." This is the sense in which negotiation is an effective dispute resolution process. Once the parties decide to do business with each other, the end of their dispute is at hand. This is the stage at which their *dispute* becomes a *deal*.

The settlement of a lawsuit illustrates this transformation quite clearly. In the preparatory stages of a lawsuit, the parties gather evidence to support their competing claims, determined to defeat one another in battle. At some point, one or both of them tire of the struggle and its disruption, or notice that the costs of litigation have started to exceed the amount in controversy, or decide that they can't wait another five years to get a courtroom. So they start to think about settlement.

At this point, the arguments they were going to use in court become bargaining chips in their negotiations with one another. "Any jury that heard this evidence would award me punitive damages and put your client out of business," each contends. That is, the persuasiveness of their arguments and the weight of the amassed evidence are used as *tools for predicting* what would happen in the future. This allows each side to assess the risk—and the cost—of proceeding to that future. As a result, each side is able to assign a monetary value to its case and to the risk of losing it.

Now, instead of arguing about who is right, the parties begin to haggle over the price of being wrong. "If I lose, I might have to pay you fifty thousand. If I win, it will cost me another ten thousand in legal fees. There's a high probability that I will win, so I will offer you only what I would have to pay my lawyer to achieve that result." And so on.

At Marin, the bargaining centered on issues like when to conduct the training of students in peer mediation, how they would select student participants, how many teachers and parents would be involved in the program, and the size of the budget to be underwritten by the local school council. The important point here is that once they started negotiating the details of the program, it was clear that the conflict was safely contained. It would just be a matter of tying things up.

Less than a month later, Marin had graduated its first class of peer mediators. Within its first week of operation, the peer mediation program had resolved successfully half a dozen difficult arguments that might have become violent. After two years of preparation, students were taking a direct hand in bringing order to chaos, and it was working. By the second year, one of Marin's peer mediators was honored as Student of the Year for the entire city.

4. MASTER THE FINAL INCH. A great deal has been written about the various techniques of negotiation, so the subject won't be covered to any extent here. But there is one aspect of the negotiation process that is of particular concern in cases of conflict. That issue is the tendency of even a well-contained conflict to reappear in the final stages of a negotiation.

The summer after I graduated from high school, I sold encyclopedias door to door. The experience taught me that you can spend all night selling the product, but it doesn't put any money in the college account if you don't close the sale before you walk out the door. Resolving a dispute ultimately means getting a signature on the bottom line—even if that line is metaphorical.

Anyone who has ever played or even watched football is familiar with a phenomenon called "the goal line stand." The ball can be an inch away from the goal line after the offensive squad has quickly marched ninety yards down the field, seemingly without opposition, yet they are turned back as they try to cross that final inch. All the forces of resistance that were nowhere to be seen just moments ago now seem concentrated in that small and impenetrable space.

So it is with conflict. I once mediated the divorce of a wealthy couple who effortlessly agreed to the exchange and disposition of millions of dollars of assets—several homes in various parts of the country, boats, an airplane, investments, and substantial sums of cash. At the last minute, just as I was preparing the final documents, they calmly told me that the deal was off.

"She should pay my legal fees," the husband asserted. This amounted to a couple of thousand dollars. The wife smiled, and refused. She had decided that the deal wasn't fair at any level. It would have to go through the courts as a contested matter. I was dumbfounded.

In other cases, parties have suddenly become bitterly antagonistic over a favorite painting, the last fifty dollars of a ten-thousand-dollar lawsuit, and even a cooking pot. That final issue, no matter how trivial, becomes the symbol of the entire conflict. No matter how many significant concessions have been made throughout the negotiations, the resolution of the "one last thing" seems, in the minds of most disputants, to determine who won or lost.

It is at this point that arbitrary processes play a useful role. To borrow a Solomonic device, many disputants agree to "split the baby"—to share equally in the last move to the middle. Sometimes a coin toss will work, sometimes a more elaborate scheme is required. In complex cases that have reached impasse, it is often useful to submit the final, narrowly defined issue to an arbitrator. Such processes are readily employed when the parties have sufficiently reduced the risk of some outrageous outcome, and are resigned to accepting a decision within a preestablished range.

The best negotiators, however, are those who see the final move as an opportunity to be generous. After a hard-fought struggle to reach an agreement, a graceful concession at the end can buy an enormous amount of good will. Insisting on winning the last point, on the other hand, can be perceived as overreaching and may generate resentment all out of proportion to its value. The old adage that "what goes around, comes around" holds true a surprising percentage of the time.

The final inch is also where we meet our resistance to "moving on." Once the deal is closed, this chapter in life's book is also closed. Letting go of a familiar problem can sometimes seem more painful or frightening than facing the unknown world that is waiting beyond it. The simple recognition that the struggle over the final inch is just our resistance to getting on with life usually breaks its hold.

CREATING THE CONTAINER

Most of us tend to think of courts and judges and arbitrators when imagining the ways in which conflict is contained. In fact, the possibilities for containment are endless. Each conflict is unique and presents an opportunity to create a container by which it might be processed to a satisfactory conclusion. Most mediators agree that the most rewarding part of the practice is designing new vehicles for resolving conflict.

All human interactions take place within some sort of container. The container is defined by the rules of the exchange. The rules, in addition to those that are made explicit, consist of the roles, relationships, and expectations of the participants. When a father gives his daughter advice on dating, for example, he is creating a context both for his relationship with her and for her experience of dating. The restrictiveness of the container will be determined by his use of authority, whether guidelines are being imposed or a dialogue is invited, and the range of outcomes that are permitted.

Similarly, office meetings and conversations are contained by issues of authority and resistance, by levels of cooperation and creativity. Requests may be made casually, by a memorandum or by implication. Employees may be managed closely or not at all. Groups and individuals may be held accountable for their performance or never questioned about their actions.

In all these exchanges, there is much that is vague and unspoken. In many situations and with most organizations, we tend to take our cues from circumstance rather than defining our expectations, aspirations, and capabilities. Rarely do we stop to consider the range of the game in which we are playing, and whether we are playing to win, for recognition, to advance within the structure—or because we have discovered the joy of the infinite game. Instinctively, we allow our uncontained reactions to determine what kind of game we play. Our effectiveness in resolving conflict will expand geometrically once we decide to take control of the process of creating the game.

THE CONFLICT GAME

It may be easier to imagine the process of creating a useful container for a conflict if we think of ourselves as employees of a large toy manufacturer, hired to create a new game for the holiday season—

"The Conflict Game." The purpose of the game is to engage all players in a step-by-step interaction that fits their motivations, challenges their intelligence, requires the suitable exercise of skill, and allows them to make reasonable use of their negotiation leverage.

There are three basic rules for designing a game board to contain a hot conflict. First, the game must be one that the participants are willing to play. Second, the game must be capable of including all the essential players and their issues. Third, the game must incrementally move those issues toward resolution in a way that keeps the parties engaged.

How do you discover what game the parties will play? By *asking*. Would you be willing to meet me for a drink? Would you like to get together with me and Fred from Personnel to talk about our disagreement? Is there something you have in mind? Do you think that this could be worked out by our lawyers? Should we hire a facilitator to run the departmental meeting? What do you think about using the electronic bulletin board to run this past all the field offices?

One of the most important factors in designing a conflict game is what might be called the "tightness" of the container. The container may be like a sieve or a permeable membrane, on the one hand, or like a vault or steel drum, on the other. How tight you make the container will determine the nature of the interaction that takes place within it. The tighter the container, the greater the energy that flows between the participants, catalyzing exchanges and generating reactions. Loose containers permit greater freedom of movement and self-determination, but may not stimulate a definitive response.

A courtroom trial is a very tight container. Each action can be assured of producing a reaction, even if ritualistic. The judge has almost absolute control over who may speak and what they may say, how the lawyers must dress, and whether they should sit or stand. The judge tells the jury what they can consider in making their decisions and what they must ignore—even if they saw the evidence with their own eyes and heard the testimony from the stand.

The jury, at least in theory, is not allowed to create its own alternatives to what is presented. An essential part of the judge's role is to reduce the entire drama to a choice between two or three well-defined options. One way or another, there will be an outcome.

A conversation at the water cooler, on the other hand, is very loose. There are no rules except what the parties wish to impose on themselves. Generally, the conversational guidelines are implicit, unstated, and unenforceable. The parties can introduce any subject, rely on any authority, and arrive at any mutually agreed destination. However, if they are attempting to resolve a conflict and don't reach agreement, the looseness of the container means that the process can end without producing any movement or change.

If there is no response to your efforts to establish a purely voluntary game, then the container will have to be made tighter. The influence of a third party or recourse to authority may be required. The first step in initiating hostage negotiations, for example, is establishing a secure parameter around the scene. While it may not be possible to force the terrorist to talk, the elimination of escape routes narrows his useful alternatives.

Creating the right degree of confinement can be a relief to all the players. Parties who are engaged in particularly hostile exchanges sometimes secretly welcome the court order that forbids them from further contact. Even a small child appreciates the limits set by parental authority. Adults who throw legalistic tantrums are similarly calmed by the knowledge that they will not be allowed to roam too far from civilization.

It is normally apparent in any situation that there are a number of alternative games in which the parties may engage. Some of those games are preferred to others. The key is to engage in the game that is of greatest benefit to the whole whenever possible, rather than pursuing only that option that promises you quick or decisive victory. The more obvious it is to one's adversary that a given game may be played to his own advantage, or that the game itself will be worth the effort, the faster he will be to join in it. We aren't normally too enthusiastic about playing games we are likely to lose.

The game cannot be played without all the necessary players. Anyone who has the power to void the game's outcome must be included in the game. Similarly, the game must include all the pieces to the puzzle. Whatever issues are regarded by the players as essential must be included unless a player can be persuaded to abandon or postpone that issue until some subsequent game.

The importance of learning how to create new versions of The Conflict Game cannot be overstated. It is too serious an undertaking to be left to the experts.

PLAYING THE GAME

There was a time when it seemed that all social institutions, including those that managed our conflicts, were ordained and established by some unquestioned authority. Courts, lawmakers, elected officials, and the police and military were responsible for settling our differences. In the course of their work, over centuries and across continents, these institutions created and re-created The Conflict Game in a thousand different forms—through the containers of government, warfare, imprisonment, and legislation. We looked to our sovereigns and our elected leaders to tell us how to play the game and to set the rules.

But life has become too complex, too fragmented, and too dangerous to rely on figures of authority to establish order in the midst of the growing chaos of a shrinking world. Now we all must become masters in containing the conflict that surrounds us and is in us. Just as society is always devising ever smaller and ever more powerful instruments of warfare and destruction, the technology of peacemaking must constantly adapt itself to meet each new threat. And it cannot meet the challenge unless all of us get in the game.

As each of us learns to become a more active player, The Conflict Game will continue to enable civilization to withstand the forces of chaos that daily tear at our tenuous hold on the promise of justice and peace.

Making peace is no longer an optional activity.

CONFRONTING CONFLICT:
The Way of the Warrior

The only way out is through.

Robert Frost

BLIND JUSTICE

Maureen FitzGerald was a tall, extroverted lawyer who loved to play the piano. She had abandoned a career as a performer and gone to law school at the urging of her father, whom she adored. "You're talented and as smart as anyone I know, and I don't see why you shouldn't use your gifts to their fullest. You're a fighter," he told her. "Enjoy your art, but make your living with your smarts. You'll be rich and a marvel at parties to top it off."

Maureen traveled on the fast track at one of Philadelphia's largest and most aggressive firms. She was the youngest female partner and, as an employee benefits specialist, oversaw the firm's pension plan and investments. Even the most senior partners came to her for advice. Her billings were always high, and so were her year-end bonuses.

The firm recently had brought in a senior "rain maker" from another law firm across town. His client base and reputation made him a powerful and intimidating figure from the outset. Whether it was secretaries, associates, or money, Norm got his way. No one wanted to face his wrath if he didn't get what he wanted. Even clients were frightened of his anger, and rarely questioned his strategy or his bills. Norm came into Maureen's office one afternoon to talk about taking some of the pension money out of the trust account for an investment he wanted to make.

"I understand that I have to get your *permission* to invest my money," Norm scowled.

Maureen held her ground. "I'm sorry, Norm, but you can't withdraw the funds. If you do, you'll expose us to some serious taxes on the whole pension account, and we might even lose our exempt status. We can't take the chance."

Norm's face reddened. He wanted to play ball with the people at this polite, silk-stockinged little firm, but letting them hold on to his money was a humiliation he didn't intend to endure. From a *woman*, yet. It's one thing to hire them, because you practically have to. But to give them control over the money, that was a *big* mistake, as this young female was clearly demonstrating. Everybody bends the rules. That's the way smart people play the game. But this self-righteous little person was trying to pull a power trip on him, and he had no intention of letting her run his life or his investments.

Norm exploded. A secretary at the other end of a very long hall could hear him shouting at Maureen. He didn't even bother to close the door of Maureen's office. A little public dressing-down might do her some good. "Who in the *hell* do you think you are? Do you really think I intend to ask *your* permission to invest my own goddamn money?" Norm was at the top of his game. He could feel Maureen shrinking before his very eyes.

Maureen didn't blink. Norm went on for another ten minutes. All work on the east side of the thirty-fifth floor stopped. Nobody moved a muscle in a dozen offices.

Norm threatened Maureen's bonus, her client relationships, her position on the pension committee, her partnership status. "If you can't do the job—and you clearly can't—I'll bring in someone who can!"

Maureen sat silently at her desk for a full fifteen minutes after Norm left. Then she picked up her coat and her purse and walked out of her office, out of the building, and a mile and a half to her home. The afternoon breeze felt good. She couldn't muster a single thought. She was empty, clean as a sandblasted wall.

It was late afternoon. Maureen sat down at her piano, pumped the pedals for a minute, and launched into Mozart. She closed her eyes. Everything went blank. She opened her eyes. Nothing. Couldn't see anything but a dark screen somewhere. Maybe the lights were out. She slumped to the floor. Maureen was able to find the telephone after crawling aimlessly around her apartment for almost four hours. It was 7:15 P.M. when the phone rang at her father's house.

"Daddy, help me," she said. "I think I'm supposed to be at my piano lesson, but I can't find the door." They tested her for weeks. Finally, a specialist from Chicago flew in. It was a stroke. An artery in her neck had burst under stress, and she was blind. Prognosis uncertain. Could be permanent.

The firm sent her flowers. The managing partner came to visit. When he left her room, he talked the records department into giving him her chart, in violation of all the rules and state privacy laws. Looks bad. Better reassign the clients. Quietly, the firm found another benefits lawyer and started assigning new matters to him.

But within a month, Maureen was back at the office. Her secretary read Maureen's mail aloud to her and took dictation. Maureen was too tough to let this get to her. Her billings stayed even. Gradually, Maureen's sight began to return. Within six months, she had most of it back except the peripheral vision. Inexplicably, however, her billings had started to decline. The senior partners with client relationships had stopped referring matters to Maureen. The new benefits lawyer they had hired while she was in the hospital was getting all the assignments.

Maureen's year-end distribution was lower than any other law-yer at her level. She noticed that all the males with her level of experience were being compensated at a rate much higher than hers. When Maureen raised this with the managing partner, he just shook his head. "It's just a matter of the numbers. You haven't put in the hours that these other folks have billed. It's nothing personal. And it certainly isn't about your gender."

Maureen was outraged. "But no one sends me any more refer-rals! How can I bill if there's no business?"

It was clear they wanted her out of the firm. Norm was too powerful to fight.

Maureen hired a lawyer and prepared to file a sex discrimination lawsuit. When word got around, she felt the hostility of virtually every male in the firm. It got so cold at partners' meetings that she practically had to wear a sweater. She was controversial, a problem, and now an adversary.

Maureen's lawyer called me just as he was getting ready to file suit. Her firm had agreed to mediation. The publicity of a lawsuit could be damaging to their recruiting efforts. When I heard him describe Maureen's version of the events, I requested that her firm agree to have Norm attend the mediation. He seemed pretty central to the story. I met with the partner who had been designated by the firm's management committee to handle the negotiations. He had been one of Maureen's closest friends at the firm. Now it was his job to dispose of her.

"We reject the notion that anything he did caused any of her problems. It was a pre-existing weakness in her artery. Even her doctor said that *anything* might have triggered it. She was an acci-dent waiting to happen." He smiled, and continued. "Norm will *not* be in attendance. We go ahead without him, or not at all."

We talked about the expense of litigation and the embarrass-ment of adverse publicity. "I'm sure you're right. What you're telling me is the same advice I would give to any of my own clients. But we just can't let her get away with accusing us of being a bunch of sexist pigs. Maybe we were insensitive, but we didn't discriminate against her because she's a woman. Hell, she's tougher than any of us. And we won't let her make Norm listen to a bunch of baseless personal charges. He's a world-class jerk, but he didn't make her blind."

Reluctantly, I scheduled a meeting with Maureen, the management team representatives, and everyone's lawyers. The firm's insurance carrier was also put on notice.

Maureen sat at one end of a long conference table and looked straight ahead, as if talking only to me. Lawyers for both sides of the dispute sat around the table. The two lawyers from the management committee stared at their legal pads. Neither looked at her as she started to tell her story.

It was the first time anyone at the firm had heard the whole account. Someone gasped as she related the long hours trying to find the telephone, crawling in the darkness and confusion, lost in a twilight that seemed endless. Without a trace of self-pity, but in a tone of quiet fury, Maureen recounted how she felt pushed aside by the firm's concern for its own economics as she struggled to recover her eyesight, her livelihood, and her dignity.

Demands and offers were made. Maureen struggled to deal with her rage. She was reasonable, fair, and willing to put things behind her. But the sense of betrayal still had a hold on her. "I'll settle the case, and I've taken another job," she recounted. "But the only satisfaction I've gotten out of this whole thing is knowing what it must have been like for them to hear about the details of what happened. I couldn't bear to look at them. In fact, I couldn't even see them because I still don't have any peripheral vision. But I know they were watching me, and they won't forget, and no matter what they tell themselves, they'll have to live with the truth."

We met a second time and reached a financial settlement. As I sat on the plane on my trip back home, I thought about the dramatically different ways that Maureen and Norm had confronted their dispute. How Norm dealt with Maureen that afternoon in her office was the kind of confrontation usually associated with conflict—hostile, intimidating, potentially dangerous. Maureen easily could have responded in kind by pressing her lawsuit as a way to embarrass and damage the firm.

Neither response would have been as direct or as powerful as the avenue she ultimately chose—an uncomfortable face-to-face meeting in an intimate setting. There was no hysteria, no posturing, no personal attacks. And no escape.

Maureen and Norm demonstrated what might be called the "high road" as well as the "low road" of confrontation. Before we explore those avenues, however, we need to consider why confrontation is an essential ingredient in conflict resolution.

THE NEED FOR CONFRONTATION

We live in an aggressive world. Drivers curse—or shoot—at one another on the highways, the courts are filled with lawsuits, ethnic warfare has become commonplace, and civility is on the decline in business and professional exchanges. In what sense, then, can it be true that we need more confrontation?

To confront means to come face-to-face—literally, to "put our brows together." When we confront, we come to the end of our own territory and stand at the border that separates us. To confront is to find the existential frontier, to go nose to nose with the outside world.

Confrontation requires courage. To take a stand puts us at risk of being knocked over. In the attempt to reduce our risks, it is not surprising that we should feel caught between avoidance and overreaction. Either we hope it goes away, or we resolve to take care of things "once and for all." There seems to be no room for a middle ground in a complex and stressful world.

One reason that there is so much aggressive and destructive confrontation in the world is that there is too little mature, solid, and thoughtful confrontation. Parents scream at their children because they don't stop to consider how they might more constructively confront a rebellious child. Corporate managers are often more willing to terminate an unproductive employee than to confront him with the facts of his performance and set a deadline for improvement. We minimize or flee from our differences because the stress of facing our legitimate conflicts is so uncomfortable.

Perhaps it's a symptom of living in a nuclear age, when a misunderstanding or mistake might just result in total annihilation. We're liable to get mugged for our shoes or our coat, so we avert our eyes and cross the street. There's often no sense of proportion in our responses to one another.

But the price for avoiding conflict is also high. Pretending that conflict doesn't exist doesn't make it so. Repressing conflict can make it even more damaging, more insidious, less manageable. Hiding in the darkness, it retains and even builds its strength to distort our choices. As long as we submerge our conflicts, we remain powerless to resolve them.

The last chapter focused on cooling off hot conflict so it could be managed; here we consider a strategy for resolving conflict that has become an impenetrable block of ice. Conflict that is ignored or repressed becomes *cold*. Like an iceberg in the ship channel, *cold conflict* can do a lot of harm before it sees the light of day. Confrontation is the fundamental strategy through which we bring cold conflict to the surface and break it down into manageable pieces.

THE WARRIOR ARCHETYPE

Omar was a bright and ambitious real-estate developer who had accumulated an impressive portfolio of office buildings. We were meeting for lunch at his private club to discuss a lawsuit he was preparing to file against a long-time competitor.

"I've been waiting to go after this guy for twenty years," he said, describing several incidents in which he had been, in his view, defrauded by the other man. "He's a crook, and now I've got him."

"Sounds like you're looking for a fight," I observed.

Omar smiled. "Absolutely."

"Man to man? Take it to the mat?"

His smile broadened. "I can already taste it. He's cost me a lot of business over the years, and now it's my turn."

"So why let the lawyers have all the fun? They'll be taking depositions and digging through documents while you sit in your office and review their monthly statements. You won't even see this guy for another year or two. What kind of fight is that? You're not even in the arena, much less the ring."

Omar was silent.

"If you really want to fight, tell him you want to sit down to settle your differences. Hire a mediator or a referee or somebody you both trust. Tell him you want to meet face-to-face, across the table from each other. You'll get to say what's on your mind, without having to listen to 'Objection, your honor.' You can look him right in the eyes and tell him exactly what you've been thinking all these years."

Omar asked for the check. Just the thought of confronting his nemesis made him feel anxious and irritable. Besides, that's what lawyers were for—to do the dirty work. There would be no confrontation. Not until the lawyers were finished. Omar talked like a warrior, but he wasn't really ready for war.

Author and psychoanalyst Robert Moore of the Chicago Theological Seminary says that the problem with men today is not that we are *too* confrontational, but that we are not confrontational enough:

> We live in a time when the warrior archetype [or pattern] is very weak. Society is dominated by soft males who are either passive-aggressive or tyrannical. We live in a time of spoiled little boys, not mature men who are willing to stand up for what they believe in. Men today want approval more than respect. The warrior in us, which is encoded in our bones and our DNA, has almost disappeared. If we don't get it back, we will have lost the capacity to protect those who need protection—the weak, the planet, our children, and our women.

We can either run from confrontation, or we can approach it with appropriate caution. There is an old Masai story that illustrates what happens when we trust our fear and not our courage.

The Masai, who are fierce and proud African hunters, say that when the antelope are scarce and the hunting is difficult, the old lions, whose jaws are weak and whose teeth are blunt, hide in the tall grass at the mouth of the valley. The young lions, with sharp teeth and strong jaws, place themselves at the other end of the valley. The old ones wait for the herds to come. When the antelope cross into the valley and begin to graze, the toothless old lions suddenly leap up and roar with all their might. The antelope, over-powered by fear, dash from the thundering voices of the old lions and flee into the valley. In their panic, they race into the waiting jaws of the strong, young lions. To the young warriors the Masai elders said, "Go for the roar."

We often tell ourselves that confrontation is wrong, or selfish, or should be avoided in the interest of protecting others from our own needs or expectations. While it obviously is true that there are times when provocation would be destructive, confrontation should not be delayed indefinitely simply because we are unwilling to face the reality that underlies it. This is part of the meaning of one of Hinduism's great scriptures, the *Bhagavad-Gita*.

The Lord Krishna, a divine power in human form, had failed in his efforts to establish a peace treaty between two contending branches of a great family, and the lines were now drawn for battle. When the story opens, one of Krishna's disciples, a formidable warrior named Arjuna, is struggling to determine the morality of the impending war as he looks across the valley and sees the faces of his family members—his teachers, his grandfather, his closest cousins. He considers the terrible consequences of fratricidal war-fare and despairs:

> *I do not see how any good can come from killing my own kinsmen in this battle, nor can I, dear Krishna, desire any subsequent victory, kingdom, or happiness.*

Arjuna decides to lay down his arms so that he might be killed rather than commit the terrible sin of harming his own family. "It would be better to live in this world by begging than to live at the cost of the lives of great souls who are my teachers."

Krishna, however, instructs Arjuna to stand up and fulfill his duty and nature as a warrior, without concern for how events play themselves out:

> O son of Kunti, either you will be killed on the battlefield and attain the heavenly planets, or you will conquer and enjoy the earthly kingdom. Therefore, get up with determination and fight. Do thou fight for the sake of fighting, without considering happiness or distress, loss or gain, victory or defeat—and by so doing you will never incur sin.

In other words, don't think you're doing anyone a favor by avoiding a necessary confrontation. The balance of life requires that we take care of business—for our own sake as well as for others. What must be done cannot be avoided without adverse consequences.

WHAT DO WE CONFRONT?

There are at least four different objects of confrontation: (1) *other people*; (2) our own *circumstances*; (3) *questions* raised by those circumstances; and (4) *ourselves*. Many of the problems associated with confrontation are caused by aiming our arrows at the wrong target—say, engaging in a personal confrontation when we really needed to deal with a difficult fact of life. Knowing what or whom to face is just as important as having the courage to confront in the first place.

As a general matter, it is usually best not to get "personal" when confronting a conflict. Human beings invariably get defensive and unpleasant when we feel personally criticized or diminished. Gang wars and civil wars have been ignited by small acts of disrespect. Personal honor is primal turf. We threaten it at great risk.

Nevertheless, there are times when conflict becomes nothing more than a raw struggle for power between persons, groups, and nations. There is no moral issue to be resolved, no factual dispute, no question of principle. It's you or me, us or them. Kill or be killed.

We therefore start with *personal confrontation*.

THE DARK MIRROR:
CONFRONTING THE ADVERSARY

It is likely that each of us, at some time in our lives, will acquire an enemy. It may be a competitor, a former spouse, an employee who was terminated right before the holidays, someone who envies our success, someone we betrayed, an ideological opponent, or the cranky guy next door. The closer the connection, the more intense the feelings.

Often, it comes as a shock that another human being actually hates us and wishes us ill. This discovery can be a blow to our self-image. We may begin to doubt ourselves, and wonder: Who am I that I have inspired such animosity? We fear to confront because we don't want to say something that cannot be forgiven.

Obviously, not every opponent is an enemy. Lawyers and athletes know that a worthy opponent can become a good friend or a valued colleague. A true enemy, on the other hand, threatens our survival, pushes our buttons, inflames our passions. The enemy inspires hatred. We may wish to defeat an opponent, but we dream of *annihilating* the enemy.

It is axiomatic in psychology that what we most detest in others we hate—and deny—in ourselves. The enemy is the inner demon made manifest. He carries our "shadow" side and forces us to confront what otherwise we would have rejected. The enemy is the dark mirror in which we behold depths that are too dangerous to acknowledge in ourselves.

Such soul-searching may provide little relief, however. Once the adversary has gone into action, we must respond. Self-doubt can cripple us just when we need every bit of confidence we can muster. Like the besieged Psalmist, we devoutly wish for a little divine assistance:

Hear, O Lord, a just suit; attend to my outcry. . . . My rav-
enous enemies beset me; they shut up their cruel hearts, their
mouths speak proudly. Their steps now surround me; crouching
to the ground, they fix their gaze, like lions hungry for prey, like
young lions lurking in hiding. Rise, O Lord, confront them and
cast them down; rescue me by your sword from the wicked, by
your hand, O Lord, from mortal men. —Psalm 17: 1; 9–14

Psychological analysis alone will not solve the problem. How, then, are we to protect ourselves from the ravenous jaws of the enemy? There are two approaches; they might be called the *high road* and the *low road*.

THE HIGH ROAD

There are times when we benefit enormously from the struggle against opposition. We become stronger and more uniquely defined as a result of the resistance provided by the adversary. Confrontation brings out the best in us. In the course of the contest, we discover and reveal our nascent character. Conflict is the crucible in which the soul is tried, tempered, and transformed.

To travel the high road means that we acknowledge the strengths of our adversary and hold her accountable at that level. We both rise to the challenge. "Defeat me, if you can," we seem to say, "but in this place, by these rules, with these weapons." The high road still brings us to confrontation, but it is an honorable one, premised on mutual respect for the capacity each brings to the battle.

Maureen FitzGerald, the young lawyer we met at the beginning of the chapter, chose the high road. She could have fought her battle in the newspapers, where she had many sympathetic friends. She could have pressed ahead with her lawsuit, or sought publicly to embarrass her former partners. Instead, she challenged them to meet her in a private arena, to speak openly and to be forced to listen carefully. Neither side could hide behind legal arguments or a veil of pleadings. And the firm responded. No admissions, no apologies—but no evasions, either. There was dignity in the en-counter, uncomfortable as it was for everyone.

Confrontation is important not only for its ability to bring under-lying issues to the surface or to change the dynamics of conflict but because we ourselves may be transformed by the experience. The paradox of confrontation is that it unexpectedly empowers those who muster the courage to pull the sword from the stone.

When we confront what we would most prefer to avoid, we are changed. Who we have been up until that moment is annihilated, to be replaced by the person who emerges when the dust settles. The shift can be subtle or very dramatic. We might become just a bit more assertive or a whole lot less aggressive. Confrontation liberates us from whatever we once feared to face.

Confrontation frees us from fear precisely by bringing us into an encounter with the source of our fear. The essence of all ancient forms of male initiation is the young boy's experience of his own terror—when he faces his fear in a ritual setting, it awakens his slumbering masculine nature. In the course of the encounter, he discovers his manhood. Now the tribe can count on him to confront external danger without being defeated by self-doubt. The process of giving birth endows women with a similar kind of fearlessness.

When victims of crime are given a safe way to confront those who have harmed them, they are given some measure of freedom from their victimhood. When we confront our own past, our own mistakes or malice, whether in therapy or confession or in a prison cell, we are changed. This is true catharsis. The shame is that so few victims have the opportunity to face those who have harmed them.

Most of us fear confrontation. Like an actor in the wings, we get butterflies in anticipation of being so exposed. Once done, however, most of the anxiety disappears. Legal processes that drag on for months and years require us to carry an unhealthy level of confron-tation anxiety. Until the confrontation has been completed, we carry that stress in our system. Like an infected appendix, it could cause serious damage if it bursts at the wrong time.

Confrontation has the power to make us hysterical if we lack the presence of mind to ground ourselves before the electricity is turned on. Not everyone has the capacity to withstand a confrontation, no matter how moderate or well-intentioned. To disagree directly can sometimes feel like an affront to our dignity, or even an invasion of our personhood. Once, during settlement negotiations in a difficult construction case, a sophisticated corporate litigator became apoplectic when the other lawyer described his analysis of the case. "Your client is nothing but a . . . a . . . pig!" she shouted, to the obvious surprise of everyone in the room.

Confronting an enemy can play a vital role in the development of our psyche. Perhaps there is something with which we ourselves will be confronted. Friends may be too polite to draw our attention to it, and strangers are simply indifferent. But we can count on the enemy to reveal our weaknesses and show us hidden parts of ourselves.

Carlos Castaneda, whose accounts of the mystical Yaqui "way of knowing" achieved great popularity in the seventies and eighties, reports that his shaman-teacher Don Juan spoke glowingly of the benefits of patiently enduring the endless demands of a tyrannical personality. Through the torments of a self-absorbed enemy, we can actually learn to abandon many of our most objectionable traits. "The more petty the tyrant, the better. This will make you a man of power."

So we must approach the encounter with awareness of the paradox that the enemy somehow is serving us by his opposition, much as Jacob's biblical angel fought him in order to strengthen him. Even in the heat of the struggle, we must stubbornly honor our enemies, for they are carrying what we tried to cast off.

THE LOW ROAD

We don't always have the opportunity to meet the adversary on the high road, however. He may already be committed to another route, and cannot easily be induced to change altitude. We may have to confront him where he is to be found, whether we like the neighborhood or not. When we take the low road, we knowingly employ coercion to force the adversary's hand. When we embark on the low road, we carefully determine the weakness of our adversary and turn it against him.

The low road may be the only route available to us if the other side refuses to be accountable for its behavior, won't negotiate, won't comply with court orders, defies official sanctions, breaks agreements, or exploits a truce. The low road is the path we follow when there is no honor or code to contain the adversary.

The adversary signals his choice to travel the low road by initiating coercive or deceptive acts. We respond to this tactic by discerning the enemy's vulnerability and defeating or redirecting him with it. Rather than appealing to his higher instincts and elevating the exchange, we meet the enemy at his darkest place and expose him to the consequences of his choices. We do not fight him with our own darkness, but neither do we pretend that his conduct is better than it really is.

Walking the low road requires balance. When we are hurt or humiliated by a ruthless adversary, it is easy to become trapped by an insatiable desire for revenge. At some point, if we become obsessed with destroying the enemy, we may forget why we are engaged or what we hoped to accomplish. Even a total victory may feel empty.

Norm, Maureen's senior partner, decided to take the low road of confrontation when he realized he had to deal with a junior female colleague in order to cover an investment. For reasons of his own, he elected not to acknowledge Maureen's authority over the pension fund or to rely on a rational dialogue about the limits of its acceptable use. Instead, he chose the first strike option, and humiliated her within earshot of a dozen other lawyers and secretaries. He chose coercion over persuasion.

Norm knew that Maureen's status as a junior partner would keep her from going toe to toe with him and that her sense of dignity would prevent her from screaming back at him.

Had Norm's partners not agreed to meet with Maureen to settle her claim, she would have been entirely justified in taking the low road herself. While there is a tendency among persons of high moral standards to prefer martyrdom to conquest, like Arjuna in the *Bhagavad-Gita*, some battles simply must be fought.

THE CODE OF CONFRONTATION

Ethics and common sense must inform our recourse to the low road, because coercion always involves some degree of invasion of another. If we are to follow this route, it is important to know that we have tried to adhere to the high road but have found the way obstructed. We should take the low road only if the adversary refuses our repeated invitation to go to higher ground. Remain open to shifting back to the high road if and when an opening appears. Remember yourself.

Following the low road requires a kind of discipline to keep ourselves in balance. This discipline consists of the following three elements:

1. RESPECT. Despite our passions and opinions, if we treat the enemy with respect, we will avoid becoming ensnared in a web of reaction or vengeance. This allows us to maintain an awareness of the better side of the other person, even when the enemy forgets his own dignity. Respect for the adversary is made possible by practical humility—the recognition that we may not see the full picture.

2. COURAGE. Fear is the principal cause of self-destructive behavior in the world. When we act out of fear, we abandon reason. When we engage in fearless confrontation, we deny power to the enemy. Courage is the willingness to risk, without which defeat is certain. Be confident, and let the chips fall where they must.

3. PATIENCE. Impulse is not the best guide to determining when confrontation is most likely to be effective. Rather, we must wait for circumstances to deliver the occasion when intervention

will have the greatest effect. Patience counsels us to watch, to learn the enemy's rhythm, and to act only when the best outcome is possible. Patience gives us distance. It creates an emptiness in which the process itself can assert itself without too much interference from the players.

Gandhi, himself a lawyer, was the pioneer in using civil disobedience, a dignified low road strategy, as a means of confronting his British adversaries with the logical consequences of their repressive policies. The object of his disruptive maneuvers was always to bring the other side to the table, where matters could be resolved through negotiation. Gandhi believed in confrontation. The essence of *satyagraha*, the use of nonviolent resistance, was to fight in such a way that the truth would be revealed. Avoiding a necessary confrontation was a betrayal of the truth.

There are conflicts that never rise above the low road, as when an opponent will not or cannot come to terms except through the power of the courts or a superior military force. This is Cain's legacy and a basic theme in the human tragedy. Wishing it were otherwise is simply naive and can be dangerous to those we must protect. In such cases, nothing short of victory will suffice.

This was a lesson I observed when a friend of mine went through a hotly contested divorce. His wife resisted his efforts to mediate a custody agreement, and pursued litigation with limitless energy and reckless abandon. She repeatedly violated the temporary parenting order and threatened him with a bloody custody battle unless he gave in to her financial and emotional demands. It was all-out war. They went to court a dozen times on the most trivial issues. Each time, the court rejected her demands and reconfirmed my friend's position. After my friend prevailed in court, he expected his wife to explode or try to even the score. But just the opposite occurred. Paradoxically, every time she lost, his wife immediately became reasonable and even cordial. Being confronted by the power of the court seemed to have a calming effect on her rage.

Indeed, confronting authority can be a relief when conflict gets chaotic, as we saw in the previous chapter. It gives structure and definition when things get out of control. Too much confrontation can overheat a situation, requiring the use of a containment strategy. If you're acting like a Ping Pong ball, a backboard comes in handy.

There are times when the low road is not a calculated strategy intended to influence the behavior of another, but an instinctive response to injustice. The time for resolving the matter has passed. We want revenge, to even the score. We want *justice*. How can this be reconciled with a desire to evolve beyond Cain's animal aggression? Through a commitment to *accountability*.

ACCOUNTABILITY

The animating dynamic of aggression is *blame*. The goal of confrontation, on the other hand, is *accountability*. When someone is seeking to make us morally culpable for our actions, we resist more vehemently than when the moral charge is absent from the discussion. This is because moralism, as described in the first chapter, is an assault on our character or even our being. We are more likely to accept responsibility for our conduct if to do so does not imply condemnation of who we are. In other words, I am more willing to say that *"what I did* was wrong" than acknowledge that *"who I am* is wrong." Psychologists sometimes refer to this as the distinction between guilt and shame.

To be accountable is much easier than to accept blame. Blame implies a loss of "face." Accountability actually restores our sense of integrity. As a result, if accountability is established without the additional burden of moralism, we are often relieved to have the opportunity to come to terms with our mistakes.

Most errant politicians in recent years have underestimated the strength of the public's need for accountability, or have confused it with a desire for blame. When Richard Nixon decided to "stonewall" the Congress and the press, his presidency came to an abrupt and otherwise unnecessary end. Gary Hart's political career was destroyed by his arrogant and obviously untrue denial of promiscuity; Bill Clinton, on the other hand, was forgiven because he acknowledged that "there were mistakes" in his marriage. As long as a public figure refuses to be accountable, he or she will be hounded by the media in search of "the truth." A little bit of accountability can deflate the self-righteous moralism that so often motivates adversaries to expose each other's hypocrisy.

Most physicians, who are regarded as gods but live in the midst of mortal error, know about this. Several years ago I gave a lecture to an ethics class at a medical school. The fourth-year students were asked how best to respond to a patient's family in a hypothetical case in which a surgeon had caused the patient's death by using the wrong type of blood. A few answered that "you just tell them there's been an untoward result," but most instinctively understood that a doctor should immediately explain that a serious mistake was made. If the doctor is honest, and reveals his or her own true feelings, it is very unlikely that a lawsuit will be filed. When the doctor holds himself accountable, he usually ends up with the family in the waiting room, sharing the experience of grief, rather than in the courtroom, arguing about blame. To be accountable means to set the accounts straight. It's more a question of math than morality.

The legend of Hercules' Labors is an instructive myth of accountability. Hera, wife of Zeus, had always hated Hercules and was determined to punish him in some way. One day, Hera succeeded in putting Hercules into an enraged trance in which he brutally murdered his beloved wife and children. The vengeful goddess then wickedly restored his sanity as Hercules stood over their bodies, blood dripping from his hands.

In his horror, Hercules longed for suicide, but, on the advice of the oracle at Delphi, Hercules sought out an appropriate punishment. His penance was known as the Twelve Labors, each of which was all but impossible. His twelfth labor literally required Hercules to overcome death by descending into Hades. Once the labors were completed, Hercules knew that he had been held accountable for his misdeeds and was free to go on with his life. Even the gods don't ask for more.

I remember being asked to mediate a "post decree" case involving two Chicago police officers who had been divorced for several years. Their decree had been entered, but they couldn't seem to work out the day-to-day disputes involved in raising their daughter. The father objected to the haircut her mother had given the child, and the mother objected when the father had the little girl's ears pierced. This was clearly a matter of an unresolved conflict that would continue to generate disputes until confronted.

After some probing, it turned out that he had been having an affair during his wife's pregnancy. She was still depressed and felt worthless. In private, I asked the tough-looking cop if he had ever apologized for hurting her so deeply.

"Of course I did. Many times. But that was long ago, and I can't help it if she's still holding a grudge against me."

"But she'll make your life difficult until she feels like the score is even."

He nodded. "But what can I do?"

Accountability is not just a matter of words. Sometimes the psyche demands a tangible demonstration of sincerity. "Is there anything you could give her that, if coupled with an apology, would make her feel that you really meant it?" I asked. He needed a few days to think about it.

I met with his ex-wife. She was still beautiful, but the years and the sorrow had taken their toll. "Are you ever going to let him off the hook?"

She smiled weakly. "I'd like to, but I just can't seem to forget what he did to me. We would never have had that child if I had known he was with someone else."

"But if he ever found a way to take full responsibility for his conduct, do you think you might be able to let go of the blame?"

"Yes. If he really meant it. And I don't just mean words."

So she went home to think about what she could give to her ex-husband to show that she was burying the hatchet.

They came back the next week. Both were nervous. He turned to her and told her the whole story. About how he hadn't told her about the other woman because he was going to try to stay, and about how he thought having a child would bring them back together. "I know I've told you this before, but I'm sorry. From the bottom of my heart. You're a good woman, and a good cop. I admire you. I couldn't want a better mom for that little girl." Then he looked at me. His ex-wife was crying. The weight of the hurt was coming out in sobs. She was starting to let go. "So I tried to think about what I've got that I could give you to let you know that I'm serious about this. It's been too many years, and we need to get on with our lives. So I brought this—you know what it means to me."

He pulled out a large picture frame. It was an original Norman Rockwell print. One with the Chicago Cubs in it. He had always loved it, and he was fighting to hold back the tears as he put it on the conference table.

The flood gates opened. She put her head on the table and just cried and cried. I asked him to leave the room so that she and I could talk in private. When the door closed, she wiped the tears away. "I don't know what to say. That picture is the most important thing in the world to him, next to our daughter. I spent all week trying to think what I could give back, and I couldn't come up with anything. I don't own much, just pots and pans and a video camcorder that doesn't work."

Now she really felt terrible. He had finally settled his account, and she was the one who was in the hole. After a few minutes, she lifted her head and smiled. "Bring him in. I just thought of something."

He sat down, arms folded across his chest.

"Honey," she said, softer than I had ever seen her, "I don't have much. But there's one thing I own that I know you would love. I forgive you, and I want you to have this." She pushed the Rockwell across the table. The account was even.

TRUTH AS MEDICINE: FACING FACTS

There are times when it is not a person that we need to confront, but unpleasant facts or circumstances. We find ourselves in conflict because we are having trouble acknowledging that our business is losing ground, that the deal isn't going through, that the marriage isn't working, that our health is declining, or that we made an irredeemable mistake somewhere along the line.

When we resist facts, we often resent anyone who points them out. There is a tendency to "kill the messenger" when the news is bad. As a result, it is easy to become engaged in a personal conflict when we don't want to confront the darker side of our human condition.

Facts do not inherently require a response. They just are. Facts demand acceptance, understanding. They compel us to reorganize our thinking to reflect the new knowledge. But they don't necessarily bring us into contact with an adversary. Even if the fact of the adversary's existence is what we have been resisting, the process is an internal one. The feeling of conflict is resolved when we fully integrate the painful facts into our perspective of the world.

The process is usually poignant. The key to confronting life's difficult realities seems to lie in recognizing the price we have paid for avoiding the truth. Instead of finding protection in our self-deception, we may find that we have suffered unnecessarily. The prayer of Alcoholics Anonymous is to "accept the things I can't change." When you fight reality it's not hard to know who will win. There is a sense of relief in giving up a losing battle. The realization that we hold the key to our own suffering, and to our own release, can be bittersweet.

An essential turning point in most conflict comes when we come to terms with facts or insights that we have resisted or that have been hidden from us. When we fully face the reality that a job or a lifestyle or a relationship has been lost, or understand the truth of our own complicity in harming ourselves or others, or discover the true genesis of our suffering, the irrepressible human urge to "get to the bottom of things" can finally be laid to rest.

When I taught at a law school, I started each semester by writing the words "truth" and "justice" on the blackboard. By the time I turned to face the class, the level of snickering and outright laughter was usually so high that it took a few minutes to get the class back under control. It had taken only a few months of intense "training" for these bright young minds to become cynical about the basic principles that sustain the social order they soon would be sworn to protect. When I asked whether they believed that the legal system was based on these two ideals, the students would answer, "You can't be serious!"

As law students quickly learn, the law is premised on something called "legal truth"—that is, what can be *proved* to be true. Any advocate knows that a falsehood that can be proved to be true often serves just as well—or better—than the real truth. This is exactly the kind of sophistry against which Socrates railed and that continues to infuriate innocent litigants every day. People hold lawyers in contempt not because lawyers are malicious but because the law is so promiscuous. It seems willing to entertain even the most absurd versions of reality and has no inherent regard for the truth. This violates our basic sense of decency and reduces our most passionate conflicts to a game of chance or blackmail.

Psychotherapy—and even common sense—recognizes that truth is essential to resolving life's difficulties. We insist that our children tell the truth, and warn them about the consequences of lying. The therapy for which we pay millions of dollars each year is essentially a process of discovering the truth about the past or present—or at least a part of it—so that it loses its unconscious hold on us. However painful, we trust in the power of truth to heal, to restore our sanity, to help us find solid ground. Truth is the only reliable antidote in a world of betrayal, deception, and wishful thinking.

FACING RESPONSIBILITY:
UNCERTAINTY AND THE UNKNOWN

Life's circumstances sometimes raise challenging questions that call for a response. Once we have accepted reality, it may present us with issues that must be confronted. Now that I know I have a child from a casual relationship, what is my responsibility to her? Knowing that I can't pay my loan, how should I deal with the bank? Since it is apparent that my partner can no longer manage an important client, how should we handle the account? Now that it is clear that the recipient of our economic foreign aid intends to disclose military secrets to a local drug lord, how should we respond?

Confronting these issues requires that we respond effectively to the outside world. The best response may not involve confronting but rather circumventing an adversary. Personal confrontation may distract us from formulating or instituting a meaningful response.

Conflicts about life's questions are best resolved through *principle*. In a legitimate legal dispute—for example, whether the Constitution prohibits the regulation of abortion or permits school prayer—it does little good to confront the *person* of one's adversary. In fact, the judicial system is intended to be an impersonal and equitable forum, and judges frequently condemn the ad hominem arguments increasingly made by lawyers in court proceedings.

Law, philosophy, and theology strive to elucidate impersonal and universal principles to guide us in making wise decisions. At their best, they aspire to elevate our thinking above the level of reactive, aggressive behavior. Too often, we instinctively pursue vengeance rather than examine our assumptions or investigate the truth. Operating on the basis of principle forces us to replace our powerful passions with dispassionate logic. The elements of what is known as "principled negotiation" are elegantly described in Fisher and Ury's bestselling book *Getting to Yes*, which single-handedly has changed the way conflict is managed around the world.

It is often the case that nurturing personal animosity distracts us from having to make difficult choices that we would rather avoid. When we displace our attention and energies by personalizing the conflict, it usually survives—and is even stronger than before. A humiliated adversary often develops an excellent long-term memory. "What goes around, comes around" is his mantra of vengeance.

Even litigation, which is often described as the classic form of confrontation, is more typically an expensive form of conflict avoidance. It shifts responsibility for decision-making away from those who are directly involved in the matter to those who could care less.

But, properly framed, confrontation can provide an excellent vehicle for changing a raw struggle for power between adversaries into a rational process in which the merits of each position are fairly weighed. Remove such a confrontation, and in the privacy of our own thoughts and in the comfort of our own office, we can convince ourselves that the matter is black or white. When we confront the other side, however, something interesting occurs within our own internal process. This strange phenomenon is called *equity*.

THE BALANCE OF EQUITY

Social psychologists have recently undertaken the study of how people who disagree with one another are able to reach decisions that they both regard as "fair." This inquiry is based in what is known as "equity theory." What equity theory tells us is that each of us has an internal moral gyroscope that keeps us in balance with the outside world. It becomes distorted when we feel that others are benefiting at our expense or when we are unfairly benefiting at someone else's expense. We can maintain our sense of balance either by equalizing the costs and benefits to both sides—or by refusing to consider the costs or benefits to others. In this sense, ignorance can indeed be bliss.

Naturally, it is more convenient for us to see only how others are exploiting us without noticing how our behavior impacts on *them*. As long as we are the victims, equity can be restored only by getting more of what we have been denied. We are not quite so eager to measure things the other way around. Why? Because the internal gyroscope will create discomfort, guilt, and awkwardness until equity has been restored, whether our "rational self-interest" likes it or not. Even Charles Dickens's character Ebenezer Scrooge was relieved when he made things right with poor Bob Cratchit.

It is precisely to avoid having to "make things right" that we often keep ourselves uninformed about the conflict *as the other person experiences it*. We don't want to hear about her pain ("After all, it was *her* fault to begin with!") or notice that we may not be the only victim in the room. Knowing all the facts, seeing the matter from both sides of the table, means that our own sense of fairness will override our desire to claim all the equity for ourselves. We can't argue so passionately once we see the larger picture. The clarity of black and white starts to retreat as we begin to distinguish various—complicating—shades of gray.

Equity theory is not based on how others would decide a case after they have heard both sides. That approach at least allows us to cling to our own extreme position. Rather, it explains an internal mechanism that adjusts our own evaluation of fairness and inevitably brings adversaries closer together. As we learn more about the suffering of the *other* person, we reexamine the depth of our own losses. We become open to a resolution that includes both of us.

This, indeed, is the purpose of mediation—to acquaint each side with the suffering of the other. There is a wonderful film of a mediation conducted, almost wordlessly, by the great therapist Carl Rogers. In a meeting of perhaps fifteen Protestants and Catholics from Northern Ireland, each relates stories of his own pain as Rogers listens intently. One by one, they speak of the sister who died in a bombing, the brother who was imprisoned for years without trial, the father who disappeared one night and never returned. By the end of an hour, they are literally embracing one another—they who had been mortal enemies.

Mediators see similar transformations every day. I remember working with a teacher who had sued her principal and the school board for sexual harassment. The school was located in a small Illinois farming town, and the "good old boys" had no compunction about relating dirty jokes to her, despite her complaints, and spreading rumors around town about her alleged sexual activities. In the course of the lawsuit, which dragged on for nearly a decade, both the teacher and the principal became outcasts in the town—the teacher for suing and nearly bankrupting the town, and the principal for causing the problems in the first place.

In the course of mediation, the principal finally apologized for his comments, bringing the teacher to tears. "I've waited ten years to hear those words," she said. "Now I feel like I can move back to Florida and get away from all this."

But then the principal added, quietly, "But you're not the only one who's been hurt by this thing. My wife nearly divorced me and nobody in town will talk to me anymore. I feel ostracized and alone. They'll probably fire me when this thing is over. At least you've got somewhere to go. I've got nothing."

The teacher looked at the man. She was speechless. She had hated him for so long she couldn't even imagine caring about the price he had had to pay. For a moment, they just looked at each other. The truth hung in the air, and the room suddenly seemed too small to contain us.

I talked to the teacher later as she lighted up a cigarette. "That was just an act," she said. "I don't believe he's suffered a single bit— at least, not any more than he deserved." But she couldn't look me in the eye, and I knew she knew.

Ignorance is bliss because it allows us the extravagance of our own illusions. Confrontation takes away those illusions. It helps us to see things as they are, not as we want them to be. Buddhist monk Thich Nhat Hanh, active in promoting an end to the Vietnam War, today leads meditation retreats for American veterans. He says:

> *During any conflict, we need people who can understand the suffering of all sides. . . . When you see that your enemy is suffering, that is the beginning of insight. When you see in yourself the wish that the other person stop suffering, that is a sign of real love. But be careful. Sometimes you may think you are stronger than you really are.*

Confrontation with the adversary takes courage, because we know we will be changed.

Jungian analyst Robert Johnson in *Owning Your Own Shadow* invokes a medieval image called a mandorla to depict the confrontation of one adversary with another. The mandorla (Figure 1) is quite simple—two circles that intersect, forming an almond-shaped

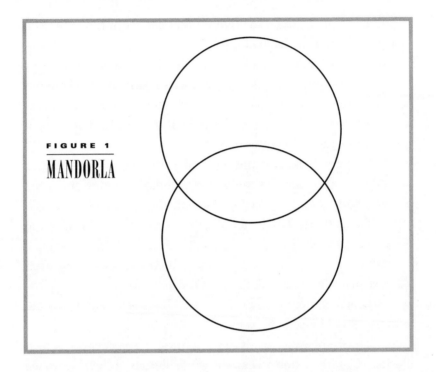

FIGURE 1

MANDORLA

common ground. The area of intersection is that which each shares with the other. The deeper the confrontation, the greater the shared space.

Johnson says:

> *Our own healing proceeds from that overlap of what we call good and evil, light and dark. It is not that the light element alone does the healing; the place where light and dark begin to touch is where miracles arise. The middle place is a mandorla.*

CONFLICT ADDICTION HOW

Some people are extreme in their willingness to be confrontational. They feed on the shadows that are raised by the process of facing the adversary, and they seem to regard everyone as an adversary. There is a dark attraction to confrontation that can best be described as an addiction.

This may come from the fact that confrontation is an assertion of power. When we face that which we fear, we are supported by a rush of adrenaline and an afterglow of self-confidence. We may find ourselves roaming the landscape of our own lives like mercenaries, looking for an engagement, longing for the inflation that an encounter will bring. The need to "prove ourselves" can become quite destructive, as evidenced by the growing presence of gangs and the apparent inevitability of warfare. When we are unsure or untested, confrontation may appear to answer the inner doubts.

Addictive behavior manifests in more subtle and sophisticated forms in many of our social institutions that are set up to solve problems. We have a tendency to maintain organizations long after they have accomplished their stated goals. Solutions are hazardous to the health of problem-solving organizations. Such groups may look for ways to create conflict to continue their own existence. Confrontation, rather than collaboration, keeps them in business. It can be hard to go back to gardening once the war has ended.

An environmental activist described this dilemma for me as we toured an area of the South that had been the scene of prolonged struggle between chemical manufacturers and local residents. "I keep telling them that [environmentalists] have to find another way to stay in the game. All these industries are in compliance now. So what do we do? We don't know where the battle field is anymore. Either we find one, or we're out of business."

Without endless conflict and confrontation, lawyers and mediators also are out of business. So are lobbyists and most community organizers. Our media are dominated by practitioners of "combat journalism." We live in a world where society encourages us to "do good," which often depends on the continued viability of someone whom we believe to be doing wrong. There's an old saying: "When there's only one lawyer in town, he'll starve. But when there's two lawyers, both will prosper."

We know how to wage war. The armaments business—what

COMPASSION:
The Power of Silence

With compassion one becomes courageous. Compassion brings triumph when attacked; it brings security when maintained.

Tao Te Ching

Compassion is a mind that removes the suffering that is present in the other.

Thich Nhat Hanh

COMPASSIONATE ADVERSARIES

In the heat of battle, we don't often think kindly of the enemy. Although we may intellectually recognize that the other side is suffering, we harden our hearts to their tribulations, some of which we may have engendered and can readily justify.

A hard heart is not always our best ally. It can blind us to the motives of our adversary and obscure our understanding of the reality in which she operates. It is not necessary that we agree or sympathize with our enemy, but it is foolish not to understand him. When we cut ourselves off from our natural tendency to feel compassion for others, including our enemy, we reduce our effectiveness because we insulate ourselves from valuable information. Conflict polarizes us, so it is not surprising that we rarely see the whole picture.

Compassion is not the same as sentimentality. Rather, it is the discipline to resonate with another person, to feel what she feels, to connect, to move beyond the limitations of our own prejudices and opinions. It guards us against hurting ourselves through our unwillingness to hurt others. But compassion does not mean that we should surrender to their desires or exhibit weakness. It simply means that we will not stop being human just because we are engaged in conflict.

Conflict takes place in an environment of mistrust. Compassion helps to restore some measure of basic trust so that some form of functional communication can take place. When that communication occurs, we usually will learn something essential for the resolution of the matter. We already know what *we* think. Compassion allows us to understand what *they* think, and why.

The way in which compassion is most commonly and usefully expressed in the midst of conflict is through *listening*. Not just the kind of listening we do while we are waiting to speak, but *real* listening. When our listening becomes as passionate as our speaking, we are then able to invoke the transformative power of silence. It is only in silence that real change takes place.

THE ALCHEMY OF LISTENING

Medieval alchemists regarded life as a process of refining and strengthening the soul as it moved closer to the divine. The soul was like iron. With the proper magic, it might become gold—precious and easily shaped into objects of beauty.

Adversaries tend to take positions that initially seem ironclad. Like two heavily armored knights, they circle one another, and the sound of metal against metal rings out in the arena of combat. A court alchemist watching their stiff and heavy-handed struggle from the shadows might wonder how to transform their iron protection into apparel of pliant gold. Caught by the regal brilliance of one another, might not the adversaries approach the controversy differently? Listening has the quality of the wizard's alchemy. It has the power to melt armor and to produce beauty in

the midst of hatred. Writer Brenda Ueland, a friend of Carl Sand-
burg, described the transformative properties of listening in
Strength to Your Sword Arm:

> *When we listen to people there is an alternating current, and*
> *this recharges us so that we never get tired of each other. We are*
> *constantly being re-created. There is this little creative fountain*
> *inside us that begins to spring and cast up new thoughts and*
> *unexpected laughter and wisdom. If you are very tired,*
> *strained, have no solitude, run too many errands, talk to too*
> *many people, drink too many cocktails, this little fountain is*
> *muddied over and covered with a lot of debris. The result is you*
> *stop living from the center, the creative fountain, and you live*
> *from the periphery, from externals. That is why, when someone*
> *has listened to you, you go home rested and lighthearted. It is*
> *when people really listen to us, with quiet fascinated attention,*
> *that the little fountain begins to work again, to accelerate in the*
> *most surprising way.*

One of the greatest gifts a parent can give a child is to listen. As
every parent knows, most warnings are forgotten and most advice
is ignored, but the times we listen to our children—to their fears
and problems and victories—are treasured moments that never
seem to fade.

The parent who can listen to a child recognizes that birth is a
lifelong experience. We are constantly emerging from an intangible
womb, discovering hidden aspects of ourselves with each new
interaction or challenge. When a parent listens with genuine interest to a child's cries of hunger, to his first words, to his frustration
at school, the child receives a vitally important message: "I care.
You matter."

This kind of acceptance is precious because it is so rare. The
world can be a cold and hostile place, seeming to reject everything
we value about ourselves. Listening creates an island of safety. As we
mature, those who listen to us make it possible to explore that

island. Those who hear us become our best friends, our lovers, our mates. They literally help bring who we are into being.

The need for listening is never greater than when we are in conflict. Long-distance charges go through the ceiling when a relationship sours. Endless community meetings follow the announcement that developers plan to build a high-rise or a half-way house near an established neighborhood. In times of conflict, lawyers and therapists prosper. Families and friends are drawn close.

Unfortunately, much of the listening we are afforded by others in times of conflict is of marginal value or is even destructive. Friends and family members often take advantage of our vulnerability by providing unsolicited opinions and projecting their own issues into the picture. Lawyers often prefer to strategize than to listen, which they often dismiss as mere "hand-holding." Everybody would rather give advice than allow us to come to it on our own. When someone is in trouble, the immediate reaction is to talk rather than listen.

When we are engaged by conflict, we naturally want to be heard. In dealing with our adversary, however, the need to be heard often becomes a struggle to convince the other person that we are "right." We want the adversary to cry "uncle" before we graciously make a concession. This is the point where conflict can most easily spin out of control. In our campaign to be right, it doesn't occur to us that our energies might more effectively be spent by listening to our adversary rather than in arguing. We are still influenced by a four-year-child inside us who deals with conflict by putting his hands over his ears and shouting at his older siblings. We still secretly believe in the power of the tantrum.

Why is it essential that we become effective listeners to resolve conflict? It is because a change of heart is almost always required before a conflict can be put to rest. Something must shift to end the impasse. Arguing—the assertion of the superiority of our position—is not generally an effective way to change your adversary's thinking. Did arguing work the last time you couldn't agree with your husband about which movie to see? Did it work when your kids refused to go to bed? Did it work when your client questioned last month's bill? Did you really change his mind, or did someone simply give in?

An old adage counsels: "If in family matters it ever turns out that you are right, immediately apologize." There is always a price to be paid in establishing our moral superiority. There's nothing wrong with being right, but it's rarely worth the cost of getting someone else to cry "uncle." Being right is a private matter. It's enough that *you* know.

Listening is far more effective than arguing as a way to resolve conflict. Listening opens new routes past the impasse by creating a "place" for change to happen. A good listener is like an engineer dealing with a river that floods after a heavy rain. Only a fool would try to defeat gravity by attempting to push the river back upstream. The wise engineer makes gravity her friend. She builds a canal and holding ponds at the proper place and lets the water flow of its own accord.

Listening allows change to take place without forcing it. Any attempt to impose a solution is likely to be met with resistance. It is the nature of free will to remain free. Like gravity, free will instantly reacts to any attempt at coercion or manipulation. Listening respects the speaker's sovereignty. It is unnecessary to be defensive in the presence of genuine listening. Listening is one of the few human interactions that reduce rather than increase resistance. For confrontation or containment to be effective, it is often necessary that we also engage in an active campaign of listening.

A good listener is an attentive companion as the speaker is led to his own conclusions. The mind shifts when the awareness that "something's gotta give" is no longer blocked by the need to justify our feelings or actions. Once we stop being defensive, the mind is free to become creative. Change then happens naturally.

The challenge of listening to one's adversary can be daunting. After all, many of the things that will be said are probably hostile and directed at the listener. But the light it sheds is worth the heat you'll take.

Adversaries seldom convince one another of the merits of their own positions, but by listening they can convince each other of their good faith and constructive intentions. Once the parties believe that the other is acting in good faith, the likelihood of finding a solution is greatly improved. Being heard means that I no longer need to fight to make my point. By listening, my adversary shows that he or she acknowledges my right to take a stand, even if I'm wrong. We cannot both listen to our adversary and at the same time perceive the conflict in terms of winning and losing.

This is why bitter adversaries resist sitting down together. To listen to your enemy implies that you accept his right to have a voice. To have a voice assumes personhood and vitality. For the Israelis to meet directly with the Palestinian Arabs, for example, means that both already have recognized the legitimacy—the legal existence—of one another. The rest is details.

Keeping in mind that good listening is a rarity even within families or among close friends, it is not surprising that we would strongly resist listening to our adversaries. Nevertheless, one of the most powerful tools of conflict resolution is the application of what I call "deep listening" to one's opponent. Listening completely rewrites the script, as illustrated by a medical malpractice case with which I was involved several years ago.

A QUESTION OF MANHOOD

Ken, a sixty-two-year-old bank vice president, had recently gone through a heart bypass operation. The increased blood flow had worked wonders for his sexual appetite and performance. For the first time in years, he and his wife were enjoying a healthy and regular physical relationship.

His annual medical examination suggested that Ken was, however, a good candidate for prostate surgery. Dr. Barrington, a highly recommended urologist, also advised Ken that he might want to remove a nondescended testicle that probably was precancerous. It was nonfunctional, the doctor noted, and its removal would have no impact on Ken's sexuality.

Immediately after the surgery, while Ken was still coming out of the anesthesia, Dr. Barrington realized, to his horror, that he had removed the wrong testicle. He had taken the functioning testicle, the one that continued to produce sperm. Barrington promptly advised Ken and his family of the mistake, and waived all the medical bills, but Ken was enraged. He had been castrated.

A lawsuit was brought, but Dr. Barrington's insurance company wanted to see if a settlement could be reached without going through years of depositions and medical examinations. Remembering Ken's open hostility, Barrington was hesitant to participate in any negotiations. On two occasions, Barrington even cancelled the settlement meeting at the last minute and went golfing in Florida. His lawyer began to doubt that Dr. Barrington had the stomach for a face-to-face confrontation with his former patient.

Finally, however, Dr. Barrington showed up for a mediation conference with Ken, his wife, the lawyers, and the insurance company representatives. Ken wanted half a million dollars to settle the case. Dr. Barrington had been coached in listening by his lawyer and the mediator before the meeting. "Don't get defensive. Don't try to argue with him. Just let him tell his side of the story. If you have to go to trial, that's when you'll argue about what happened. This is Ken's opportunity to get it out of his system. Consider it part of your medical care of him to permit him to say whatever is on his mind."

Dr. Barrington understood. He put aside his fear and anxiety and feelings of incompetence and gave Ken his full attention. It wasn't easy. Barrington listened intently as Ken detailed the humiliation, the frequent trips to the sexual dysfunction counselor, the loss of his manhood. Ken's wife also spoke at length. They could hardly stand to look at Barrington, but he took it all in.

Ken's anger was so fierce that it seemed to hang in the air like a sword. We took a break to allow everyone to breathe. Ken turned to me, looking despondent. "I don't think he heard a word I said. He hasn't said a thing about all this since the day of the operation and probably just figures that it's the insurance company's problem now."

Dr. Barrington came back from the break and sat down. His medical file was in front of him. "You know, I can't tell you how many times I've stayed awake at night, wondering 'How did this happen?' This isn't what I went to medical school for. I want to make people better, not have them leave the operating room . . . worse than they entered it."

Now Ken was listening. His wife, for the first time, looked at Barrington as he spoke. Maybe Dr. Barrington had heard what they said, after all.

Dr. Barrington made no attempt to excuse his error but was able to identify precisely what had gone wrong, having to do with a test he should have conducted on his own instead of relying on the hospital's workup. "And Ken, Sally, I don't blame you one bit for how you feel about me. In the same circumstances, I'd feel the same way. All I can say is, I'm sorry this happened. Truly sorry."

There was silence. Ken stared at his hands for a long time. He seemed lost in an old memory. Holding a picture in his mind like a photograph, he silently returned to the recovery room when he had first come back to consciousness after the operation. He remembered the doctor's face that day. The doctor's remorse had been there since the beginning. Ken could see it more clearly now. It had just been obscured by his own anger, the anger of his wife, and the anger of his daughter as the two of them stood next to his bed. And by the doctor's fear of what might happen. The anger and the fear had been making the decisions long enough.

Finally, Ken spoke. "Doctor, I think the time has come for us to get on with our lives." His voice dropped to a whisper. "This may seem hard to believe, and maybe my lawyer doesn't want me to be saying this, but I . . . forgive you. You made a mistake, and I have suffered, that's true. But I know that you're a good doctor. You meant me no harm. I wish you none."

The urologist was near tears. Together, they stood up and, to the amazement of their lawyers, shook hands. Although he might have left at any time, Dr. Barrington waited in the reception area of my office for six more hours, until the final details of the lengthy negotiations between the lawyers had been ironed out. Ken and Sally weren't the only ones who had been released of a heavy weight.

THE BASICS OF LISTENING

From the time we first start making gurgling sounds, all human beings are constantly taught how to talk. How to make words, how to make speeches, how to make sales presentations, how to argue a case to a jury, how to ask for what we want.

But there isn't much room in the curriculum for listening, and most of us don't come by it naturally. The focus of our educational system is on expression—how to write or say what we wish to communicate. We spend 30 percent of our communication time speaking, 9 percent in writing, 16 percent in reading—and 45 percent of that time in listening. Listening is used the most and taught the least. And listening is by far the most difficult skill. In fact, listening is so rare a quality that it sometimes seems to belong in the exclusive domain of the professionals—therapists, clergy, and talk show hosts.

Philosopher Mortimer Adler gave a speech on listening in the 1950s that compared the relative difficulty of listening and speaking: "I have discovered that I can easily give a college lecture for four hours without stopping. But to listen, intently, for even an hour is exhausting."

What is exhausting about listening is the effort to restrain our own incessant inner chatter and desire for attention. All it takes is a decision to give that attention to the person speaking. Being polite is not enough. We must be willing to clear away the debris until the muddy water gives way to the pure spring beneath. "Tell me more," we must learn to say.

The late therapist Carl Rogers observed:

> *The major barrier to . . . communication is our very natural tendency to judge, to evaluate, to approve (or disapprove) the statement of the other person or the other group. Real communication occurs, and this evaluative tendency is avoided, when we listen with understanding. What does that mean? It means to see the expressed idea and attitude from the other person's point of view, to sense how it feels to him, to achieve his frame of reference in regard to the thing he is talking about.*

Rogers's point was not just that listening makes for a clearer understanding of another person's views, although this is certainly so. *Listening actually changes the person to whom you are listening.* Based on his extensive experience as a psychotherapist, Rogers concluded that "listening with understanding is the most effective agent we know for altering the basic personality structure of an individual." If it works in therapy, it can work for me and you.

Listening, then, is a communication. What we communicate by effective listening is that we have heard and understood the content of what is being said. That means that the message doesn't require the speaker to engage in repetition, clarification, or elaboration. The speaker has completed his or her task. This shifts the energy of the conflict. It is no longer driven by the speaker's need to be heard. The first speaker can now become a listener. The big picture—composed of all sides of the question—can now emerge.

To communicate effectively the listener's message that "I have heard and understood what you have said," the following elements are required:

1. ATTENTION. Put everything else aside. Make eye contact. Suspend your critical, judgmental side and open yourself so that everything can flow directly into your inner self without obstruction. Become a vessel. Fill up.

2. EMPATHY. Allow yourself to be touched. Permit the other person to find the chord in you that resonates with what is being said.

3. MIRRORING. Repeat what has been said so that the speaker knows that the content of the communication has registered. Don't interpret or diminish it. Don't subvert it, twist it, or respond to it. If you are really good at listening, you may be able to restate it better than it was originally said, but this can be dangerous if the restatement is perceived as a sneaky way to undercut the speaker's point. Mirroring is successful only when the speaker is able to say: "That's exactly right. That's what I was saying." A good listener is like a good journalist: No matter what one's own opinion, listening means being able to report the other's views fairly and objectively.

The key to "listening with understanding" (as Rogers calls it), or "deep" listening, is to have and communicate the *intention* to listen. The degree of your intention will determine how effective you are. If your intention is clear, the technique will fall into place.

THE PRACTICE OF LISTENING: GOOD AND BAD LISTENING

Dr. Barrington, in the story that opened the chapter, showed good listening skills, even though it was difficult for him to hear all the charges being leveled at him by Ken and Sally. Barrington had been advised by his lawyer that the surgery was a mistake but probably wasn't medical negligence, so it would have been easy for Barrington to be defensive or argumentative. He could have been angry at Ken for suing him or otherwise could have attacked Ken's motives. Many times, those who have been sued devote a lot of time to this kind of counteroffensive. But Barrington did not.

Dr. Barrington showed that he was interested in everything that Ken and Sally said. He didn't sift through papers in his file or cross his arms or make faces at his lawyer when he heard something that might have overstated the case. Nor did he play the tough guy. It was clear that Dr. Barrington was touched by what Ken said. He allowed himself to empathize with his former patient and the obvious distress that had followed the surgery. The doctor did not formally "mirror" what Ken and Sally said, but he clearly signaled that he had gotten the message. Moreover, he communicated that he had himself been troubled by the outcome of the surgery.

Our lives are filled with examples of bad listening. Parents who act as if their children are not entitled to their own feelings and opinions. Employers who don't want to know what their workers think. Customers who won't listen to their vendors and vendors who are more concerned about the profit line than the product line.

When the purpose of communication is argumentative, there is very little room for deep listening, the purpose of which is to see what is burning in the deepest reaches of another's heart. In arguments, one listens only enough to learn what positions to rebut. The kind of listening that happens in lawsuits and other disputative contexts could be called "shallow listening." When a person feels attacked and responds defensively, very little listening will occur.

We resist listening to one another when we assume that by listening we are being asked to solve or do something about the matter. Especially if our conduct is being described, it is natural to want to respond. It takes practice and discipline to listen faithfully to one another without feeling a need to agree, disagree, or do something about it. Every communication does not have to be a debate. Listening can be an opportunity for a friend or spouse simply to express a feeling, or to come to terms with something that isn't likely to change or be solved, or maybe to solve it herself. Good listening requires enormous discipline. Some come by it more easily than others, but all of us can benefit from the conscious practice of our listening skills. Sooner or later, someone will test our abilities.

Community conflict is an excellent place to learn how listening works—or doesn't work. A number of years ago I was appointed to chair a commission to advise the new mayor and city council of Phoenix whether to sign a proposed development contract that had been negotiated by the prior administration. The developers planned to raze all buildings in a one-square-block area of the downtown area and replace them with more-attractive commercial and retail structures. It would mean the relocation of a number of marginal businesses as well as one or two prospering concerns.

When we were scheduling the commission's public hearings, one of the city planning department employees warned me to expect a filibuster from the wife of the owner of a major department store who was threatening litigation if the city went ahead with the proposal. "Don't worry about that," I was advised by John Goodson, a fellow commission member. John, a creative and inspired lawyer, promised to guide me through the hearings. "I'll show you how to eliminate her hostility and come out with an even better proposal," John promised.

"How will we do that?" I asked.

"By listening to her. *Really* listening." John smiled as if he knew something mysterious.

Sure enough, at every meeting, she showed up and took her place in line to speak against the proposal. We had considered setting a five-minute time limit on presentations, but John insisted that there be no limits. "She gets to talk until there's nothing more to say. We will invite her to discuss all of her concerns, in detail, until she's ready to sit down on her own."

At each meeting, John made certain that the woman from the department store did not leave the microphone until she had said everything that was on her mind. If she made a general statement, John invited her to go into detail. If she brought documents or photographs, John asked if they could be incorporated into the record. Even when the rest of us became irritated or impatient, John's attention never flagged. And he always thanked her for her contribution.

It was near the end of our third or fourth meeting. Following John's coaching, I had said, for perhaps the twentieth time, "Is there anything else you would like to say? Anything at all?" A smile appeared on the lips that had been so tightly pursed for weeks on end.

"No," she said. "I think that's all I have to say." And she sat down. John looked over at me and grinned.

Now, for the first time, I could work productively with the woman and her husband and get their input on the project. They would be guaranteed a store location in the heart of the new development at bargain prices. Perhaps they would even be allowed to invest in the project. Nothing more was said about bringing a lawsuit.

Listening doesn't always mean that opposition can be eliminated, of course. Differences will remain, no matter how effective the listening. But deep listening, listening that is patient and unhurried, provides an excellent vehicle for removing the emotional obstacles to dealing with the differences. Listening makes it possible to talk about solving a problem rather than simply maneuvering to undo one another.

It is easy to forget to listen. When we get too focused on achieving our own goals or making a point, listening is the last thing that comes to mind. The moment we begin to regard others as incidental, as obstacles to our progress or a blank slate on which we must write, listening becomes impossible. A tyrant has neither the desire nor the capacity to listen.

In a collaborative process that we'll discuss at length in a later chapter, I found myself behaving like a tyrant. I was coming to the end of an intense consensus-building process on an environmental matter. Twenty-five participants had labored for weeks to put together a comprehensive program for dealing with the state's solid waste problems. To everyone's amazement, we had managed to reach unanimous agreement on virtually every point and were drafting the final report. The Christmas holidays were approaching and I had promised to have everyone out of the meeting by 4:30 P.M.

It was nearly five o'clock, and the participants were starting to put on their coats as we made final arrangements for a formal signing and press conference at the state capitol. One of the quieter participants spoke up. He was haggard but determined. "I can't sign this. No way. It's too imbalanced. This will take weeks to finish."

We were all in shock. We all shared the same homicidal impulse as it began to dawn on us—all that work, down the tube. There would be no agreement, since we had imposed a rule that any document we might create would have to be approved unanimously. And I was responsible for the failure. As facilitator, I must have overlooked his resistance or neglected to include him along the way.

I lost it. "Is there some reason you want to subvert this group?" I demanded. I had my theories. There would be little he could say. He must have some kind of agenda. There were reports that he might try to scuttle the process as a way to get revenge on one of the participants who recently had made an unfavorable ruling on one of his projects. His timing was impeccable.

The man, an introverted engineer who had genuine difficulty expressing himself, looked shocked. Then all the other participants started taking potshots at him. I broke up the meeting and stepped into a corner of the room with him.

"Look, I know that you support what we have put together. There must be something I don't understand. What do you need to be able to sign off on this?" I looked into his eyes. He really didn't seem to be enjoying himself. This wasn't a charade. He was genuinely uncomfortable with something.

One of the other participants came up to us. She and the engineer had shared rides to the meetings. She had joined in with the engineer when he objected to signing off on the document. "It was that article this morning. The one that accused us of participating in 'secret' meetings with private industry and the government. How do you think this looks to all those people we have to report back to?" The engineer nodded.

So that was it. They were both concerned about being accused of selling out their position to folks who wouldn't be able to understand the compromises or the victories.

"What if you didn't have to sign it? Could you still agree to the report and to being listed as a participant?" I asked.

"Sure. No problem," he replied.

We announced to the group that there would be a press conference but no formal signing. Everyone breathed a sigh of relief and
went home to finish their holiday shopping. And I reminded myself
to remember to look—and listen—before leaping down someone's
throat.

Learning how to listen is more than mastering a technique or a
formula. Good listeners develop the deeper aspects of their character that give power to the quality of their listening. Good listeners
prepare themselves for the experience. They take the process seriously. They know how to set everything else aside and attend to the
emergence of the unknown. Listening requires respect for the dark
mysteries that can come forth from another person.

Listening is a conscious matter. We must quiet our own
thoughts, release our expectations, and become aware of our own
feelings. Listening requires patience. We must wait for the thoughts
to take shape in another person's being and give time for the words
to form and find expression.

LISTENING AND FAIRNESS

Listening changes not only the one to whom we listen, but the
listener as well. To listen is to subject ourselves to our own sense of
what is fair. When we listen, the grip of our passion and prejudice is
loosened.

As we saw in the last chapter, equity theory demonstrates that
we automatically adjust our inner sense of what is fair (and, conse-
quently, our own "bottom line" position) in proportion to the cost
to our adversary of the underlying experience or event. In short,
empathy equalizes. Listening allows us both to confront the adversary in a nonthreatening way as well as to bring us both closer to a
reasonable middle ground.

I have observed this countless times in mediations. One party
will explain that the case cannot be settled because there is no
reason for either side to change its position. But once they are face-
to-face, they can no longer regard one another as numbers or a file or

an anonymous enemy. They can no longer pretend that the injustice has been one-sided. There are two sides to every coin, we are told. Once we see this to be true, the basic human impulse of fairness begins to alter our sense of what we want to achieve in the transaction.

This explains why stubborn people are bad listeners. We might learn something that changes our view of the matter! It also explains why propaganda (which vilifies the enemy and restricts access to information about his suffering) is important to our ability to conduct long-term warfare. When the enemy is human, and we cannot deny his pain, we feel the longing to be just.

SUMMARY

Of all the tools available to us in dealing with conflict, none is more important than attentive, intentional listening. Listening helps reduce resistance and opens our thinking to creative solutions. Listening not only clarifies the message but changes both the messenger and the listener. Listening makes it possible for both sides to have a change of heart.

Listening doesn't happen by itself. It takes a conscious decision and a willingness to release the distraction of "being right." In learning how to listen, we develop the virtues of patience and even humility. Ultimately, listening teaches us to resolve conflict by letting it resolve itself.

COLLABORATION:

From Partisan to Partner

*In great teams conflict becomes productive. The free flow
of conflicting ideas is critical for creative thinking, for
discovering new solutions no one individual would have
come to on his own.*

Peter Senge, *The Fifth Discipline*

*Victory creates hatred, defeat creates suffering.
Those who are wise strive for neither victory nor defeat.*

Maha Ghosananda

THE SOLID WASTELAND

Bob Perciasepe had a problem. The Maryland General Assembly
was about to convene its annual session. As Secretary of the Department of the Environment, Perciasepe would be called upon to
testify about the usual array of legislation—bills calling for bans on
incinerators, bills to loosen the regulation of incinerators, bills to
reduce his budget, bills to increase his regulatory responsibilities.
How to manage the state's solid waste problems—trash—was becoming a controversy he could no longer control. Already, there
were 110 citizens' groups throughout the state's four major bio-

regions that had solid waste on their agenda, and the legislative session was shaping up to be a nightmare.

Perciasepe had appeared before the Assembly countless times before. He was always somebody's target. This year, he just didn't have the heart to go back. There had to be a better way. "They tell me that there's something called a 'charrette' we can use to bring everybody to agreement about solid waste," Perciasepe said, looking straight at me, as if I knew what a charrette was.

"Right. I'm sure it would work," I answered. Naturally, I had no idea what a charrette was.

It had something to do with people talking to each other, I was sure. So, chances were, this "charrette" process would help people in Maryland decide what to do with their trash. I looked up the term as soon as I got back to Chicago.

Charrette. *A contest of speed and endurance by medieval architecture students to complete their design projects and deliver them to their professors before the deadline. So called because of the chariot-like vehicles in which they transported their models, sometimes resulting in ceremonial races around the courtyards of the university.*

This definition didn't make any sense to me, so I called Timmie Daugherty, the Director of Community Relations for Perciasepe. "Why a 'charrette'?" I asked.

"I know you think that this would be a manageable project if you worked at it for six months," Daugherty responded. "As you must have figured out by now, a charrette is an eleventh-hour rush project—and it's eleven fifteen on the legislative count-down. We only have six weeks before the Assembly meets, and Bob wants an agreement before then. You're going to have to push the cart pretty darn fast if we are going to be ready by January one." So it was a race against time.

The goal of the charrette was simple: To reach agreement on as many controversial issues as possible. Participants in the process included representatives of state and local government, a variety of business interests, waste disposal companies, legislators, and environmental organizations. Within days, all groups had selected their delegates, twenty-five in all. Many of them were veterans of years of skirmishes, protests, and studies.

Veronica, for example, headed a powerful environmental group that had prevented a local steel plant from expanding its facilities for the past twenty years. Sam, the company's vice president for governmental relations, sat coldly next to her at our first meeting. Other participants were also wary. "There's no way we'll ever agree about anything," said the retired chemist from western Maryland. "But it's always nice to know who your enemies are." Everyone laughed, a bit nervously.

It was a daunting task. Each group at the table had a long list of priorities. Many of them conflicted with the others' lists. Some of the environmentalists wanted to outlaw incinerators; others on the same negotiating team came from communities that wanted *more* incinerators and fewer landfills. The local governments wanted less legislation and more money to enforce what they already had. And everybody wanted the Department of the Environment to do more than its budget allowed.

Before we tackled the substantive issues, we needed to prepare ourselves. At our first all-day session, everyone participated in a series of training exercises to assess our communication styles and improve our negotiation techniques. We worked through a complex theoretical environmental problem to practice our skills—the only twist being that everybody played a role that was "out of character" for them. Environmentalists took the part of big business, which in turn took the part of government, whose representatives became environmentalists. They played their parts with amazing enthusiasm and humor. The walls quietly started to come down.

By the next session, participants started to report that they were now using their new conflict resolution skills to settle neighborhood disputes and to improve their communications with difficult colleagues at work. It was at this point that we started to address the substance of the work before us.

The first step was to establish our ground rules. Listen; don't interrupt. Show respect. Confront tough issues, don't back away. Speak candidly. No talking to the press until we're done. Finally, we agreed to what was obviously an impossible guideline: All decisions and recommendations of the group would be *unanimous*. Nothing would be approved without the consent of every single person at the table.

The discussions began. Six weeks later, just before Christmas, the group issued its unanimous report, containing more than fifty separate recommendations to the Maryland General Assembly. Once committed adversaries, together these disparate groups had created a remarkable document called the Solid Waste Planning Accord, the vision of which was to make Maryland "the leader in environmentally and economically sound solid waste management by 1996." Perciasepe would appoint an advisory commission to carry the work of the Accord forward.

Bob Perciasepe had made his peace. Rather than becoming lost in a pitched battle for legislative advantage, the Accord participants had found a way to redirect their energies to building a collaborative vehicle that carried all of them where they needed to go. The press conference at the state capitol felt like a victory party. Adversaries had become colleagues. And, in many cases, friends.

LABORING TOGETHER

Collaboration among adversaries defies logic, and so warrants careful analysis. The word "collaboration" has two principal meanings. The first definition is to "labor together." We collaborate best when each of us brings something useful to the enterprise. Together, we are more competent than we are apart. Your strengths compensate for my weaknesses, and vice versa. This is the essence of teamwork.

There are five different ways in which people habitually tend to respond to conflict, based on our personality and training. These are competition, cooperation, accommodation, compromise, and collaboration. As we will see, collaboration is *qualitatively* different from the other four approaches. Although it is generally easy to collaborate with our friends and colleagues, but something we resist attempting with our adversaries, collaboration is often the most effective way to work our way through—or around—conflict.

Collaboration resolves conflict by reconstructing the way people connect with one another. It adds something or catalyzes the parties to produce something new. Unlike most forms of dispute resolution, which address *past events*, collaboration focuses on establishing the course of a *future relationship*. Collaboration is concerned with action, rather than on resolving issues or assigning blame for past events. The conflict is not so much worked out as passed by. Collaboration is the vehicle by which we can escape conflict's gravitational pull.

Collaboration, in which we are working with the other person, is usually considered to be the polar opposite of *competition*, in which we are trying to defeat him. But collaboration can include elements of competition, as well. For example, a corporate project might benefit from competition among various departments to control costs, enlist new customers, or develop the next company slogan. Competition *in the service* of collaboration can be invigorating and even fun.

Collaboration is not the same thing as *accommodation*. To accommodate means to give in, to submit. When I accommodate my adversary, I simply abandon my own needs or opinions and yield to her superior power or bombast. Accommodation is retreat. While appropriate and even necessary in certain situations (when, for example, you are completely outflanked by the other side and to resist would risk extinction), accommodation is not bilateral. The submissive person brings nothing to the party. Chances are, this makes for a boring party.

Nor is collaboration the same thing as *cooperation*—"I'll scratch your back if you scratch mine." Cooperation is often a big improvement over competition, but it has its limits. Cooperation can take the form of an exchange of equivalent values or an agreement not to get in each other's way. Most popular negotiation strategies are studies in the effective use of cooperation to manipulate others into giving us what we want, either by persuasion, opportunism, or by cleverly assessing their needs and giving them what they want. It moves things around more efficiently, and can produce consensus, but doesn't necessarily generate new resources or ideas out of the exchange.

Collaboration may involve some *compromise*, but it doesn't stop there. Compromise is a tactic of convenience in which logically justifiable outcomes are forsaken in the interest of expediency. We agree to split the difference, flip a coin, take half a loaf, or take up Solomon's offer to "cut the baby in half." It is the very arbitrariness of compromise that is its saving grace—if the outcome is arbitrary, no one really wins or loses. It allows both sides to save face. Compromise may therefore be an excellent way to preserve a collaborative relationship when there is no other way to negotiate an impasse. It involves a short-term sacrifice for a long-term gain.

Collaboration, on the other hand, implies a *relationship*, which demands much more from us than mere agreement or the surrender of dissent. Collaboration is a living, dynamic process that constantly moves forward. It is open-ended, in contrast to the closure that is the natural outcome of consensus. Collaboration is an on-going dialogue, not a final pronouncement.

There is a second, and darker, meaning to the word collaboration, which may explain partly why adversaries tend to resist the process. A "collaborator" is often one who works secretly with an enemy in order to serve private welfare at the expense of family, friends, or the national interest. Adversaries naturally are reluctant to embrace a process that makes it appear to their colleagues, clients, or constituents that they have "sold out" to the enemy.

The power of this resistance was brought home to me once when

I was asked to facilitate a large meeting of corporate executives and environmental spokespeople on the issue of racism in the siting of toxic facilities. The studies seemed to show that low-income black and Hispanic neighborhoods usually ended up with most of the waste dumps and pollution-causing industry, and various stakeholders had begun to marshall their troops into the battle lines on the issue. In the face of this controversy, I was impressed that industry was willing to sponsor what clearly would be a heated exchange.

The symposium was suddenly cancelled when several influential environmental and community leaders threatened to organize a protest of the event. "There is no way we can allow these corporate criminals to take control of the issue," I was told.

"But they want to talk, and the environmentalists they have invited are legitimate representatives who won't be compromised," I responded.

"Anyone who shows up will be blacklisted," I was informed.

For many of us, collaboration still implies weakness and unprincipled compromise. The more moralistic our position, the more we resist mingling with the enemy. Safety lies in shunning contact with the opposition, standing by the purity of our principles, condemning those who cross the lines.

What is the price we pay by refusing to consider cultivating our common ground? In this case, environmental and community advocates lost an opportunity to deliver their message to those who most needed to hear it. And so, the battle wears on.

MAKING MUSIC TOGETHER

Collaboration has a useful analog in musical composition. In music, the word *resolution* means "the passing of a dissonant chord into a consonant chord." In this sense, conflict resolution is not so much the solving of a problem as it is the art of moving competing tones towards a deeper harmony.

Anthony J. N. Judge, a polymath who heads the Union of International Associations in Brussels, expands the musical metaphor through at least seven levels of discord and harmony. At the first level, the *monotone*, there is but a single voice, drowning out or ignoring all others; the second level features *competing monotones*, with discordant values; next comes *responding tones*, which respond in some measure to one another, though still contrasting; the fourth level expresses simple *melodies*, in which various sequences of views find resonance with one another; followed by the fifth level, which expresses *harmonious chords*, which are combinations of value complexes; and then *sequences of chords*, which provide a context in which discordant values can be fully expressed. As the progression continues, each level of interaction becomes more complex, rich, and inclusive—and more fully resolves all that it contains.

When two parties reach an impasse because both are—quite legitimately, perhaps—"right," and have no way to alter their positions, collaboration provides an opening through which they can move without having to compromise important principles. Collaboration provides a musical "score" by which both melodies may play themselves out. The conflict is resolved not through the logic of one-or-the-other but through the higher integration of both.

SYNERGY

Collaboration is not only a quality of music, but also of science. A single outcome that simultaneously solves several problems is called by engineers "elegant" or even "beautiful." Life is full of elegant solutions if we take the time to search for them. This means we have to discipline ourselves to reject apparent answers that serve one side by disadvantaging the other. When the proposed resolution of a conflict manages to satisfy the needs of both sides, it commonly is called "win-win" (even though winning, by definition, has been eliminated from the equation). This is the highest attainment of cooperation.

Collaboration has the capacity to go beyond "win-win" outcomes. Collaboration is pregnant with the possibility of something more, something that could not be predicted by the arithmetic of adding the known qualities of one side to the known qualities of the other. All natural living systems have unexpressed potential; they contain more than meets the eye. When we find creative ways to integrate their energies, we are sometimes able to generate an outcome that is *synergistic*.

Synergy, like collaboration, means "to work together." But it specifically indicates that the sum is greater than its constituent parts. Synergy upends our expectations by revealing a universe in which $2 + 2 = 5$. Buckminster Fuller, synergy's greatest proponent, defined it as "behavior of whole systems unpredicted by the behavior of their parts taken separately." Synergy is how nature is always finding ways *to do more with less*.

We see this in the operation of many chemical interactions, where the properties of the combination of drugs is completely different from anything either element possessed on its own. For example, neither hydrogen nor oxygen alone could prepare us to anticipate the refreshing taste of water on a hot day.

The goal of collaboration is to create synergistic combinations. This is often possible, and even necessary, when a dispute cannot be resolved on the terms on which it has presented itself. Once all the various parts are out on the table, there may be no apparent way to rebuild the machine—except by designing an entirely different one. The puzzle with mismatched pieces gets solved by using them for a mobile.

Synergy can apply to even the most mundane disputes. Once I was asked to help settle a grievance that had arisen over unpaid engineering fees. A prominent engineer had been retained to test the soil for a proposed recreational development on Lake Michigan that required an EPA permit. When the engineer submitted his report to the EPA, the agency refused to grant a permit because the supporting test data wasn't provided by the engineer. The developer, which already owed fees to the engineer, refused to make any payments and hired another engineer to repeat the test. The permit was promptly granted. The first engineer then sued for the unpaid fees.

As I soon learned, it appeared that the first engineer had in fact compiled all the required test data but had withheld it because the developer was in arrears on payment. Settlement negotiations about a monetary resolution were going nowhere because the developer didn't want to pay for testing that didn't get him the permit. The engineer was similarly firm, having done all the requested work.

One of the axioms of conflict resolution is: "If the pie isn't big enough for everyone to get a piece, make it bigger." This particular axiom didn't accord with what little I knew of the principles of physics or baking, but I thought I would give it a try. Somewhat sheepishly—in view of the passion with which each side pointed its finger at the other—I asked the developer, "Is there any work for which you would be willing to hire the engineer, so that he could make up the difference on the next job?"

To my great surprise, the developer jumped at the idea. "Those guys are the best in the business. I would love to have them handle the second phase of the project." The case was settled for a partial payment of the disputed balance and a contract for future engineering services. The dispute had gotten in the way of the relationship. Finding a way to reestablish the relationship—enlarging the pie— caused the dispute to evaporate.

SWORDS AND PLOWSHARES

Collaboration is a source of power. Collaboration between former adversaries can release otherwise inaccessible stores of productive energy. We have seen many examples of this in our lifetime. The United States has developed strong and productive partnerships with virtually all of our former enemies—starting with Great Britain and extending to Germany, Japan, Mexico, Spain, Italy, China, North Vietnam, and Russia.

Many of the companies engaged in mergers in the 1980s and 1990s were former adversaries. Fiercely competitive American semiconductor manufacturers have managed to suspend their corporate hostilities from time to time to work closely together to develop products that could compete with their mutual adversary—the Japanese. News of an alliance between adverse companies such as

Apple Computer and IBM on product design is always exciting and ripe with opportunity.

The greater the hostility, it seems, the greater the collaborative potential. Synergy seems to nourish itself by consuming chaos. There is an instinctive human attraction to the elegance and power of synergy. No matter how strong the animosity, adversaries always carry the seeds of collaboration. No matter where we go, or how fierce the force of contradiction, the small flame of synergy continues to burn. The possibility of relationship cannot be extinguished and, whenever the storm subsides, it quietly beckons.

The possibility of synergy is easily obscured by our usual ways of resolving conflict. The legal system doesn't ask us to imagine what might be created, but only what must be destroyed. I observed this in a dispute between an agent at a large brokerage house and a client who had lost a substantial sum when an investment failed. Even though they had been friends for twenty years, litigation was pursued as if they were complete strangers—and, in fact, they soon became estranged. Their families, once very close, no longer spoke to one another, and the situation was obviously painful for everyone. The broker lost a good account and had a stain on his otherwise clean reputation. Both sides seemed trapped in the legal machine.

After several hours in mediation, we were getting close to a financial settlement that returned to the investor a reasonable portion of his funds. But something still seemed sour. There was too little satisfaction in the settlement. I asked the broker why he seemed so disappointed. "He's my friend—at least he *was*. That's what I care about. Not the money. Money doesn't take the place of friends—and we all have too few of them."

The investor sat up in his chair. He ignored his lawyer's admonition to hold his tongue and spoke up. "I never thought he did anything wrong here—it was the firm, pushing their people to peddle a lousy product. It wasn't his fault. I know that. It was just that we had to name him in the lawsuit, or so my lawyer said. I'd give anything to have things right again."

The two men went into another office, alone. Fifteen minutes later, they both emerged, smiling. The investor agreed to restore his family's accounts—worth over a million dollars—to the brokerage firm. The broker was happy, and so was the firm. With the relationship back on track, and a renewed chance for everyone to profit from it, there was a genuine reconciliation that would never have been possible in an adversarial contest.

BROKEN MERGERS AND BAD MARRIAGES

Collaboration is not always feasible, however, and there can be great risk in attempting such partnerships if it is obvious that "the marriage is doomed." When two former adversaries have no common goal or vision, any attempt to collaborate is liable to collapse if the old hostility should surface. Collaboration doesn't happen automatically or just because someone has good intentions. There needs to be a strong container to house the conflicting energies of the old enemies. Mere determination "to work together" does not guarantee a true alliance, erase mistrust, or harmonize competing values.

I observed this a number of years ago when two prominent Chicago law firms attempted a merger. One firm was quite old and respected, and largely served institutional clients such as banks and utilities. It was managed by a former governor of the state, a respected and powerful man. The other firm did very little corporate work, but had a reputation for the ruthlessness of its litigators, especially the firm's senior partner.

The cultures of the two firms clashed immediately. They had nothing in common but a fear of their own limitations. My mediation partner, Bob Crowe, an acquaintance of the former governor, inquired whether it might be useful to mediate the conflict. Perhaps a more satisfactory decision-making process might be designed, or a new compensation scheme worked out.

"Bob," said the former governor confidently, "don't worry about this. There's nothing to mediate. *We've got this guy by the balls!*"

The next week, the former governor died of a heart attack. The merger fell apart, the clients left, the firm went into bankruptcy and dissolved. The merger that was envisioned in the legal documents didn't have the power to integrate the incompatible cultures of the two firms.

Personal relationships based on impulse often are similarly disastrous. The wisdom of arranged marriages lies in the fact that parents and matchmakers usually know enough about the demands of marriage to appreciate the need for compatibility—a quality that hormones often overlook. Compatibility is based on common values, shared ambitions, and complementary characteristics. Without it, a marriage likely will be swamped by the rolling seas of life.

Maggie, the enraged wife we met in the first chapter, was not a candidate for collaboration. In her need to inflict damage, she had lost her bearings. Like many others who become motivated exclusively by their own ambitions or inner demons, Maggie lost track of her conscience. Collaboration is not possible with those who are committed to revenge or are possessed by a simple desire to hurt others. When that is unalterably the case, we must recognize things as they truly are, and respond appropriately.

When a former friend, ally, or spouse suddenly turns on us, the change can be stunning. While we often attribute destructive behavior to psychological causes, and are misled by compassion to justify or tolerate it, it is critical to know when to fight back. An overweening desire to collaborate can be a real handicap.

WHO COLLABORATES?

Especially in working with "stakeholder" groups like the Maryland Accord, the selection of participants can be vital. Dirk Ficca, an activist Presbyterian minister who heads a large interreligious organization in Chicago, divides candidates for collaboration into three groups. The first consists of *authentic collaborators*—those who recognize the value of dialogue and have a genuine interest in a process that offers mutual gain. The second group are the *opportunists*, who may be willing to participate if they think they can obtain an advantage. The third group are the *obstructionists*, who oppose collaboration and may attempt to block any move in that direction.

Dirk's advice is invite the obstructionists, but don't let them get control of the process; strengthen the hand of the collaborators, and reinforce their leadership; and give the opportunists a good reason to get involved and stay involved.

Collaboration is most likely to succeed when the right team is assembled. There is little choice about designing the team when a dispute concerns particular individuals who speak for themselves, but when the adversaries are corporations or large entities, they must decide who will represent them.

Perhaps the most important question is the representative's capacity to participate meaningfully in the discussions. Whoever comes to the table must be able to speak with authority, or the other parties will subvert or terminate the process. "Authority" is often subjective, of course. What matters is that the other side feels that this is someone they can talk to, who can make decisions or whose opinions will be respected by their superiors, and who is at the same level as they. Everyone wants to feel comfortable that the other parties are equally serious about the matter before they will put themselves at risk.

Obviously it is essential that everyone who could veto any decision of the group come to the table. Each group knows if it is complete as assembled or if someone else needs to participate for the process to work. The convener's responsibility is to ensure that she has properly constellated the necessary players so that, at the end, the group will regard its work as legitimate. This is discussed in more detail later, when we consider the dynamics of creating "the whole."

One consideration in deciding whom to invite is what might be called "the coyote factor." In Native American mythology, the coyote is held with special regard. "Coyote stories" are always rich with wisdom and humor. Coyote is the trickster, a maverick, a contrarian. Coyote is always upsetting the apple cart. He walks his own path and isn't impressed by custom or held in check by what the rest of the animals think is best. As a result, Coyote is often excluded from important councils because the others don't want him to mess things up.

So consider inviting Coyote into the collaborative process. At best, if he isn't left outside the door, he might decide to cooperate. At the worst, you'll be better prepared to see what's coming.

COMING TO THE TABLE

The first hurdle to overcome in initiating collaboration is getting all the key players to the table. But just because someone is an opportunist or even an obstructionist doesn't mean that they won't collaborate. When it comes to conflict, there are few natural collaborators among us. Most of the time, we need to see that we'll get something out of the exchange before we are willing to participate. But even those who strongly oppose a collaborative process, whether on grounds of principle or power, can be surprised by the possibility of outcomes not otherwise available to them.

Collaboration between adversaries is possible only when both sides have the capacity to undertake the process. Only a fool will attempt to collaborate with an opponent who wishes him harm and is committed to his destruction. If she desires collaboration, the adversary must first demonstrate her worthiness to engage with him at that level. Collaboration, like love, is a risky undertaking. We are wise to assess the good faith of those who would join us. Unlike cooperation, we cannot pressure or manipulate another into collaboration. The intention to collaborate must be demonstrated, and the right to collaborate must, in a sense, be earned.

There are many ways to show the good faith required to establish a basis for collaboration. In trying to convince parties to mediate, for example, the good faith of the initiating party is often demonstrated by its willingness to pay the costs of mediation. Even simple gestures will do, such as giving the opponent the "home field advantage" by agreeing to meet in her office, or by agreeing not to file a motion or not exercising a legal right. Small courtesies go a long way in a mean-spirited world.

Adversaries sometimes ask too much of one another before they consent to a collaborative—or even cooperative—process. Generally it is inappropriate to demand substantive concessions before coming to the table, although it sometimes can be difficult to gauge what "substantive" means.

Once, in trying to mediate a resolution of a hotel ownership dispute, one of the investors refused to come to the table until the other side made an unconditional opening offer of at least $12 million dollars for his interest. Since the other party claimed that the man's stake was worth no more than $1 million, they refused to come to the table and insisted that he was overreaching. When the jury later awarded the investor $17 million dollars *and* potential ownership of the entire $250 million property, I realized that "good faith" is a matter of degree.

Insisting on too much proof of the other side's authentic desire to work things out can be counterproductive. If you require the other side to make meaningful concessions just to have the chance to explore a resolution, they naturally will be less inclined to be generous when they sit down at the table. Psychologically, we have only so much leverage to use in a negotiation. It is far wiser to use that leverage when it counts, and not deplete it on purely symbolic victories.

To come to the table, each side must see that it makes sense from its own point of view. It is fair to say that it always makes sense at least to *consider* collaboration. In most cases, nothing is lost by the effort. It is always easy to return to an adversarial process if collaboration fails. The process is voluntary, so there can be no outcome unless it is agreeable to everyone. Still, it is natural that adversaries should resist doing anything that might be helpful to those they oppose. It is only when a party to a dispute becomes more committed to his own welfare than to the destruction or disadvantage of the other that collaboration can make its appeal to reason.

It can be difficult to persuade one's adversary of the logic of collaboration. Anything that seems good to one side will be regarded with suspicion by the other. Whenever possible, it is more effective to have some neutral party make the case for sitting down together. That way, nobody looks too anxious, and neither side has to deploy too many negotiation "chips" to arrange the meeting. In practice, one of a mediator's principal functions is to convene the negotiations, overcoming each party's concerns without requiring the others to make concessions that would unfairly upset the balance.

This is not always easy. When one of my mediation partners, David Ferguson, was engaged in his own dispute, he came to realize how powerful is the human tendency to refuse to collaborate with the enemy. After Dave purchased his first house, he became embroiled in a heated dispute with his landlady over the return of his security deposit from his rented home.

He stormed into the office right after he filed suit against his landlady in small claims court. "She'll be a little more gracious when she discovers that she has to pay triple damages for keeping my money," Dave huffed.

Our other partner, Bob Crowe, smiled at Dave. "Do you think you might want to mediate this, Dave?"

Dave glowered. "To be honest, Bob, I would have to be convinced. I just can't imagine that she would ever be reasonable, so I don't think there would be much point in it."

So even the mediator wouldn't mediate. If someone as reasonable as Dave could resist the very process at which he was so adept, then it is clear to me that collaboration among adversaries may never arise on its own. Somebody must first give us a reason to put down the swords. Only then can we imagine other uses for the metal.

THE KEYS TO COLLABORATION

Collaboration does not just happen by itself. Three elements seem to be required before a vague willingness to cooperate can mature into a genuine joint enterprise. The first, *establishing a common vision*, provides the motivation and the context for engaging in collaboration. The second element is the *balancing of power*, which assures that each player has the resources to contribute to the common vision while realizing individual objectives. The third ingredient is the mechanism by which adversaries are able to calculate their moves and countermoves in a collaborative enterprise: *relational thinking*.

THE FIRST KEY: VISION ◆

Collaboration can be enormously challenging when former adversaries are involved. It requires that they reconceptualize themselves, their relationship to one another, and the nature and purpose of their actions. To accomplish this shift, they must adopt a way of perceiving their world that focuses on a shared horizon. That is, they must learn to *see together*.

TOWARD A COMMON GOAL, AGAINST A COMMON ENEMY

As we discussed earlier, vision means *starting with the destination in mind*. Collaboration puts us on a different course by plotting a new goal, one that is interdependent rather than mutually exclusive. This interdependent vision therefore must be one that requires, for its realization, what each party has to offer. It must be sufficiently challenging, urgent, and compelling to redirect the parties' aggressive energies away from each other and toward some mutually beneficial outcome.

If a proposed collaborative arrangement serves one party, but not the other, it is not collaborative—but merely exploitative. If I am sufficiently persuasive, I may succeed in convincing you to *cooperate* in a venture that helps me and not you, but this is not collaboration. Collaboration requires self-interest. If it does not further the agenda of both sides, it is as likely to fly as a bird with one wing.

For example, establishing a common vision is the first stage in mediating a divorce. It shifts the parties' attention to the future, about which they have something to say, and away from the past, about which everything has been said. The mediator might ask: What do you most want to achieve through this process? What do you want your lives to be like when we are finished? How would you describe the next chapter of your life story? In an ideal world, how would you like to see this come out?

Vision is not something that is manufactured. The artist describes it as *given*, as by a muse, not as the product of training or planning or calculation. The inventor discovers it. The mystic is pursued by it. Vision is what is *true*, existing apart from and free of the constraints of the mundane world.

Michelangelo was reported to have described the process of sculpting as making apparent that which lay concealed in marble, invisible to other eyes: "The statue is already there. I simply clear away the debris which obscures it from view."

Finding a common vision, then, is a matter of ascertaining a pre-existing but unobserved truth about shared aspirations. Like the artist, we only have our intuition to tell us if what we find there is either true or not. If it is false or contrived, we either have not arrived or have failed to recognize what is there. There is no real resolution that is false or forced. Like the artist, we must be faithful to the vision and follow it until it finally reveals itself.

On the other hand, many collaborations of convenience have their origins not in aspiration but in a shared animosity towards some person, entity, or principle. As a mediator and facilitator, I have noticed that when parties begin to regard me as their common adversary—because they object to the rules, the accommodations, or the lack of progress—they start to work more effectively with each other. Shared animosity is a powerful binding agent.

We see this every day. The common enemy of abortion has created common ground among various religious communities that historically have opposed and even fought one another—the Catholic church, fundamentalist Christians, Orthodox Jews, and Shiite Muslims. The common enemy of white bigotry built a powerful civil rights alliance between African-Americans and Jews. British imperialism unified the original thirteen colonies.

Such unions may not sustain themselves for long unless a common vision or positive purpose ultimately emerges. Collaboration based on animosity toward a common enemy lasts only so long as the enemy threatens, and therefore is usually temporary. The aphorism that "politics makes strange bedfellows" refers to the casual fling, rather than a more permanent alliance. Nevertheless, the appearance of a common enemy against which hostile energies can be targeted is often the only effective way to redirect a conflict.

This is apparent in multi-party disputes. When a single plaintiff has sued a number of defendants, they often will expend as much time and money in attacking one another as they do in defending themselves from the charges made by the plaintiff. Ironically, co-defendants are often more aggressive in pursuing their internal differences than they are in dealing with the plaintiff. Until some defendant steps forward to remind the others that the real threat comes from the plaintiff, and to organize a joint response, the defendants can become consumed by desperate attempts to blame one another for the problem. This just makes the plaintiff's case stronger against all of them.

Once the common enemy no longer binds them together, old grievances among temporary allies may reappear. When collaboration is premised on shared hostility, the conflicts among the collaborators are temporarily submerged. The marriage is one born of convenience, not abiding love. Without a common vision, collaboration against a common enemy does not usually require the parties to work out their differences. All that is needed is an agreement to act as if their own dispute, for the moment, does not exist. The differences remain and may sink the enterprise when the common enemy is vanquished or disappears.

It is very difficult to achieve a common vision without taking a hard look at our divisions, because those differences so obviously have the power to impede the vision from becoming a reality. The differences cannot just be put aside; they must be *overcome*. The vision becomes a template against which our conflicts begin to lose their authority to define our relationship, and a crucible in which they can be transformed.

A shared vision is a more lasting premise for collaboration than is the threat of a common enemy because its lifespan is not dependent on the behavior of some third person. If the vision is large enough and flexible enough, the collaboration can continue indefinitely.

A collaborative vision has three essential qualities. First, it *emerges* from the authentic interchange of the parties themselves, and is not grafted onto them from the outside. Second, it reveals a large enough *perspective* that everyone can find a place in it, and is inspired by the possibilities. Third, it gives *direction* to the enterprise as a whole, and cannot be realized without full participation.

Emergent Vision

One of the most difficult jobs a facilitator or mediator faces is getting the parties to articulate their own sense of purpose. One of the conveniences of conflict is that it provides a sense of direction—toward or against wherever the adversary happens to be. But a shared vision cannot be dependent on merely reacting to one another. So we must ask ourselves what we might have in common that could carry us away from the eddying waters in which we have been swirling.

This is hard work. At first, no commonalities will come to mind. Then, slowly, little possibilities will begin to come to the fore, but perhaps they lack the flash to attract much notice. Then something completely grandiose that is beyond the pale will have to be considered and rejected. For every good idea, ten bad ones will be suggested. It is a messy, nonlinear, and often frustrating exercise. Tempers flare. The parties start to get agitated with the facilitator for not giving better instructions. "How should I know?" they indignantly complain. "You're the expert, *aren't you?*"

But this labor involves perspiration. The parties have to sweat it out. It is essential that the facilitator, even if he sees exactly what they are trying to say, let the parties struggle to find the words. When they do, they will own them and guard them with their lives. If he supplies the answer, they will disregard it the same way we all ignore advice offered too freely. The leadership of the facilitator means seeing but not saying.

The job of the facilitator is to stand for the possibility of a vision that resolves the competing claims. All that the facilitator—no matter who plays that role—needs to do is affirm that there is such an answer, no matter how hard it is to find it. If the parties become stuck, it may be useful to suggest that there are many potential answers that are equally valid. If they need to focus their attention on problem-solving rather than on bargaining, then the facilitator may assert that there is *only one* truly right answer, at this moment, with these particular people. But the facilitator should not impose his own answer. When it comes to their own vision, the parties must be the experts.

Professor Steve Goldberg, who teaches negotiation and alternative dispute resolution at Northwestern University Law School, and has co-authored a popular textbook in the field, once described to me the importance of this principle. Steve often is appointed to mediate complex lawsuits. What applies to mediation, which is a form of collaboration, also applies to any kind of collaborative experience.

The first case I was assigned was totally outside my field of expertise, so I had to tell the lawyers honestly that I had no idea how it would come out if it went to trial. To my surprise, the case settled easily anyway. The second case was in an area with which I was familiar, so I started to argue a bit with the lawyers about how the law would go. This case was a little tougher, but we settled it. The third case fell right into the particular area of the law where I had my expertise, and I thought—Oh boy, I'll really be able to be useful on this one. The case never settled. So I concluded, the less I know, the better. Let the parties be "right"

*and have all the opinions. My job was to get them to a settlement
that* they *wanted—not one I thought made sense for them.*

Any party, even someone who seems peripheral to the controversy, can plant the flag of confidence that will allow the process of
resolution to unfold. Vision creates *possibility.* As long as the parties
believe that it is possible to reach a settlement, or to design a
common enterprise, or to solve a difficult problem, and are given a
context for finding it, they almost certainly will. A common vision
creates hope. Most conflict lingers because the parties have become
discouraged, not because they actually can't solve it.

Simple encouragement is surprisingly effective. One of my favorite mediation techniques when things have become particularly
hopeless is to smile broadly and declare, "We're really making progress now!" Either the parties think that I know some secret about
conflict—that it really *must* be true that "it always gets darkest
before the dawn"—or they laugh at the absurdity of the remark. In
either event, things lighten up enough for a breakthrough.

Perspective: The Big Picture

The role of vision is to move the parties into a new form of relationship that makes their conflict seem less pivotal than it once was.
Imagine a battle between feudal armies inside the castle walls. Dust,
smoke, and panic reduce visibility to a few feet. But from the walls
and the watch tower, one can see the surrounding rolling hills and
the lush farm lands—and maybe the advance of reinforcements.

Vision takes us to higher ground, and therefore provides *perspective.* Vision lifts up, inspires, attracts, and holds our attention. As our
perspective changes, so also does our motivation. From the vantage
point of collaboration, when we can see what is possible just beyond, conflict just doesn't seem so appealing. Vision built great
cathedrals that soared over the thatched roofs of medieval villages
and vision sent us to the moon in the midst of the Cold War. We can
see more clearly from a distance. Our best information about deep
deposits of minerals and fossil fuels comes from satellite data and

high-altitude fly-overs. We are best able to comprehend our conflicts when we observe them from above, rather than from below.

Leadership rests primarily in the capacity to provide this perspective. Leaders *envision*. The Book of Proverbs tells us that "without a vision the people perish." Without a common vision, people are drawn apart by their private fears and myopia. The leader is one who sees what is possible, who sees around corners by looking over walls. The visionary in conflict resolution is the person who most clearly sees the need to bring matters to a dignified and expeditious conclusion. It has little to do with the image we normally have of leaders as powerful or important. In fact, the visionary who sees the path to resolution is typically humble and even anonymous.

The Nobel Peace Prize was awarded in 1994 to *Chairman* Yasir Arafat, *Foreign Minister* Shimon Peres, and *Prime Minister* Yitzhak Rabin, but it was the quiet vision of a group of selfless Norwegians who made the miracle possible. Likewise, a minor defendant in a complex lawsuit, whose legal bills may exceed her potential liability, can be an effective catalyst by calling a meeting of all the other defendants to plan a settlement strategy. Friends, relatives, and colleagues can play a similar role. Even though it may be dangerous to become entangled in the conflict itself, quiet invitations to "see things differently" can be remarkably effective.

We often are energized and even inspired by the view from higher altitudes, where the air is crisp and the light is clear. Given the chance, most people *want* to do better. Finding a vision with perspective allows us to see how we might.

Getting Direction

A vision should not only emerge from the players and inspire them, but it must give them a clear sense of direction.

This can be achieved either by agreeing to a particular process—"we will submit the matter to an arbitrator if we can't decide it ourselves by four-thirty P.M."—or by describing an outcome with such particularity that it is only the steps along the way that must be identified. An example of this might be, "We will divide the assets of our business in such a way that both of us will be able to cover our overhead costs without borrowing money from the bank."

In a sense, when the vision adequately defines a direction for the discussions, the rest is details. Each potential element of an agreement can be measured against the directional standard to see whether it furthers our journey or not.

In the Maryland charrette, it became obvious on the first morning of our negotiations that we required a clear and powerful vision statement if discussions were to proceed. The need for a vision became obvious after each group described the "wish list" it had developed; the litany of controversies was mind-boggling. There was no common ground. Everything was up for grabs.

Creating a mission statement is not easy. It should capture, in a sentence or two, the essence of the group's shared aspiration. A mission statement should be big enough that it requires everyone to operate at or beyond the limits of their ability yet definite enough that, at any time, they can determine whether they are on course. The classic example of a mission statement is President Kennedy's mandate to "put a man on the moon before the end of the decade." It demanded the best from everyone. They didn't know how they would do it, but they knew that they had to function at the very top of their game if they were to have a chance to succeed.

Moving at break-neck speed, the Maryland group found their vision in an intense four-hour session. They drafted a mission statement that committed them to making Maryland "the leading state in environmentally and economically sound solid waste management" within two years. The light of that single sentence would illuminate every dispute that arose in our discussions. They committed themselves to taking whatever action was required to make it happen.

They wrestled with tough controversies like incineration of hazardous wastes and the siting of landfills. They argued and bargained and fought over words and principles. In every case, the final arbiter was the mission statement they drafted on the first day. Even before they could see where they were going, they had the vision to guide their steps.

THE SECOND KEY: BALANCED POWER

Using collaboration as a way to resolve conflict obviously implies a very different attitude about *power*. Most forms of conflict resolution involve the use of *power over* other people. Collaborative conflict resolution requires power as well, but it is *power to*, rather than power over. This means that power must be balanced among the players so that all parties can employ it to play their part in achieving the common vision they have designed.

STATIC AND DYNAMIC POWER

There are two basic ways to employ power when confronted by conflict. These might be called the *static* and *dynamic* models. The static model is coercive—it relies on force. It is adversarial, dualistic, and exclusive. If you have sufficient power, you will be tempted to adopt a static application of power, through which you may hope to extinguish, marginalize, or repress the person or system that is causing so much difficulty. This approach includes homicide, capital punishment, court injunctions, and warfare.

But why shouldn't we impose our will on others, if we have the chance? In a dog-eat-dog world, isn't it naive to believe that things will work out better if we are *nice*, and share our things? Why should we collaborate? After mastering life's educational, professional, and commercial obstacle course that brought us to positions of influence and authority, doesn't the law of "survival of the fittest" compel us to employ such power as comes our way?

The answer would only be in the affirmative if there were some relation between power and wisdom. The fact of the matter is that having power doesn't mean we understand its best use from the perspective of the overall system. The premise of collaboration is that two heads—even if they tend to butt into one another—are better than one.

When I was a young lawyer, I was involved in a complex and high-stakes lawsuit involving the development of new technology. As we waited for the jury to deliberate, a settlement meeting was convened. Wasn't there some way for the competing companies to enter a joint venture, by which both of them would profit?

The technical people found a way to work together, and the corporate people thought it was a good idea, but the decision-makers were so invested in winning the case that the proposed joint venture never had a chance. The case went to the Supreme Court twice, and both companies lost their "window of opportunity" while other competitors took the market away from them. Each side sought to use the courts to get power over each other. Only through collaboration could they have remained competitive, but the passions of litigation were irresistible.

When power is employed inclusively, it is *dynamic*. Something develops, emerges, happens. Dynamic power seeks to make the best use of all resources in the interest of the system as a whole. In this sense, the dynamic application of power is geared toward the future. It wants to go somewhere. Power is how it gets there. It focuses on the doing of something, rather than on the undoing of someone else. Collaboration requires a dynamic and inclusive use of power.

It is important to recognize that people, too, are dynamic. There may be an imbalance of power in the first stages of a conflict, but collaboration literally cannot proceed until power is brought into equilibrium. Sometimes the players have to change for this to occur—by learning to be more assertive, by strengthening their position, or by developing a more effective strategy—and sometimes the process itself must adjust.

The adage that information is power is especially true in collaboration. When one side has greater access to information than the other at the outset, this can be rectified by compelling its disclosure or by conditioning the process on information acquired by a third party who has been selected to investigate the facts on behalf of all.

Because collaboration is voluntary, the ultimate leveling mechanism is the fact that decisions cannot be imposed. In the Maryland Accord, for example, power was quickly balanced by agreeing that all decisions had to be unanimous. Everyone had the right to veto the decision of the majority.

ABSTAINING FROM THE EXERCISE OF POWER

It sometimes is necessary to *not use our power* in order to initiate or sustain collaboration. Choosing not to use power to impose our will on others is one of the most difficult challenges a human being can face. We instinctually pursue power (money, celebrity, success, influence) and are trained in its use by nearly everyone around us— parents, teachers (and the principal!), mentors, employers, competitors, spouses, and children—and almost never question it when we bring power to bear to create an advantage for ourselves. Forbearance is practically grounds for canonization or institutionalization.

A dispute of my own showed me the remarkable power of such forbearance. Although I had some background in trademark law, I didn't check the records very carefully many years ago when I co-founded a mediation firm called "Resolve." As it happened, another mediation firm in a different part of the country had registered the same trade name and planned to make use of it. Eventually, we found out about one another and, being mediators, decided to meet and see if something might be worked out.

My counterpart was flanked by the general counsel of the large organization of which she was part and by their trademark attorney. I asked her what she would like to have happen from our meeting. "It's really quite simple. We own the mark and registered it. You are infringing. We want you to stop using it, and would be happy to allow you enough time to exhaust your current supplies of letterhead and notify your clients."

For the next two hours, I pointed out that while there might be a technical infringement, it didn't matter. Our clients would never mistake us for one another; my own firm had been in business for years and had been actively using the name long before her group decided to adopt it as their corporate name. There was no loss of business, no confusion, and no reason to enforce the trademark. We would be happy to acknowledge their ownership and sign a license agreement at a nominal charge.

Nothing seemed to move her from her decision to enforce the

trademark, which would involve expensive and somewhat embarrassing litigation for two firms that prospered by keeping clients out of court.

Finally, I looked directly in her eyes. We were both uncomfortable and anxious. "Look, you can sue me, and you might well win. You have the upper hand. I think I can keep you from getting any money from us, but you probably could get an injunction. You have the power. But why use it? It won't get you any clients or protect you from losing any you already have. It will be a pointless victory— it will harm my business if I have to change our name, and it won't help yours at all. I can think of better ways to spend fifty thousand dollars than to litigate an interesting legal dispute."

To my surprise, not only did she decide not to insist on enforcing the trademark but she even invited us to serve on a mediation panel her firm was assembling to handle a government contract. Needless to say, we didn't use our firm name when we were listed!

Why did she decide not to exercise her legal rights? Because, I think, my friend recognized that forbearance from coercion might just create an opportunity that static uses of power rarely afford. She wanted to take things to the edge, where she could make choices that were not automatic or self-defeating. She sensed a chance to change how adversaries relate, and she took it.

Bob Perciasepe made the same choice when he decided to convene a meeting of all the stakeholders in the Maryland environmental controversies to create solid waste policy. He could have issued regulations, followed his own enforcement priorities, and opposed any legislation he didn't like. But he set aside his own static power options and invited everyone to engage in the exercise of dynamic power.

THE THIRD KEY: RELATIONAL THINKING ◆

Collaboration is not a matter of simple arithmetic, in which one and one make two. On a good day, cooperation will allow each of us to use the other to get what we want, but collaboration expects more of us. It pushes us beyond our private aspirations to a larger vision. In collaboration, one and one make three—or four—because collaboration is synergistic.

Most of the time, and especially when we are involved in a conflict, we tend to think of ourselves as the center of our own little universe. In fact, one of the major attractions of conflict is that it is so easy to justify the extreme self-concern it generates. When we are under attack, we can lavish attention on ourselves, our predicament, the ways we are victimized and disadvantaged. Who could argue with that?

Collaboration is seldom possible when people are thinking only about their own needs. Collaboration may involve sacrifice and putting the interests of the group ahead of my own. It is precisely because collaboration redirects our attention to "that something out there" that we can stop thinking about ourselves, and our problems, for a moment. Collaboration is life's way of telling us to wake up and smell the coffee.

What might be called *relational thinking* is the mental discipline through which we begin to see ourselves in relation to others, as part of the whole, not apart from it. Without losing our sense of individuality and without forgetting our goals, we learn to pay attention to the needs of others as a way to further our common purpose.

Relational thinking requires us simultaneously to observe three different "fields of influence"—ourselves, other players, and the overall system of which we are part. That is, we need both to stand our ground and to find common ground.

STAND YOUR GROUND

Standing our own ground is not easy, even in the course of collaboration. It requires that we know ourselves. If two parties have been in a long-term relationship and are now engaged in a conflict, they may have strong feelings, and a clear intention to dominate the other, but that doesn't mean they know what they want for themselves.

To think for yourself means to disengage from thinking about the other's reaction to your goals. That requires that we stop thinking either *on behalf of* the other ("I suppose I would like to keep the place in the country, but he would *never* go along with that . . .") or *against* each other ("I just want to make sure that he suffers for the next ten years . . ."). Instead, we must think *for ourselves*.

The kinds of questions we can ask ourselves at this stage might include: What exactly do I want? Why do I want it? What will I get? What do I have to give? What am I willing to do to get what I want? What will I refuse to do? Who have I been in the past in relation to this issue? In what ways am I willing to change in order to achieve my goals? Who do I want to be when this is over? In what ways am I open to influence from others? In what ways do I resist being influenced?

In constructing the Maryland Accord, each participant spent time meeting with other members of his "affinity group"—citizen activists, business interests, local government, and the like—before the group met as a whole. At these small caucuses, each affinity group mapped the full range of possible outcomes and narrowed their objectives down to a manageable size. The environmentalists began with a list of over two hundred issues, which they ultimately organized into seven categories of concerns. By the time the entire group sat down together, everyone knew where they stood and how far they might be willing to move.

FINDING OUT WHERE THE OTHER SIDE STANDS

Once we know ourselves, we must examine our information and attitudes about the other person. In a competitive process, our information about the other is usually limited to her weaknesses or vulnerabilities. We don't want to know about her strengths or virtues, since that would cloud the issue and might soften our resolve.

But collaboration requires that we fully and accurately assess the other and his gifts, as well as his shortcomings. We look for openings rather than reasons to remain outside. The purpose of our examination is to comprehend the qualities and interests of the other so that we can determine how they relate to our own character and goals. The point isn't to ignore those features that make him our adversary but to recognize ways in which, under the right circumstances, he might become an ally.

Ignorance of the other side's goals and aspirations is one of the great barriers to settling disputes. It isn't simply a matter of not knowing what these are, but of not even *wondering* what they are. Adversaries can become so involved in their own drama that they don't stop to ask themselves about the motivations of the person who is putting so much effort into vanquishing them.

Once we decide to understand our opponent, there are many questions we might ask ourselves. What offends me about my adversary? What do I admire? In what ways is she a worthy adversary? What about her do I envy? What do I fear? In other circumstances, how might we complement one another? What motivates her against me? What kinds of behavior influences her to change? Do I know how far she might be willing to change? In what ways is she resistant to change? Do I really understand what she wants? Is there some way to find out what she wants? What is her bottom line? What does she think I want? How far does she think I'll go to work this out?

Not only are the answers to these questions the most important that adversaries *can* possess but, in all probability, it is information that they do, in fact, possess. One of the paradoxical qualities of conflict is that it often brings us so close we can read each other's minds.

This anomaly is particularly obvious in disputes that deal strictly with money. The operative question is, "What is the other side's bottom line? What do they really need to have to settle the case, rather than go to trial?"

Negotiation then becomes a process of testing out one's assumptions about the other person's position by making moves that will induce the other to reveal his true position. Once one is confident that the other person has gone as far as he can go, short of a jury verdict, it is easy to decide whether to take it to trial or to settle. In most cases, if you truly have managed to bring the adversary to his bottom-dollar position, shorn of bluff and bravado, reaching a settlement is probably imminent.

Relational thinking allows us to discern where the other side stands so that we can decide if we are willing to stand with them. It's like testing a rope to see if we can rely on it to rappel down the mountain. If we know ourselves, where we want to go, and where our adversary is headed, making that decision becomes easy.

STANDING WITH THE WHOLE

Even if we know ourselves and our adversary, it is our relation to the whole of which we are part that creates synergy. Synergy implies "something more." When we operate in relation to something that is greater than our conflict, we discover that new possibilities can emerge.

Breaking away from our fascination with ourselves and even our concern with our competitor frustrates the ego and therefore is not easily achieved. For this reason, coaches who are able to convince talented and competitive superstars to work together are considered geniuses. They literally train their players to evolve beyond their own egos. Chicago Bulls coach Phil Jackson describes the successful application of this kind of group consciousness to encourage "selfless" championship basketball in his best-selling book *Sacred Hoops*.

When we are fragmented by conflict, we often are connected only by our *lowest common denominator*. We resort to the same kind of infantile threats, economic pressure, name-calling, demonizing, violence. In our powerlessness, we turn to anything that might make us feel in control. But this is not who we want to be. Conflict keeps us from expressing what is great in us, except when we believe that greatness can be achieved at the expense of another.

We enter into relationship with the larger system by identifying, instead, our *highest common denominator*. When we operate from the highest common denominator, we are able to engage in conduct that is dignified and even generous. It restores our higher senses and raises us to our former height.

When divorcing parents are able to focus on issues like "the best interests of the children," they can put the disputes about custody into perspective. When labor and management recognize that both sides have an interest in the survival of the company, negotiations about working conditions can proceed in a greater spirit of cooperation. When politicians feel a sense of responsibility for future generations, they can take a harder look at their legislative priorities.

THE TAO OF COLLABORATION

Collaboration requires, then, that we proceed in full awareness of ourselves, the other, and the whole. In addition, we must track the effect of each element upon the other. Even as we engage, our attention should monitor the consequences of our own actions on the condition of the other and the whole; the impact on the whole and ourselves of the other's behavior; and the demands made on us both by the whole. By taking action only within this relational matrix, we are assured of evolving toward the best possible outcome without sacrificing integrity.

As we consciously observe the relational matrix, a path will emerge for us to follow. It is not our path, or the path of the other, or even the path of the whole as we have imagined it in isolation. Chinese sage Lao-tzu called this mysterious and unfolding road map the Tao, or the Way:

> *The Tao in Nature*
> *Does not contend,*
> *yet skillfully triumphs.*
> *Does not speak,*
> *yet skillfully responds.*
> *Does not summon,*
> *and yet attracts.*
> *Does not hasten,*
> *yet skillfully designs.*
> *Nature's network is vast, so vast.*
> *Its mesh is coarse, yet nothing slips through.*

MEDIATION:
Impasse and the Third Force

> *Block the passages.*
> *Close the door.*
> *Blunt the sharpness.*
> *Untie the tangles.*
> *Harmonize the brightness.*
>
> **Tao Te Ching**

THE PARALYSIS OF POLARITY

So far, we have considered four different strategies for managing our own conflicts toward resolution. But there are times when we can't do it alone. These are the times of impasse, when, as they say, the faster we go, the behinder we get. Like spent boxers in the fourteenth round, we can do little but cling to one another to keep from falling down. Each action brings an opposite and equal *re*action, resulting in complete *in*action.

Impasse is perfectly normal. Opposing forces have a natural tendency to neutralize one another when neither side has a clear advantage. Sometimes the drift of systems toward homeostasis restores enough stability so the players can catch their breath and settle on a useful resolution, but often it simply results in a standoff that forecloses any possibility of progress.

It is at such times of paralysis and frustration that disputants will generally first consider engaging the services of a mediator, whether from the United Nations, the Jimmy Carter Center in Atlanta, a local volunteer mediation service, or a firm of professional intermediaries. They want someone to break the logjam so that negotiations can get under way or back on track. Bringing in a "third person" to move the matter toward resolution has now become commonplace.

THE THIRD FORCE

There are many kinds of intermediaries that might be brought into a dispute. The President might meet with union leaders and management and threaten to enact emergency legislation if an agreement is not reached. A trusted lawyer or accountant might be asked to sort out a dispute between two investors in a close corporation. A battalion of armed United Nations Peacekeepers might be deployed to monitor troop movements on both sides of a border. These each are an embodiment of what might be called the Third Force.

The Third Force is the power of a "non-engaged" person to catalyze changes to a static or chaotic system. Its influence is greatest at the very center of two opposing forces. This is the field of greatest turbulence, as well as the richest array of possibilities. The Third Force can turn the tide of conflict because it occupies a place at the fulcrum, where the greatest leverage can be exerted with the lightest touch.

There is an old Sufi story that a master and his followers came upon a village in which the local residents were engaged in a skirmish with government soldiers. "Master," said one of the devotees, "shouldn't we help out here?"

"Oh, yes!" said the master.

"But tell us, Master—which side should we help?"

The Master smiled. "Both!" he said.

Bill Ury of the Harvard Negotiation Project speaks about a medieval Chinese equalizer named Mu Tzu, a great general who was famous for his interventions. When two neighboring warlords

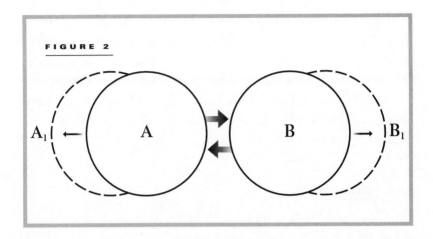

FIGURE 2

would prepare for battle, Mu Tzu would ask both sides if he might help them work out their differences. If either side refused his assistance, he would ally his own private army with the other side until matters were brought to a standstill. Then he would again ask if it was time to work out a peaceful resolution.

The presence of a mediator—whether it's your uncle, a therapist, or Jimmy Carter—can help resolve an impasse even if he does nothing more than ask each side to explain its position to him. When a third person is involved in a conversation, the dynamics of the system are radically altered. It's simply a matter of conflict resolution "physics."

When there are only two players, as shown in Figure 2, each side pushes the other as hard as possible in an effort to achieve a dominant position. This increases and reinforces the polarity: they move farther and farther away from one another. The aggressive force of either party distances the other, who both retreats to avoid the impact of that force while attempting to dislodge the aggressing party.

When both parties address a third party, however, their presentations carry a much less aggressive charge. They do not attempt to use their words to intimidate the neutral party (which probably would be counterproductive) but to win his empathy and support. Emotional displays in such circumstances serve less to dominate than to demonstrate righteousness.

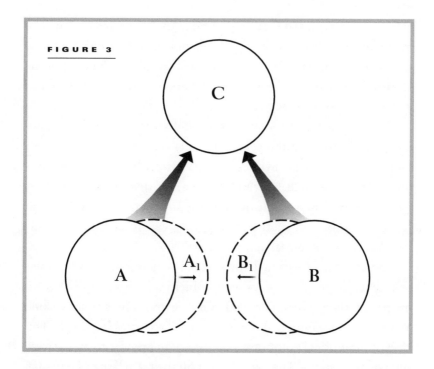

FIGURE 3

This dynamic shift also takes the heat off the opposing party, who now is free to witness the exchange from the vantage point of the spectator, rather than as target. This makes it possible to actually listen to what the other side is saying without having to erect a defensive barricade to deflect the assault.

As shown in Figure 3, this process of "triangulation" redirects the parties' attention toward the middle ground, where their positions may ultimately intersect. The flow of energy towards the neutral third party at the center cannot but have an impact on each side's direction and momentum.

MEDIATION IS THE MESSAGE

The most popular and effective form of Third Force intervention is mediation. A mediator is an impartial person, acceptable to both sides, who is without any authority or power to govern the outcome. The task of the mediator is to structure communications between the parties so that they come to their own agreement. The mediator should be free of any agenda or preconception about how the matter should be resolved, or he will risk losing the trust of the parties. The mediator must be fair and open, a good listener, and an imaginative problem-solver.

The very fact that the mediator—unlike an arbitrator—cannot impose a decision on the parties actually reinforces the mediator's usefulness. It reduces the parties' need to overdramatize their positions (since the mediator can't make a decision anyway), so they tend to become more realistic and honest when they describe their contentions. In a mediation, the parties can relax, and gradually they become less formal and positional.

The absence of external authority also communicates the message that the power to solve the problem resides exclusively with the parties themselves. The mediator's powerlessness creates a kind of leadership vacuum that demands that the parties step forth. This kind of intentional emptiness has the unique power to evoke fresh and creative energy. The parties must fill the breach that the mediator has now opened by his refusal to take responsibility for the outcome or to rescue them from their dilemma. The mediator is like the host of a dinner party. He can prepare the meal and set the table, but it is the guests who must carry the conversation if the party is to succeed.

If the mediator has no authority, then what makes the process so effective? Mediation is powerful precisely because it ordinarily employs *all four* strategies that have already been described earlier— containment, confrontation, compassion, and collaboration. The mediator is like a stage manager who ensures that each approach makes its appearance when it is most useful.

Having already described the elements of each strategy, we should now consider how mediation can be used as a framework by which they can be orchestrated. The settlement of a series of lawsuits that arose from a tragic medical error is a good illustration of the process.

ABOVE ALL, DO NO HARM

At age forty-three, Linda Hardy was a successful and well-liked communications manager at a large corporation based in the South. Energetic and attractive, Linda balanced the demands of her job with an active social life. She and her husband, Ray, had chosen to pursue high-level careers rather than raise children, and their life together was rich and intimate. Together they found time for tennis, hiking, and even bare-boat sailing in the Caribbean.

It was during a routine visit to her doctor that a mass was found in Linda's left breast. A mammogram confirmed Linda's worst fear. Cancer. The world seemed to stop when she heard the word. Cancer. Her mother and her sister had both died from breast cancer. Couldn't be. Not this soon. Please God.

Linda looked in the mirror. She had always been proud of her gentle Southern beauty and her healthy, tan body. Linda promised herself that she would save her breast, if at all possible. Her sister had undergone a radical mastectomy a few years earlier, but Linda couldn't imagine living with such a terrible deformity. Ray would try to be understanding, of course, but what if he wasn't that strong? What would happen to them if Ray no longer desired her? She couldn't bear to lose him, to have him turn away in disgust, no matter how well he concealed it.

The shock of the bad news was lightened considerably when the doctors informed Linda that she was an excellent candidate for breast conservation surgery, and that a radical mastectomy would not be required. Some radiation therapy would be needed after the surgery, of course, but the breast itself could be saved. Linda and Ray could easily live with a scar. She breathed a sigh of relief.

The surgery went well. The cancer had not gotten into the lymph nodes, and the prognosis was excellent. Linda and Ray celebrated with champagne. She never liked champagne, but this time it tasted sweet as life itself.

The radiation therapy, she was told, would be a breeze. She would receive a radiation dosage of 6,000 rads over a twenty-five-day period. There would be no shrinkage or toughening of the breast from the treatment, which would be administered with pinpoint accuracy by the hospital's brand-new linear accelerator.

After two weeks of radiation, Linda began to experience severe pain and swelling in her left breast, which had also become quite red. The doctors prescribed skin cream and remeasured her to make sure that she was getting the proper dosage. They assured her that the swelling and redness would disappear once the treatment was finished, and continued to administer the prescribed radiation dosage to its conclusion.

A little more than a month later, after repeated complaints from patients and oncologists about discomfort and redness after radiation, the hospital physicist recalibrated the linear accelerator. To his horror, he discovered that he had misread the instructions in the manual, and had re-entered a series of computer instructions that already had been preprogrammed. As a result, some twenty-five patients had received excessive radiation over a six-month period. Linda Hardy was among those who had received the highest exposure.

Linda's pain continued to worsen. A month after radiation treatment was concluded, she learned from her physician that instead of the prescribed dosage of 6,000 rads she had received more than 9,600 rads. The incision site from the surgery, which got a more concentrated dose, received over 11,000 rads.

The effects of radiation are not entirely known or predictable. Hiroshima, Nagasaki, and Chernobyl have provided a great deal of data about the kinds of deterioration that can follow excessive radiation, but each patient would have to be carefully monitored to track the symptoms.

In accordance with the strong ethic of accountability established by the hospital's board, the administration took full and immediate responsibility for the error. The head of the oncology department contacted all the other patients who had been treated on the accelerator and met with each patient personally. Although lawsuits were filed by a number of women, the hospital promptly admitted liability in a court filing and instructed its lawyers to make generous settlement offers.

The minor cases were easy to settle, since many of the patients had not received dangerous levels of radiation and probably would never experience any symptoms. But the parties were unable to reach a settlement in the four most serious cases. Among the other side effects of the radiation were a deep sense of rage and resentment, and these plaintiffs seemed determined to take the hospital through a series of costly and bitter trials.

This was not a risk the hospital wanted to assume. Acknowledged as the leading medical facility in the state, St. Luke's was still subject to all the financial pressures of the increasingly competitive health-care industry. Preparing for trial would be a drain on its resources, and the director of the oncology department would have no time for working with his patients or the physicians and nurses on staff. Trial would mean a barrage of negative publicity that it didn't need just now. The hospital's risk manager suggested they consider mediation.

CONTAINMENT AND CONFRONTATION

We scheduled two separate sessions. At each meeting, I would work with two plaintiffs and their lawyers, as well as with the hospital's lawyer, risk manager, and claims representative. My fees would be shared equally by all the parties, and everything we discussed would be confidential.

The confidentiality agreement provided assurance to both sides that it would be safe to speak candidly about the case and to recognize the limitations of their own legal positions. As a relatively informal proceeding, mediation provides a setting that is open enough for the plaintiffs to feel comfortable about describing their injuries and the heartbreak that accompanies such experiences. But the container is rigid enough that certain protocols of courtesy must be followed, which make it possible for the defendants to listen carefully without feeling attacked.

Face-to-face with the head of oncology and the physicist who miscalibrated the radiation device, the women were finally given the opportunity to confront those whose actions had caused such suffering. Linda described the constant pain she lived with, the thickening and hardening of the tissue in her breast, terrible itching, the pain she feels when she is exposed to the sun—even wearing several layers of clothing—and severe pain in her chest cavity. As her husband sat close by, Linda struggled to make sense of the dramatic and irreversible changes in her life. Driving the car was increasingly difficult. Going outside was impossible.

"The overradiation has dominated my life and my consciousness since I first learned of it, two years ago," Linda said as she struggled to keep her composure. "The overradiation is much worse than the cancer ever was," she said in her soft Southern accent. "The cancer couldn't be avoided. The radiation could have been. It didn't have to happen. And that's what I keep thinking about. *It didn't have to happen!* Now, even if I wanted to, I couldn't have a mastectomy. There isn't enough healthy skin. I've been on all kinds of pain medication, and the only one that works is so strong it can destroy the liver. The pain makes it impossible to think about anything else. And I feel deformed—it's hideous."

Linda explained that constant fear is the worst part of it. Like other radiation victims, Linda worried about the greatly increased risk of developing a sarcoma, leukemia, lymphodermia, spontaneous rib fractures, or coronary disease.

Barbara Kauth, another plaintiff, softly explained that she was already beginning to experience some of those symptoms. A quiet country woman, her condition had degenerated so far that it had become impossible to work at any job for more than an hour without becoming completely exhausted. The bank where she had been employed for ten years graciously decreased her responsibilities but finally had to let her go when she couldn't even sit at a desk for half a day. "I just hope I can live long enough to teach my twelve-year-old boy how to cook for himself," she whispered.

Barbara suffered from overwhelming depression but resisted

psychotherapy for religious reasons. Linda, who had spent two years in a therapist's office, was at least able to find the motivation to go to work. "But I battle with fear and depression every single day," Linda said. "I know what Barbara's dealing with, and it makes me so mad sometimes I could just explode. Twenty-five women! If they had just listened to us when we told them about the redness—but they're doctors. So they know better, right?"

COMPASSION

I turned to the hospital's lawyer. She looked right into Linda's eyes, and then at Barbara. "My name is Marilyn Vance and I represent St. Luke's Hospital. I'm here because we know that we made a terrible, unforgivable mistake. I've listened to you both, and I've read all the documents on your cases. I've talked to the doctors, and I've asked them to come here with me, and they'll also have something to say. I just want you to know that on behalf of the hospital and the people who operate it, I deeply, deeply apologize and ask for your forgiveness."

The room was silent. None of us was accustomed to hearing such a sincere and heartfelt display of compassion, especially from an attorney. Marilyn turned to the men sitting at her side. Both the head of oncology and the physicist who miscalibrated the linear accelerator spoke of the distress they had experienced in trying to grapple with the mistake.

The physicist had trouble finding the words. Finally he looked up. "I know you may never be able to forgive me. My error has damaged your lives, and there's no way I can make up for that. I will think of you every day of the rest of my life."

THE CAUCUS

Mediation provides one device for reaching agreement that no other form of conflict resolution can offer. This is the *caucus*—a private meeting with each party to explore its concerns, objectives and expectations.

Many mediators use the caucus as a way to create doubt in each party's mind about its own case by dissecting their positions. Other mediators attempt to get each party to disclose its own "bottom line." I take a more direct approach. I simply ask each side to tell me what it believes *the other side's* bottom line is. All subsequent offers or demands are then designed to determine whether those assumptions are correct.

By focusing on a strategy to get the other side to bargain to its bottom line, each party can make whatever moves it thinks will induce the greatest movement from the other. This shift in emphasis reduces the need to repeat or reinforce positions or arguments that don't inspire movement from the other side.

The caucus is also a good opportunity to work through issues that a party does not want to discuss with the other side. Once I mediated a lawsuit brought by the parents of a fourteen-year-old boy named Kevin who had drowned at a church outing. Despite several offers from the insurance company, the parents simply refused to negotiate. Kevin's father, Karl, was a gruff German immigrant who had rejected every approach I could imagine.

Finally, I asked all the lawyers and insurance people to leave so that I could speak with Kevin's parents in a private caucus. Karl sat with his arms crossed, defiant and silent.

Lucy provided the first opening. "One of the reasons it's so hard for Karl to compromise is," she said, looking at Karl, "that this is not the first time he has had to go through something like this. Before we met, when he still lived in Germany, he was married before, and he had another son. His son was crippled, but Karl loved him. He suffered through his son's slow death, as the disease twisted him up and finally killed him."

Karl's eyes started to fill with tears as he now spoke to me. "When Kevin came along, he became my whole life. He was such a good boy. Everybody loved him. Me, I don't have many friends. I keep to myself. With Kevin around, who else did I need? He was so easygoing, he's always telling me, 'Pop, relax. Everything it will be okay.' "

Karl stopped to get his voice back. With the heel of his thick hand he pushed the tears back. "And we'd go fishing all the time. He never cared whether we caught anything. He just liked being with me. I never knew a boy like that—he was always hugging me, even with his friends around. He made me laugh so much. He was like sunshine to me. And now there's no sunshine. I think about him all the time. It's like he's not really . . . gone."

I struggled to hold back the tears that started to stream down my face, listening to this strong man with the heavy German accent speak about the light of his life. I thought of my own children, and how precious they are to me. But Karl held himself in check. It seemed to take all his strength just to keep from drowning in his own grief.

I moved my chair close to Karl's. "Karl, I want you to come on a little journey with me. Just close your eyes for a moment, and relax your body. Imagine yourself walking in the woods—your favorite woods, a fishing pole in your hands. Now you're camping beside a river. The campfire is warm, and you feel very good. Someone is with you at the fire, and you are talking."

A tear slowly rolled down Karl's cheek. His eyes clenched and his face reddened. "Who is it, Karl? Tell me who you're talking to."

"It's Kevin," he whispered. The tears came faster now.

"What is Kevin telling you, Karl? What is it that he wants?"

Lucy was crying, too. Her face was buried in her hands. The sound of her sobs touched something in Karl. It was hard for him to speak. "He wants me . . . to go on. He wants me to let him go. He says that he's happy where he is, that we don't have to suffer for him. Oh, my God, he's such a good boy."

When the tears finally stopped, with Karl and Lucy holding hands for the first time since Kevin died, it was no longer so important how the lawsuit would be resolved. The time had come to let go of Kevin. The lawsuit was a life-support system, and the time had come to disconnect.

CLOSURE

After caucusing several times over the course of two hours with all parties in the radiation cases, the hospital managed to reach agreement with both Linda and Barbara. When I returned several weeks later, the other two cases were also concluded within a day. The payments were substantial but quite reasonable, and everyone was able to avoid the stress, expense, and risk of an unpredictable trial. There was a sense that life could now go on, that accounts had been put in order. Both sides were lifted by a subtle feeling of elation.

At the end of that first session, after handshakes all around, Barbara's lawyer pulled me aside. He had been more than a lawyer to her. In the small town where he practiced, it was expected that an attorney also be a friend and good neighbor, and he had worried about Barbara's psychological condition as much as he was concerned about her deteriorating physical condition.

"The most amazing thing just happened!" he said incredulously. "My client just smiled! This is the first time she's done that since the radiation treatments ended. She even told me she'd go to see a therapist! Just that one smile made it all worthwhile. She knows her boy will be taken care of, and that has to mean a lot to her."

The hospital's representatives were just as pleased. Nearly three million dollars of business had been transacted in two days, but a trial might have been much more expensive. And its reputation for holding itself accountable was intact. There would be no bad publicity. The hospital's policy of acknowledging its failures as openly as it promoted its successes had paid off.

COLLABORATION

After the settlements were announced, the lawyers and clients quickly agreed to keep confidential the amounts for which the matters had been resolved. In fact, they would have honored almost any reasonable request the other side made, because the barriers of adversity had disappeared. Buoyed by the grace of closure, the patient-doctor relationship had been restored, and I overheard one of the women say how glad she was to be able to return to St. Luke's for further treatment.

In many cases, the process of drafting a final settlement agreement can be the foundation of a new and healthier relationship. In the "turf war" between two doctors described in the Preface, the settlement agreement established the ground rules for their communications when disputes arose. The process of negotiating those ground rules provided an excellent occasion for Thurston and Rebecca to actually work together successfully. It gave them confidence that they could do so again in the future.

In most settlement agreements I draft, I include a comprehensive dispute resolution provision that was originally created by my own mentor, John Goodson, many years before. It has never failed me. This novel dispute resolution mechanism provides that, as a first step, if either party has any reason to believe that the other has violated any part of the agreement, they would meet for no less than an hour to talk about it directly. If they wanted, they could invite an agreed-upon third person to attend their conversation as a witness, but without power to resolve the matter. A supervisor or someone from the personnel department is an obvious candidate, but it could as easily be a mutual friend.

This definition of the dispute resolution "triggering event" is far broader than lawyers typically include in the remedies or default provision of most agreements. It is designed to call attention to a problem before it gets serious, even as early as the moment a party starts to get uncomfortable or suspicious.

Once the general counsel of a large corporation told me that she always inserts a provision in her contracts that requires the presidents of both companies to talk for at least two hours if either company felt the agreement has been violated. "Their time is too valuable to be wasted, so they always settle the dispute before they leave the table. We've never had a contract dispute go to court so far."

The second step of the dispute resolution provision requires the parties to hire a mediator—me or anyone else they agreed to—if they didn't work out their differences informally. This would add a cost to the process, and while still voluntary, it would begin to impose restrictions on their freedom.

The goal of a good dispute resolution provision is to add an increased cost, and restrict the freedom of the parties, at each step of the process. That way, armed with the knowledge that their failure at one stage will result in less control and greater cost at the next, the parties will be motivated to reach an agreement at the earliest stage possible. When such provisions are used, people rarely get even to mediation and have never, in my experience, gone beyond it to a more coercive stage. But it is essential to provide such a procedure, for its deterrent effect, if nothing else.

The logic of this kind of incremental approach is well known to most major league baseball fans. Under the collective bargaining agreement, certain highly paid players are eligible for arbitration of their salary demands if they cannot work out an agreement with the management of the team. Most cases settle without an arbitration hearing because the adversarial process is so damaging. Winning usually isn't worth the resentment it causes, even when big money is at stake.

STYLES OF MEDIATION

Although there are basic tools and techniques that all mediators share in common, there are two schools of thought on the best way to bring parties to an agreement. One approach is called *directive* and the other is known as *non-directive* mediation.

A directive mediator gets overtly involved in steering the process toward a particular conclusion. In private caucuses with the parties, a directive mediator looks for ways to destabilize their positions through cross-examination and frank feedback about weaknesses in their positions. A directive mediator is willing to argue, cross-examine, and influence parties in the direction of compromise. To be an effective directive mediator means that the parties come to trust the expertise or judgment of the mediator and are willing to have their arms twisted.

In the overradiation cases, a more directive mediator might have quickly formulated an opinion about the settlement value of the claims, based on initial interviews with the parties. Recognizing that the hospital wanted to avoid litigation and that the plaintiffs didn't want to endure the arduous task of testifying to a jury, a directive mediator might have reached his own conclusions and then worked on the parties to get their concurrence.

But it was our goal to have the parties themselves work out their own agreement, without undue external pressure, so that everyone felt that justice—precisely as they themselves envisioned it—was done. This is more likely to occur if they struggle and stumble along until they strike a suitable deal of their own design.

The danger with directive mediation, of course, is that the mediator won't have the ability to convince the parties to see things her way, and will lose credibility by having staked out a position. Most judges who become mediators after they retire from the bench quickly learn that their opinions about the facts or law carry considerably less weight when they are no longer able to issue orders and empanel juries. Most lawyers—as well as other adults—are inclined to trust their own judgment over anyone else's. It can take a lot of persuasion to convince them of the error of their ways. This can be exhausting, time-consuming, and aggravating all around.

But there are some very successful directive mediators who have the knowledge, charm, and theatrical ability to orchestrate settlements among resistant adversaries. Through humor and hard work, they manage to win the respect even of those whom they have pummeled into agreement.

A non-directive mediator has a different sense of what it means to achieve the "right" agreement. For him, fairness is in the eye of the beholder—if the parties agree to a particular outcome, the non-directive mediator is likely to regard it as a just resolution. The non-directive mediator manages the process so that the parties can discern their own goals (if they aren't already clear about them) and achieve those objectives to the greatest extent possible. With few exceptions, the only requirement is that the agreement be sufficiently solid to survive the period of "buyer's remorse." If they are willing to stand by the agreement when they have to explain it at the office, to their husband, or to themselves, it's fair.

The non-directive mediator makes no attempt to convince a party that her analysis is faulty. Rather, knowing that both parties have the power to veto any unacceptable proposal, the mediator encourages each party to negotiate for its best possible outcome. Only when it fails to win agreement—and the proposing party therefore is more receptive to suggestions—will the mediator begin to explore other, more realistic approaches. That way, the process itself brings the parties down to earth, and the mediator doesn't have to be "the heavy."

Moreover, this is a more efficient way to get to an agreement, because the mediator doesn't have to argue with either side. "If it will work—if you think the other side will agree—give it a try," he says. The non-directive mediator is more like a coach than a referee. He wants both sides to succeed—within the limits of what is possible. He works to develop alternative strategies and to test the limits of each side's flexibility.

But this kind of non-engaged intervention can be very frustrating when a party is unable to assess the merits of the case or has no way to know whether one outcome is more reasonable than another. Every mediator is frequently asked, "So what do *you* think is fair?" A non-directive mediator, like a psychotherapist, is likely to respond, "Well, what do *you* think?"

An effective non-directive mediator is also likely to be very subtle. He listens a lot and asks an occasional, probing question that shifts the conversation in a new direction before anyone notices. The word I like to use is "transparent"—the parties should be able to see each other clearly without the distortion of the mediator's interpretation or opinion. The mediator should command very little attention for himself so that the focus of the energy is on the problem that must be solved.

This presents a bit of a dilemma for the successful but subtle mediator, however. By the time the case is resolved, the parties may feel so much ownership of the process that they will have a hard time remembering exactly what it was that the mediator did. They recall moving in and out of rooms and struggling to find some middle ground but can't put a finger on exactly what role the mediator played. It all looked too easy. And when it comes time to refer friends or colleagues to a mediator, they might find it difficult to explain why the low-key guy is any better than the showman. "If it was that easy," they say, "I guess it was something I could have done myself!"

THE LIMITS OF MEDIATION

Like all human interventions, mediation is not appropriate for all conflicts. There are times when it will fail, and even times when it makes matters worse. The problem is, it is almost impossible to predict such failures.

From my earliest days as a mediator, and being something of an iconoclast by nature, I took great pleasure in mediating cases that I was told could not be resolved except by force. I recall meeting with the legal staff of a large chain of department stores. The head of its torts division, who was responsible for managing all the cases involving accidents on store property and other forms of personal injury, flatly declared that "mediation might be fine when everybody wants to cooperate and they have an ongoing relationship, but it will never work for tort cases. These suits are just about money. The parties will never see each other again. Why would they want to settle?"

I didn't have an answer, since I had never handled a tort case before. But I thought of him often in later years as the list of settled tort cases approached the one thousand mark.

Then we were told that, well, maybe you can settle a personal injury case, but never a product liability case. Too complicated. Had to know a lot about how products were designed and how careful a manufacturer was required to be in building and selling them. But these were much the same as the other tort cases. Within a few years, we had settled hundreds of product cases, from malfunctioning hospital anesthesia equipment to poorly designed table saws.

Well, maybe personal injury cases and products cases could be settled, the skeptics said, but never could you mediate cases involving medical malpractice. Or legal malpractice. Or cases involving death. At least, cases involving the death of children. Assault and battery cases? Rape? As each conflict found its way to resolution, the conceptual barriers continued to drop. There seemed to be no way, in advance, to declare any category of disputes off limits.

Nevertheless, there are limits. One obvious limitation is the willingness of the parties to participate in mediation. If there isn't a way to get them into the same room (or adjoining rooms, anyway), there's not much that can be done. And even if they come into the same room, they have to be willing to hang in there through the rough spots, when it looks hopeless. Not everyone can muster that much optimism or faith. But getting the parties to the table is properly the mediator's function, and most mediators are quite skilled at it.

The second limitation is more difficult to evaluate. There are times when a disputant is incapable of accepting any resolution not imposed by force. Agreement is not an option. Perhaps a voluntary settlement would represent a failure of principle or courage. Perhaps the person has a tyrannical nature or is incapable of compromise. Some people are not sufficiently socialized to recognize or accommodate the legitimate needs of others, and who would only exploit the process to gain an advantage.

These are the times when only a clear victory or defeat will resolve the matter. For example, it may be essential to prosecute a serious crime before attempting to mediate a victim-offender reconciliation. The law may be used to effect an accounting before forgiveness has any meaning. To advocate mediation when clearly coercion is required would be foolish or naive. Mediation can be employed in such cases only when firmer forces have paved the way.

Once I had the opportunity to have dinner with a former member of the Tibetan government in exile. Formerly both a Buddhist monk as well as an officer in a Tibetan unit of the Indian army, my guest was an open, warm man who displayed a balance of practical and spiritual qualities. The conversation soon centered on the Chinese occupation of Tibet and the role of non-violence in resisting that occupation.

"What role might non-violence, a basic tenet of Buddhism, play in such a struggle?" I asked.

"For a strategy to work, it must be understood by the enemy. The Chinese do not understand non-violence, so they do not comprehend the nature of our response to their actions. They think we are foolish and weak. So they crush us. Non-violence in such circumstances is romantic and ineffective.

"This is very difficult for us. But I think the answer must be a balance of force and non-violence. We need to find a way to put them at risk, to create consequences, before they will see the logic of negotiating with us. Until that happens, they are at the mercy of their own affliction. They simply do not know when to stop."

There was a time when I would have argued that coercion is never justified. My experience as a mediator eventually taught me otherwise. An awareness that an involuntary outcome will be imposed, if there is no agreed-upon resolution, is a dependable catalyst of productive conversation. The world of conflict is generally filled with human beings seeking to satisfy human needs, not saints seeking to transcend them. Even saints must learn how to deal with sinners.

Force has its place. Without a willingness to employ coercive measures when voluntary processes are refused, most intractable or emotional conflicts would linger without any prospect of closure. The "enlightened" party's reluctance to employ force in such cases is a great advantage to the uncooperative party, who can then abuse the other without having to account for her behavior.

I recall attempting to interest the dean of a business school (which, ironically, provided an excellent program in conflict resolution to its graduate students) in mediating a tenure dispute with one of his faculty. The professor wanted to avoid litigation and adverse publicity to the school, and had decided not to retain an attorney unless he had to. To my great amazement, the dean refused to mediate.

"Why?" I asked.

"Because we don't have a dispute," he said, smiling. Meaning, until the professor hires a lawyer, there may be hurt feelings, but there's no coercive threat to the university that would require the dean's attention.

As in all things, the application of force is a matter of balance. Whenever possible, mediation should be considered and attempted. If it fails, there are other options, none of which will have been precluded by the effort. Indeed, even if mediation fails to produce a full accord, it virtually always can resolve the current impasse, refine the issues, narrow the area of controversy, and improve the channels of communication.

But if mediation won't avail, it may be time to polish the armor and sharpen the sword. My Tibetan friend reminded me that, during the the eleventh and twelfth centuries, as holy wars were waged between Muslim and Christian armies over control of Jerusalem, a unique order of warrior-monks called the Knights Templar came to prominence. The Templars provided safe passage to pilgrims, nurtured diplomatic relations with many Muslim leaders, and fought valiantly when the peace failed. "Perhaps we need more warrior-monks in the world," he suggested with a smile.

The relationship of force, social change, and conflict resolution brings us to consider whole systems and how the parts might work together. In the chapter that follows, we examine the phenomenon called *confluence*.

CONFLUENCE:
The Politics of the Whole

*In every organized whole, the parts perfect themselves and
fulfill themselves.*

Teilhard de Chardin

*We need the vision of interbeing—we belong to each other;
we cannot cut reality into pieces. The well-being of "this" is
the well-being of "that," so that we have to do things together.
Every side is "our side"; there is no evil side.*

Thich Nhat Hanh

SYSTEMIC CONFLICT

While conflict often arises out of our direct, personal relationships,
it can as easily be a reflection of the nature of the organizations and
social systems in which we live and work. The way these organizations operate, and the roles we play in them, may generate conflicts
that have nothing to do with our individual passions, history, or
concerns. We are simply responding to impersonal forces that we
cannot affect, much less control. This might be called *systemic
conflict*.

Systemic conflict often appears in the guise of individual conflict,
until someone notices that the issue is beyond the capacity of the

disputants to resolve on their own, or until it becomes apparent that the same kind of issue is causing havoc throughout the system or organization. Settling individual disputes simply can't resolve the real conflict when it is the system itself that is generating the tension.

We all belong to a variety of systems. Some are obvious—our families, friends, work environment, nation, religion, and ethnic group. But there are many other groups to which we unconsciously pledge our allegiance as well, which invisibly form around our attitudes and values—groups consisting of loyal or fickle fans of the local sports team, drinkers of alcohol or opponents of drug use, those who have equivalent earning potential, those who share our views about television, crime, and the role of the federal government. When members of one group encounter followers of another, conflict can arise.

We may not be wearing gang colors or carrying flags, but we immediately sense that the presence of "the other" threatens the security of the system, and we feel the urge to defend it. We fall back on an instinctive tendency to dominate and control, without noticing that we are acting under the influence of unknown forces. As Shakespeare observed, there are times when we all are players in a larger drama that we do not understand. The world is a stage, and we struggle just to follow the script.

Understanding conflict within or between groups and organizations requires us to examine *the whole* in which the conflict is occurring. The individual cases of conflict are helpful clues, but it is the big picture—what psychologists call "the gestalt"—that we need.

It is an adage of the market place that one should avoid talking about politics or religion when conducting business. Nevertheless, in this discussion we will turn to a dramatic illustration of group behavior that features both politics *and* religion. The occasion was an historic congress of people of all religions and cultures who came together to consider how they might jointly address some of the world's most pressing problems. Although the scale of the Parliament of the World's Religions was larger than most routine organizational experiences of group behavior, it embodied many of the dynamics that govern virtually all social systems, from the local PTA to the United Nations.

THE WORLD WAS IN ONE ROOM

At the end of a warm August in 1993, the world came to Chicago and checked into the Palmer House Hotel for a week. For the second time in history, the great spiritual traditions of East and West came together in a Parliament of the World's Religions.

Originally planned as a hundred-year commemoration of the first Parliament, which was held during the Columbian Exposition in 1893, this event attracted almost nine thousand religious believers and practitioners from around the world. Every religion was fully represented by high-ranking officials and large delegations of followers. His Holiness the Dalai Lama spoke at an open-air event and hundreds of leaders from every major faith tradition were invited to endorse a document called "The Declaration of a Global Ethic" that set forth a set of moral principles to which all people of faith might subscribe. There were over seven hundred speeches, demonstrations, spiritual programs, concerts, and major events in the course of eight days.

As I took the train downtown from my home, I kept seeing the image of a giant lotus flower blossoming in the middle of the Loop. I glanced down the sidewalk as I entered the Palmer House Hotel on Wabash Street, where the elevated train runs. The marquee on the tavern next door read "Welcome! Leaders of the World Religions." They were going to be disappointed. Not the the usual convention business. The bartender watched a lot of television that week. But, at the Palmer House itself, life in all its variety was in full bloom.

The first time I stepped off the elevator at the Palmer House I was almost knocked over by the sheer energy of happy pandemonium. The outside world instantly evaporated and I entered a buzzing carnival of human diversity, the likes of which I had never before seen. Walking over to get my staff registration materials, I nearly stepped on the naked feet of a darkly bearded yogi in regal saffron robes who sat cross-legged on the floor. Smiling bands of Buddhists from Cambodia and Japan bowed and greeted one another like brothers. Lutheran ministers and papal delegates stood in line together at the registration counter as devout Jains and Muslims pored over the thick program catalog. Turbaned Sikhs mingled with New Age mystics. The whole world was in one room. And it was having a very good time.

The Parliament was one of the most complex events ever conceived. Hundreds of presentations addressed the critical issues facing the global family—the deterioration of the environment, challenges to human rights and social justice, the role of science and technology, threats to culture and community, and the prevalence of religious violence. Elaborate productions showcased dance, music, and the arts. Workshops in meditation and prayer were conducted from the earliest hour to the end of the day. While all this was occurring, two hundred and fifty of the world's most prestigious religious leaders met separately, under tight security, down the street at the beautiful Art Institute, to discuss what they might accomplish together.

On just a few weeks' notice, we had assembled fifty of the leading facilitators from around the country and several European nations to ensure that all registrants had an opportunity to be more than spectators at the event. We were expected both to facilitate the meetings of the elite Assembly of Religious and Spiritual Leaders as well as to bring thousands of grassroots participants into some form of orderly interaction. Inspired by the vision of futurist Barbara Marx Hubbard, we quickly invented a process called "the Parliament of the People" that would be open to anyone who wished to participate. The facilitation team also was expected to help mediate controversies that arose among the participants. Given our small ranks, we decided to conduct a wide assortment of trainings for the participants in conflict resolution and dialogue— just in case we needed help.

It soon became apparent that the job of the facilitation team was beyond our ability to manage. We discovered that although the event had been planned over the past five years, the Assembly of Religious and Spiritual Leaders had no real agenda. There was no opportunity to debate the merits or language of the Declaration of a Global Ethic and no provision to introduce legislation, to discuss the critical issues, or to address the Assembly as a whole. Except for a brief period of "open microphone," dialogue was limited to private discussions among groups of ten at each table.

This was a recipe for disaster. We couldn't imagine how the Parliament organizers expected important dignitaries to travel across the world, only to sign a Declaration that someone else had written, without wanting to say a word or two. They didn't become leaders by simply signing off on someone else's work.

While we worried about the Assembly, the Parliament of the People grew beyond our expectations. Each day, thirty or forty facilitated groups simultaneously convened in the huge Red Lacquer Room to construct a complex road map for grassroots interreligious cooperation and social action. We began our sessions with prayer and music or silence or inspiration. Every single participant was invited to summarize his views on notecards, which were organized and posted on a giant wall for all to read. At the close of each session, each group sent a representative to speak to the whole. Anyone who was unable to address the Parliament of the People directly was invited to make a recorded statement to one of the video crews around the room or could submit his thoughts in an "instant newsletter" called *Your Voice*, which was published several times a day and distributed throughout the Palmer House.

It was a remarkable sight. Assembly leaders were invited to participate in the Parliament of the People, and many did. Great and venerated leaders of nonviolent social movements from across the world sat in intimate circles with humble community organizers from Cincinnati and San Francisco. Protestants and Muslims and Neo-pagans worked together to imagine a common vision that would serve all while affirming the unique identity of each. It was loud and spontaneous and full of hope.

From the first day until the last, everything happened at once. The Sikhs were verbally attacked by representatives of the predominantly Hindu Indian government for criticizing its policies in Punjab, and a prominent Sikh speaker had to be escorted from the stage for his own safety. The Assembly of Religious and Spiritual Leaders erupted from all directions when it became clear that the delegates would have no input on the Global Ethic. The Roman Catholics nearly withdrew when the Native Americans were allowed to request a vote on a resolution condemning the Church for a fifteenth-century papal bull. The Orthodox Jews withdrew when Nation of Islam leader Louis Farrakhan made anti-Semitic remarks in his presentation, and the Greek Orthodox withdrew when the Wiccans were allowed full participation as a legitimate religious tradition. And an activist promised a group of homeless people they could get free food by attending a lecture on the homeless—which they were promptly asked to leave.

It became clear that while the open process in the Parliament of the People was working, the tightly controlled Assembly had run aground. After meeting with the Parliament Chair, we were given clearance to use the same interactive process at the Assembly that was guiding the Parliament of the People. The participants loved it. Using a system called "messaging," British facilitator Tim Casswell built a veritable wall of three-by-five index cards—which recorded the views of every participant—on one side of the very formal Board of Trade room where the Assembly met, and a complex mosaic of common aspiration began to emerge. When printed as the final edition of *Your Voice* newsletter, it became the final record of the Assembly's discussion.

When the facilitation team met each morning with Barbara Bernstein, the visionary Program Director of the Parliament, each of us reported on the prior day's events. It seemed that everyone was everywhere at once, with virtually no form of centralized coordination. Billie Mayo had worked out the situation with the homeless people. The incident with the Sikhs was resolved when the entire room of a thousand people spontaneously burst into "We Shall

Overcome" and were led in a great circle dance by Native American elders. Nadia McLaren and Robert Pollard stayed up all night getting copies of *Your Voice* distributed throughout the hotel. Tim Casswell and his team organized thousands of three-by-five cards that contained the words of participants in the Parliament of the People into a series of huge hallway displays that simultaneously were published in the newsletter.

Everything worked virtually without direction, without anyone to issue orders and dictate assignments. The group had a mind of its own. The group as a whole knew more than any individual could possibly grasp, so the group determined what was needed and who needed to do it. Things, quite literally, were out of control. And everything got done. We were "in the flow" and it was *really flowing.*

This is the experience of *confluence.* It emerges when a group learns how to think collectively—to be guided, not by individual ego or even by explicit agreement—but by what is called *group mind.* It occurs when a constellation of individuals crystallizes into a *whole.*

It was not just the facilitation team that felt the confluence. The entire Parliament floated in it. Every time the elevator doors opened, it released a chattering microcosm of the world into the lobby of the Palmer House—smiling, laughing people from distant ends of the earth literally rubbing shoulders and finding the experience delightful. The event was so complex, and the variety of programs was so rich, that it was impossible to stay isolated among one's own little group or to chart a solitary course through the dizzying array of performances and presentations. The sheer magnitude of the event made the experience of community inevitable.

FLOWING TOGETHER

In a world of differences and disagreements, is it possible to go beyond resolving conflict, and even past the common enterprise of collaboration? Is there a way in which people not only can learn to tolerate one another, not only to cooperate, but to flourish together? Is there some higher purpose for the differences we experience as conflict? If so, do our conflicts merely disguise a more profound order? What is the relationship of the many and the one?

These are the ancient questions faced by prophets, philosophers, and mystics of every age. Those who attended the Parliament found an answer in the experience of confluence. The word "confluence" is used here to express the profound intelligence that is available to us when we touch the dynamic unity that holds us together in the midst of our adversity and fragmentation. Confluence—"flowing together"—is the experience of life moving forward, as one.

What the human soul ultimately desires is its own individual fulfillment, which, it seems, is possible only through differentiation from *and* union with others. We long to feel our waters flow like the river of life, not in isolation from other streams but together. It is a paradoxical image; when two rivers flow together, in what sense are they still "two"? But that is the point of paradox. There is no simple answer—just an image that won't stay still.

A person who experiences confluence is able to go with the flow, yet retain her increasingly unique identity. She is both part of the larger stream and a stream unto herself. Her consciousness holds both images at once. Whatever enters the stream touches her, enriches her, becomes part of who she is, is changed by her, yet does not take away her true nature.

Confluence flows like grace from the center of our being, confirming that what is at the center of all of us together is also at the center of each apart. Charlene Spretnak probes the mystery of this union in *States of Grace*:

> *When we experience consciousness of the unity in which we are embedded, the sacred whole that is in and around us, we exist in a state of grace. At such moments our consciousness perceives not only our individual self, but also our larger self, the self of the cosmos. The gestalt of unitive existence becomes palpable.*

At the place of confluence, identity undergoes a profound redefinition. There is no longer an issue of contradiction, of threat, or defense. The only question is: Which way? Where do the waters flow at this turn? Beneath the rocks, into the caverns, through to the sunlight, into the valley, across the desert?

Confluence requires that we learn to read the movement of the waters. I am reminded of the Colorado River, which thunders through the Grand Canyon for over two hundred miles. Lava Falls, its biggest challenge, is one of the most spectacular patches of white water in North America—a swirling fury of standing waves and crashing water. Before attempting to navigate a passage, you climb the rocky cliffs and study the flow of the river as it hurls itself over a barricade of hardened lava and on toward Nevada and California. You consider the twisting eddies and chart the ribbon of currents that weave through the maze of hidden obstructions. But then you take the ride. You study the water, take a breath, hold on tight—and definitely take the ride. Life flows. Conflict pulls us into the roiling waters of life, and whether we find the flow or fight it will determine our survival. As individuals and as a species.

Our capacity to experience and sustain confluence is largely determined by the social structures and institutions through which we relate to one another. In the same sense we earlier used the word "contain," these institutions *contain power.* One model of power tends to be highly individualistic, while the other views power as residing in the group *as a whole.*

HIERARCHY AND PANARCHY

Society arises from chaos. The process is a continuing one; times of social transition and transformation are especially chaotic. Social systems must reestablish themselves in response to the energy of incipient change or chaos will sweep us away. The resulting social systems can emerge either as *hierarchy* or *panarchy.*

We live in a world where our response to social conflict is largely managed through a hierarchical model of power. A *hierarch* is a high priest, someone with special access to the sacred instruments of power. A hierarchy is a closed system, like a pyramid, with the vast majority at the base and a few at the pinnacle. Power comes from the top, and is incrementally stepped down at each succeeding level. Hierarchy celebrates personal power and the domination of the many by the few.

This is the basic model of religious institutions, the courts, the military, government, and corporations. It tells us whom to salute and when to genuflect. It is based on a static concept of power—that the purpose of power is to consolidate the ability of those *with it* to *keep it*. Power is balanced in a hierarchical system by the assertion of rights, possessed either by individuals or groups. There is no authentic experience of the whole—just a collection of largely autonomous parts, each vying for its own interests by competing with the others.

Panarchy is a word I have coined to describe a social system in which there are no high priests. "Pan" means "whole." Governance in a panarchy is based on the ongoing creative interaction of the whole human ecosystem. Power comes from the *center* of that system, which is not its lowest common denominator but its highest. It moves society and the individual forward together rather than accepting current limits and positions as the full range of the possible.

Panarchy is dynamic and interactive. Everyone has a stake and a voice, but each person must be willing to adjust his expectations and opinions in light of the needs of the whole and in response to the emergence of new information. The goal of panarchy is to discern the intelligence of the whole as clearly as possible and follow its lead. Social systems are containers that facilitate that process but are not ends in themselves.

THE HIERARCHICAL PYRAMID

As shown in Figure 4, hierarchy is established, disestablished, and reestablished through the process of *revolution*. Revolution is the foundational event of hierarchy. In the face of social chaos—change, fear, disruption, threats from the outside, loss of authority—revolution overturns the prior order and demands a new order.

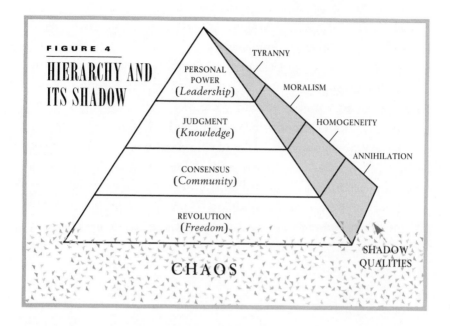

FIGURE 4

HIERARCHY AND ITS SHADOW

PERSONAL POWER
(*Leadership*)

TYRANNY

MORALISM

JUDGMENT
(*Knowledge*)

HOMOGENEITY

ANNIHILATION

CONSENSUS
(*Community*)

REVOLUTION
(*Freedom*)

CHAOS

SHADOW QUALITIES

Notwithstanding its disruptive appearance, revolution almost always confirms and even reinforces hierarchy. "Sacrifice your bourgeois individuality for the sake of the revolution—freedom is just around the corner." In the place of old authority, new authority arises.

Revolution has its positive and negative aspects. On the one hand, it is capable of overthrowing tyranny and establishing freedom. More typically, it annihilates or deconstructs the social order without reestablishing a new or improved form in its place. Revolution often lacks the structural integrity to resist chaos, and typically incorporates into its very fabric chaotic elements that it cannot quite shake.

The process by which revolution becomes institutionalized is consensus. The social contract in a hierarchical system is based on the consensual grant of authority to "leaders" by the governed. This contract essentially assures that decisions will be based on the lowest common denominator of the governed. Even if there is no explicit legal right to vote in a hierarchy, the tacit consent of those who are members of that system is always required for its continuation. If the people truly refuse to be ruled, they cannot be. Neither, in a hierarchical system, can they easily rise above the limitations of their base common denominator.

Consensus elects politicians who promise sweeping change—and then promptly creates an impasse so that it becomes nearly impossible to advance beyond yesterday's failed solutions. Consensus gives us a Democratic President and a Republican Congress.

One of my favorite examples of consensus politics is the issue of statehood for the Commonwealth of Puerto Rico. Puerto Rican political parties are distinguished from one another largely on the basis of their position on statehood—one party promotes statehood, one party wants Puerto Rico to continue its unique status as a commonwealth, and a small third party advocates independence. The voting margins on the issue are so close that it guarantees a deadlock on the statehood question—which keeps all the politicians safely in business. Consensus protects the system from change.

Consensus operates in the marketplace, as well. It decides what will appear on television and in the shopping mall and in the restaurant. It cannot create, because creativity is dynamic and threatens the static order of hierarchy. Instead, it absorbs threatening cultural movements and gets merchandising rights to it. Consensus takes black "gangsta rap" from the ghetto and moves it into the suburbs. It co-opts what opposes the status quo so that the structure of society stays in place.

Static power exists to sustain the status quo. But, as Buddha and the Greek philosopher Heraclitus observed, *everything changes*. The use of static power to maintain what cannot be held in place is an expensive and ultimately pointless exercise, as Buckminster Fuller points out:

> It is evident that 99 percent of society is now preoccupied positively or negatively only with status quo, ergo, with non-reality ergo, ignorantly.

The dark side of consensus is that it results in *homogeneity*. If we agree about everything, then life becomes mindless and boring.

When we drive past the same fried chicken outlet or department store or manufacturer's "outlet" in every town in America, it's hard not to worry about the vitality of our culture. Consensus kills culture. It also makes meetings tedious and of doubtful utility. Consensus discourages further revolution but often at the expense of distinction. Consensus never discovers the dynamic "whole" that lies beneath the parts, because it consists only *of* the parts.

On the other side of the ledger, consensus is essential to *community*. We must have some commonality to our values if we are to hold together. Consensus makes it possible to live together long enough to consider revealing our differences. As Communitarian Amitai Etzioni argues in *The Spirit of Community*, life together is possible when our relationships are based on responsibility, as well as on rights:

> *The times call for an age of reconstruction, in which we put a new emphasis on "we," on values we share, on the spirit of community. . . . When Communitarians argue that the pendulum has swung too far toward the radical individualistic pole and it is time to hurry its return, we do not seek to push it to the opposite extreme, of encouraging a community that suppresses individuality. We aim for a judicious mix of self-interest, self-expression, and commitment to the commons—of rights and responsibilities, of I and we.*

The third component of hierarchy is *judgment*. Judgment is the means by which hierarchy manages conflict when consensus cannot be achieved. It is linear, rational, critical, analytical. It makes sense. Costs are weighed against benefits. Choices are made in accordance with impersonal principles. The process is open to reason and insight. Order is established through discernment and debate. Judgment means that the parties are governed by what is "right." While a decision may take the form of a win or loss, its impact on the parties is secondary to upholding the determinative principle.

Even in hierarchy's most primitive forms, there is a sense that its actions have a logical explanation, even if the "leaders" refuse to provide it. Mao Tse-tung's Cultural Revolution, for example, was presumed to have some purpose—although it may in fact have been nothing other than an evil whim. Mao never clearly said what he hoped to achieve, but the Red Army operated as if they knew anyway.

Law is the classic form by which judgment is applied to conflict. The basic premise of the legal system is that when particular facts are systematically evaluated in the light of certain pre-existing rules, a rational outcome will naturally suggest itself. Thus, disputes can be concluded on the basis of the objective merits of the case, rather than by virtue of the parties' respective power or resources. The same reasoning underlies ethics as a means for determining right behavior.

When judgment correctly discerns truth, we acquire *knowledge*. With knowledge, we can distinguish between what is valid and what is an illusion. However, judgment is also capable of turning into *moralism*, which abuses others with the "rightness" of a position. We often crush one another under the weight of our principles, losing sight of the persons who struggle with real-world dilemmas. Acknowledging this tendency, lawyers often console their clients with the old axiom that "hard cases make bad law." That is, when a dispute is too close to call, principles don't seem to help. Another familiar saying is "The law is an ass." Most litigants would agree.

The fuel on which a hierarchical system operates is *personal power*. Personal power may be derived from inheritance, office, or popular election. When reason fails, power comes forward to resolve our differences. The king is in charge. Authority is exercised from above—it issues from a board of directors, an executive decree, legislation, an encyclical, the home office. Some rule, others obey. There is a polarity of "us" and "them" at every level.

When conflict is resolved through power, decisions are made unilaterally. Differences are resolved by force. Power is a closed system—"because I said so." There is no need for discussion or collaboration. The goal is established from the outset. It's just a question of getting there. The other person is merely an obstacle that must be overcome.

Power in the hands of the enlightened can be an effective and gracious way to resolve conflict. When power is joined to wisdom, and is recognized as such, it can be a great relief for the parties to have the matter concluded. Personal power can create great leaders. Figures of authority, such as parents, teachers, elected officials, judges and corporate executives, play an important role in the functioning of society. When leaders fail to exercise authority when it is appropriate to do so, chaos quickly takes the helm.

The dark side of authority is, of course, *tyranny*. A narcissistic leader uses power only to satisfy her own needs, without regard to others. As a society, we have become so accustomed to dealing with the abuse of power that we have nearly forgotten its proper role. Not all power is tyranny. Power is essential to order. Without power, we would be incapable of overthrowing tyrants. And when we must, we again employ revolution.

All the elements of hierarchy were in operation at the Parliament of the World's Religions. In fact, some futurists who attended the event considered it to be the final flowering of the hierarchical model. Every religious tradition was represented by its dignitaries. The elite, who conferred with one another behind closed doors away from the Parliament itself, had very little contact with the thousands of grassroots participants at the Palmer House. Decisions were made by a small executive committee, without the benefit of the views of most Assembly members.

This was illustrated most tellingly by the Parliament's handling of its signature piece, The Declaration of a Global Ethic. Two or three local organizers had reworked a draft document prepared by famed Swiss theologian Hans Küng and presented it to their guests without any opportunity for debate or modification. "If they don't like it, they don't have to sign it," one of the local drafters told me. (His own official church representative was one of those who later refused to sign the document.) A huge parchment text was ceremoniously displayed for Assembly members to endorse but not to discuss.

When Assembly members were informed on the first day that there would be no opportunity for debate or modification, they nearly overthrew the sponsoring conveners. Some walked out; many more just shouted at the moderator in frustration. Finally, in an effort to rescue the document from oblivion, facilitator Landrum Bolling sagely suggested that the title be modified to read "*An Initial Declaration Towards a Global Ethic.*" The Assembly promptly accepted, and a crisis was averted. The Parliament organizers seemed genuinely surprised that their unexamined hierarchical approach to "consensus" had caused such an uproar.

Is there another way to make decisions in a diverse and potentially conflicted body politic? Just as hierarchy is a closed system, panarchy is an open system. It operates from the grassroots, from the center of social activity. It is dynamic, flowing. Neither decreed from above, nor ignited by sectarian revolution from below, panarchy instead *evolves from within.*

To understand an *evolutionary social order*, we need first to consider the process of evolution.

EVOLUTION AND CONFLICT

One of the great pioneers of evolutionary thinking was the French scientist and philosopher Pierre Teilhard de Chardin. Teilhard viewed evolution not merely as a physical process (which he described as the development in complexity of the "without" of things) but as a phenomenon of human consciousness (the "within"). As a species, we have come to a point in the process when what happens to our bodies is much less important for the continuation of life than what happens to our capacity to think about and comprehend nature itself. Thinking beings can intentionally cooperate in evolution.

Consciousness, Teilhard says, has been the focus of evolution even at the physical level for millions of years. In the animal world, nature has concentrated its efforts, above all, in advancing the development of the nervous system, culminating in the unique human capacity of *reflection:* the power acquired by consciousness to turn in upon itself. This ability acts like a super-charger of the evolutionary process, as Teilhard explains in *The Phenomenon of Man*:

> *The being who is the object of his own reflection, in consequence of that very doubling back upon himself, becomes in a flash able to raise himself into a new sphere. . . . Man discovers that he is nothing else than evolution become conscious of itself. . . . The consciousness of each of us is evolution looking at itself and reflecting upon itself.*

Evolution is not the prerogative only of the elite or the powerful. Humankind is a *species*—even our physical distinctions are genetically insignificant. Through the phenomenon of consciousness, we are drawn closer than is imaginable in any other life-form. We are intimately connected to one another, brought closer every day by our vast and instantaneous network of communications technology. Advances anywhere in the globe are quickly reproduced everywhere. We spread our evolutionary genes, not through our chromosomes but through fertile thoughts. We propagate through propaganda. We evolve not so much our physical structure but the "within"—the invisible spiritual center through which we all derive our human identity.

We cannot evolve, then, at the expense of the other. The laws of nature declare that we move ahead together, or not at all. Teilhard continues:

> *The egocentric ideal of a future reserved for those who have managed to attain egoistically the extremity of "everyone for himself" is false and against nature. No element could move and grow except with and by all the others with itself. . . . Life does not work by following a single thread, nor yet by fits and starts. It pushes forward its whole network at one and the same time. . . .*

From man onwards, thanks to a universal framework of support provided by thought, free rein is given to the forces of conflu- ence. . . . *To be fully ourselves it is in the opposite direction* [from separation], *in the direction of convergence with all the rest, that we must advance*—towards the "other." [Emphasis added.]

It is through the encounter with the other that evolution is carried forward by conscious humanity, but in accordance with the laws that it follows throughout. The most significant of these is called *coevolution.*

COEVOLUTION

Evolution is not a solitary act. Each of us is constantly adapting to one another. At one moment we challenge and obstruct the move- ment of those around us, while at another we support and encour- age their progress. As each organism evolves, it affects other organisms, and must then respond to their responses. Flowers evolved to be fertilized by bees, and bees evolved to consume the nectar of flowers. As the cheetah got faster, so did the gazelle. This relationship of mutuality is called *coevolution.*

Teilhard observed the motivating force of evolution in this pur- poseful dynamic of conflict :

> *To jolt the individual out of his natural laziness and the rut of habit, and also from time to time to break up the collective frameworks in which he is imprisoned, it is indispensable that he should be shaken and prodded from outside. What would we do without our enemies?*

If we eliminate those on whom we depend for our own evolu- tion, the process will come to an end. Thus, from an evolutionary point of view, it is in our interest to obtain the best result from a transaction that does not endanger the viability of the system as a whole. As the Chinese say: "Take another man's rice, but don't break his rice bowl." Or, put differently, what goes around, comes around. Do unto others, even when locked in combat. The Golden Rule, in one form or another, is found in virtually every surviving culture and religion on earth.

Philosopher James Carse might have been talking about the dance of coevolution when he wrote a brilliant little book called *Finite and Infinite Games*. All human interaction can be understood as voluntary participation in a game, Carse suggests, even though some of those games are deadly serious. The purpose of a finite game, he says, is to win, and thus bring the game to an end. The purpose of an infinite game is to continue play. For a finite game to work, its rules may not change in the course of play. For an infinite game to continue, however, its rules *must* change as the game is played. Only by changing the rules, such as our expectations and definition of success, can we keep everyone in play.

Evolution, whether on a personal or planetary scale, is an infinite game. It is always expanding our boundaries and moving us beyond old limitations. If we choose consciously to participate in the evolutionary process, we must train ourselves to transform finite games into creative opportunities for coevolution. That means moving beyond the desire to eliminate our adversary so that we might win the game. By adjusting the game as we play it so that all the players stay on the field, we ensure that coevolution will continue to evolve each of us and the whole of which we are part.

Conflict always presents us with a choice between entropy—that is, the degeneration of a system—and evolution. The impulse to dominate is not just bad manners—if unchecked, it can defeat the process of complexification that ensures the continuation of society. Evolution doesn't simply sit on the sidelines, cheering for the "fittest" to win a decisive victory. Evolution depends on the widest possible variety of survivors. Without diversity, life has nowhere to turn when change is required. Life sees to it that the rains fall on the good and evil alike, so that the game plays on.

Perhaps this accounts for the emptiness that often comes with winning. *The Wall Street Journal* followed the fortunes of several

American Olympic athletes who experienced profound depression after achieving remarkable success at the Games. The source of their unhappiness, it seemed, was that they had lost themselves in the quest to prove themselves superior to their peers. They had forgotten that it was "just a game," and that it was the game they loved more than its outcome. Many of us go through similar disappointment when a long struggle ends in the very victory we had been seeking. As Carse says:

> *The more we are recognized as winners, the more we know ourselves to be losers. That is why it is rare for the winners of highly coveted and publicized prizes to settle for their titles and retire. Winners, especially celebrated winners, must prove repeatedly they are winners.*

If we shift our focus from ending the game to playing the game well, the experience of conflict resolution will be quite different. We can begin to relax a bit. We learn to appreciate our adversary as more important to the quality of our inner sense of order than the solace of friends and the support of family. Mutual respect becomes more rewarding than the praise of partisan observers.

The depth of our character can be measured by the capacity to understand and include the needs and aspirations of others, even of our enemies. While it may be good negotiation tactics to satisfy another's interests so that she will satisfy yours, it is also essential to the continued viability of the system that sustains you both. Coevolution requires that we develop the ability to think on behalf of the whole system, and to make choices that keep us moving toward our goals without ending the game.

Through coevolution, we begin to notice the ways in which we are part of the same whole, branches of the same living tree of life. It is the experience of the whole that radically shifts our framework from self-centeredness to self-realization. This encounter is so far beyond our logical categories of thinking that to grasp it the mind must break free of its terrified isolation and open wide to the entire universe.

IN RELATION TO THE WHOLE

What happens when what we want for ourselves has consequences that don't serve our community, our family, or our environment? How can we think about our goals except in a very self-centered way? Is it possible for human beings who are caught in conflict to become motivated by larger considerations than the impulse to get what we want?

Fortunately, there is a counterbalancing force that seems to beckon us to "get over ourselves," as a wise friend used to say. This voice is much quieter than the ego, but equally persistent. It reflects the idea that we are part of something larger—a "world" or even the "universe." Determining the nature of that "something larger" and how we relate to it is one of the fundamental challenges of the human experience. For some, it is a family, a neighborhood, a church group, a political party, or a corporation. Others are satisfied only by a more universal affiliation, and aspire to a relationship with God or to an encounter with the Absolute.

Learning to see ourselves in relation to the whole, however we describe it, is one of the essential achievements of the evolving person. Teilhard points out that "at first sight we are disconcerted by the association of an Ego with the All. The utter disproportion of the two terms seems flagrant, almost laughable." But this is the relationship from which civilization is derived. The whole is what holds us together. It is the metaphor that contains our disparate energies and imaginations. Being in relation to a world creates a basis for social accountability.

When urban children join gangs and become entangled in endless cycles of murderous revenge, it is because the adults have not initiated them into "the world." This loneliness is too great, too frustrating. Whatever the price, they must enter. So they answer the voice by constructing their own world, with powerful affiliations and terrible consequences.

Understanding the whole and our place in it is what gives life *meaning.* Without meaning that comes from the big picture, we are liable to make decisions strictly on the basis of short-term gratification or simply because they confer a relative advantage over another. Wholeness is the gateway through which we can obtain an accurate sense of direction. Without it, we are lost—whether we know it or not.

Our search for the whole is often filled with dead ends and disappointment. When we attempt to collaborate by engaging in a process or by joining an organization that fails to satisfy the condition of wholeness, we are likely to become isolated and cynical. So we participate halfheartedly, or simply meet our own needs, or we abandon the enterprise. We leave the church because it has no room for nonconformity. We leave the corporation because it demands homogeneity. We leave a marriage because it stifles our personality.

Operating in an environment of wholeness makes us complete. Each individual tends to mirror the complexity and richness of the system in which she operates. Thus, even though we may more readily concur with the decisions made by an organization in which everyone is just like us, the consensus may be shallow and ephemeral. It gives us nothing we don't already have. There is no meaning, because the whole is not present.

GROUP MIND

However, when there is an experience of the whole, it allows us to access a kind of intelligence that far exceeds our usual capability. We can see connections and possibilities that previously were obscure, hidden in a block of marble like Michelangelo's masterpieces. The origin of this intelligence is what might be called *group mind.* Group mind emerges when people engaged in a common project lose track of their independent frame of reference and begin to think on behalf of the whole.

The most common form of group mind is the experience of falling in love. Looking into the hypnotic eyes of the beloved, we lose track of our separate boundaries and "fall" into the boundless, timeless world where two become as one. Together, we become more beautiful, more self-confident, and infinitely more creative. What seemed inconceivable alone becomes effortless in partnership with one another.

Thomas Merton, a wise Trappist monk, understood this better than most married couples:

> *When people are truly in love, they experience far more than just a mutual need for each other's company and consolation. In their relation with one another they become different people: they are more than their everyday selves, more alive, more understanding, more enduring, and seemingly more endowed. They are made over into new beings.*

The experience of group mind, even in professional settings, is not so different from falling in love. When soldiers stand side by side and face death together, it creates a bond much like love. Even working long hours to finish a difficult project by an impossible deadline can create a feeling of intimacy and joy that transcends the mundane dimensions of corporate success. The rare experience of real teamwork is transformative because it has the unique capacity to make us over "into new beings."

The experience of group mind can include those against whom we are engaged in struggle. Skillful competition is a genuine pleasure when we respect our opponent and share a commitment to the highest values of the contest. The game brings us closer, especially when we are most deeply involved in pursuing victory. In this sense, what looks from the outside like competition is actually collaboration. Each of us needs the other to press against us to trigger the release of our own excellence.

A friend once described for me a case in which he represented the father in a custody battle. He doggedly questioned the mother at her deposition and meticulously explored all her weaknesses. Unlike most witnesses in such circumstances, however, she looked him in the eye and answered every question, even over the objection of her own attorney. On the night before the trial, she conceded the case and agreed to allow the father to have custody of the children. This was extremely hard for her to do, since she was moving out of the state and rarely would get to see them.

My friend received a telephone call from the woman the next day, asking him if he would join her for a drink. After consulting with his client, he agreed to do so. He was stunned by what she said to him. "I don't entirely understand this, but I am incredibly attracted to you. You were overwhelming in pursuing your case, but absolutely respectful to me even while you took my kids away. You made me examine everything I thought I knew about their best interests. I should hate you, but I think I may have found the ideal man instead. It's strange, isn't it?"

Such anomalies alert us that something larger may be afoot than meets the eye. We find a contradictory logic at the very center of conflict, when we have pushed past the posturing and the pathos and the power struggles. When we have at last journeyed all the way to the very heart of conflict, we know that we have reached a new boundary, called *the edge of chaos*.

THE EDGE OF CHAOS

This is the stage in nonlinear systems—and human interaction— that approaches chaos but does not yield to it. All sides have fully played their hand and set in motion the full dynamics of opposition. Everything appears headed for mutual annihilation. This is the place of creativity, where the static and dynamic principles maintain a volatile and uneasy truce. It is called the *edge of chaos*. It is here, and only here, that life—and confluence—are possible.

In his excellent treatment of complexity—the new science that is emerging in the wake of chaos theory—Mitchell Waldrop describes the edge of chaos as "the constantly shifting battle zone between stagnation and anarchy, the one place where a complex system can be spontaneous, adaptive, and alive."

Under these conditions—"spontaneous, adaptive, and alive"—higher levels of order are able to make an appearance. The goal is to remain flexible enough to respond to external influences without being knocked into the void of pure chaos. Life requires complexity; it cannot emerge when the elements are homogeneous or incapable of staying within shouting distance of the edge of chaos. A static, linear system inevitably dies; the right amount of chaos, however, makes it possible to adjust to changing circumstances and move ahead as needed.

Evolution constantly moves life to the edge of chaos, where the options for survival always first appear. As it adjusts to external threats and challenges, life at the edge becomes increasingly complex and more highly integrated. Evolution is a process of *complexification*. Adaptations that expand the system's capacity to respond to the outside world will survive; less effective options are discarded by the process of natural selection. Evolution is like a self-correcting computer program that continually creates new applications as it debugs the old ones.

The impulse to assert control over others in the midst of hot conflict reflects an instinctive aversion to edges. Naturally, we prefer comfort, familiarity, and security. Life at the edge is dangerous. If we can only get control over the adversary, it is hoped, life will return to normal and we can avoid having to make unpleasant changes. We want things to stay the same, to be simple. But life can't sustain itself except by becoming more complex.

We can't alter evolutionary principles, but it may be possible to acquire a taste for edges. As cultural historian William Irwin Thompson explains in *The Time Falling Bodies Take to Light*:

Edges are important because they define a limitation in order to deliver us from it. When we come to an edge we come to a frontier that tells us that we are now about to become more than we have been before. As long as one operates in the middle of things, one can never really know the nature of the medium in which one moves.

SYNTROPY: THE EVOLUTION OF THE WHOLE

When we live at the edge of chaos, our boundaries are always in doubt. From this vantage point, it becomes easier to observe the nature of our interdependence, to see the operation of the whole in the interaction of the parts. We see that there is no way to manage chaos except by expanding the social forms through which we contain it.

Social capital—the capacity of human organizations to manage problems—cannot expand except through evolution. Evolution, as we saw, is based on opposition and demands the proliferation of competing and opposing alternatives. In turn, Teilhard tells us, it is precisely through life's struggle to preserve essential differences even as it unites them that humankind moves forward in the face of social evil:

> *[We must face] the evil of growth, by which is expressed in us, in the pangs of childbirth, the mysterious law which, from the humblest chemism to the highest synthesis of the spirit, makes all progress in the direction of increased unity express itself in terms of* work *and* effort. *[We live in] a particular type of cosmos in which evil appears necessarily and as abundantly as you like in the course of evolution—not by accident (which would not much matter) but through the very structure of the system.* [Emphasis added.]

Evolution is not conducted in some laboratory or private meeting room where the scientists and scholars of the world gather secretly to plot our future. Rather, it takes place in our encounters with one another—in the marketplace, the bedroom, and the court-room. When we clash, when we "strike together" in conflict, change is afoot. With change comes the prospect of advancement or de-cline. It is in the dust and blood of conflict that we make decisions that matter and that determine what it means to be human.

Conflict is nature's fundamental tool in the evolutionary game. We cannot eliminate it. But we have the power to alter our relation-ship with it by becoming increasingly aware of the nature of the whole system of which we are a part, and by operating in service to that whole. Confluence occurs only when the individual person is aligned with the whole, which necessarily includes all other persons. Paradoxically, it is only through such "whole systems" thinking that the individual is able fully to self-actualize.

Buckminster Fuller observed that nature is not only entropic—that is, tends to disintegrate—but that it also regenerates itself through the organizational principle he called *syntropy*: the ten-dency of nature to create whole systems at every level, by reorganiz-ing the fragments produced by entropy into higher orders of complexity. If conflict is entropic—that is, turns our well-ordered world into waste—then the sensible solution is to look for ways to convert the waste back into order.

How does this happen? Fuller called it the "honey-money" prin-ciple. A bumblebee is driven to pursue the nectar of flowers, and inadvertently picks up and delivers male pollen along the way to the plant's female organs, "thus unconsciously participating in a vastly complex ecological interaction" that helps sustain the total life system. It is the "side effect" of the bee's visit to the flower that is most important to nature.

Money is the "need" that drives humans to our interactions. But, again, to understand what we do in terms of the entire system, we must look at our behavior not in terms of our own conscious mo-tivation but in terms of the impact we have "ninety degrees" to the side of our intended trajectory. We seek money, and build cities to create it. We seek money, and create microchips and lasers and genetics. We pursue honey, but leave flowers in our wake.

In the case of conflict, it is only by operating out of the framework of "the whole" that we can grasp the real meaning of adversity. But it is more than a framework. A wholistic perspective informs each player of his true role and provides a center from which new solutions might emerge. There are no solutions in a win-lose polarity; only the whole can provide the answer that is unseen by the parts.

How do we find the whole? Not with the linear thinking that keeps us fragmented and in opposition. The truth is that we are *found by* the whole, and this only by maintaining ourselves in a state of radical openness. We must, as the poet Rilke commanded, "live the question" until it draws out an answer from the mists of human experience. The whole is never fully found, never circumscribed, always emerging and evolving. We sense its presence intuitively, search it out, reflect and embody it, and release it to redefine itself again and again.

THE PANARCHY VORTEX

If hierarchy is modeled after a pyramid, panarchy is more like the swirling vortex depicted in Figure 5. A vortex, of which a whirlpool is an example, is a dynamic system that is organized through the power of its center. What is at the center of a vortex? *Nothing.* The movement of the vortex's energy field creates a vacuum at its center, toward which everything in the system is drawn. At the center is stillness—the eye of the storm.

Panarchy's first response to social chaos is not revolution but *evolution.* It is founded not on the substitution of one static organization for another but on the process of orderly emergence. Panarchy moves *toward.* It doesn't flee from chaos but rather seeks always to align itself right at the edge of chaos. Panarchy harnesses the energy of chaos and puts it to work in the development of higher levels of integration and individuation.

As in all social systems, panarchy has its light and dark sides. The risk of panarchy is entropy—the container with which it harvests

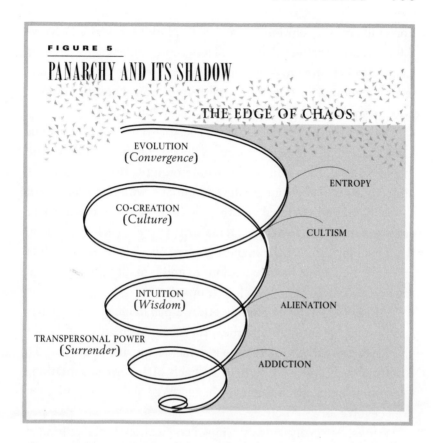

FIGURE 5

PANARCHY AND ITS SHADOW

THE EDGE OF CHAOS

EVOLUTION
(*Convergence*)

ENTROPY

CO-CREATION
(*Culture*)

CULTISM

INTUITION
(*Wisdom*)

ALIENATION

TRANSPERSONAL POWER
(*Surrender*)

ADDICTION

chaos can be so loose that nothing ever takes shape. I remember organizing a series of meetings of leaders of the men's movement with the purpose of engaging emotionally mature men who had done trainings and workshops in an explicitly political venture. Our discussions were great, there was a surplus of enthusiam and energy, but it soon fizzled out. It was too open, too undirected to sustain its own momentum. Entropy got the better of us.

The positive side of evolutionary social organizations is their unique ability to generate *convergence*. Such organizations are open and inclusive. They invite all the players into the fold, whatever their stand or attitude. Anyone who wants to get on the field can play the infinite game of evolution. At some point, all will converge, or come together. The greater the variety, the more powerful its common action. Through the establishment of incongruous and ironic alliances, evolution "eats chaos." Nothing is wasted, every-thing is reused and recycled. Conflict becomes the energy source for an evolutionary system—it keeps the players engaged and commit-ted long enough to transform their interaction. Evolution knows how to say "yes," and it knows when to say "no."

The presumption of evolutionary social systems is that each of us has a place. No one needs to be excluded for the welfare of the whole. In fact, the good of the whole requires that we have the opportunity to realize our greatest potential—within the context of the whole. The individual and the whole meet at the place where each person has the freedom and maturity to make each decision on the basis that "it is for the highest good of all." There is no conflict when the individual has the wisdom to find himself in the center of the vortex, where he meets all of humanity.

With evolution as its guiding ethic, a panarchic system creates and sustains order through the process of *co-creation*. It is not enough just to agree. Co-creation is dynamic, moving us beyond the comfortable stability of consensus. Each of us brings something interesting and alive to the interchange. We catalyze one another. We coevolve as we co-create.

Writers, especially, know the joy of co-creation. In the writing of this book, I spent many happy hours discussing its principles with my brilliant and loving partner, Barbara. As we sat over dinner or walked to the post office, I would ask her a question and she would respond. Until I asked, she didn't know that she knew the answer. My job was to ask the right question. Hers was to fit it with its most perfect rejoinder—to imagine its highest intellectual match. Alone, I wouldn't have asked the question. Alone, she wouldn't have realized she could access the information. We literally *thought together.*

At its best, co-creation is the means by which *culture* is devel-oped. All culture is a dynamic response to what is no longer alive. Culture is what people do in response to the outdated forms of their socially mandated activities. Society consists of our obligations; culture is what we create. Because culture always emerges in distinction to the staleness of what is, it is evolutionary. Culture moves us ahead.

The dark side of co-creation is *cultism*. When imaginative people are drawn together by a powerful vortex, they can become so excited by the feeling of being "on the frontier" that they unconsciously collapse into antagonism toward "the outside world." This leads to defensiveness, even paranoia. What once was dynamic becomes frozen at its embryonic stage and never matures. Cults are failed evolutionary experiments.

Just as judgment was the linear form of discernment used in a static model, *intuition* is the intelligence of dynamic panarchy. The whole cannot be grasped by reason, as St. Thomas Aquinas realized upon the completion of his medieval masterpiece of logic, the *Summa Theologica*. The whole is sensed by nonlinear mental faculties. We must rely on synchronicity, coincidence, a hunch. We can perhaps follow the tracks of the whole, but we cannot know exactly what it is that we pursue. The whole, by definition, cannot be apprehended by any single part. If it is experienced, it cannot be described. Intuition tells us if we are moving in the right direction, but it cannot explain itself to the rational aspect of our thinking mind.

Intuition can bring us to *wisdom*, which is more profound than mere knowledge. Wisdom knows what it does not know. Wisdom is self-aware. *It knows.* Intuition is able to sense the whole through an inexplicable wisdom that is able to determine whether the whole is present or whether someone or something else must be included to make the process complete.

Intuition can also be incredibly lonely. Its shadow is *alienation*. Many times, those who receive powerful intuitive messages from an incomprehensibly deep source are left troubled or disturbed. A "religious experience" can produce a schizophrenic as well as a saint. In indigenous shamanic traditions, the would-be "medicine man" must first leave his senses and travel to "the lower world" before he develops the power to heal. In modern society, this experience is usually diagnosed as a psychotic break and results in institutionalization.

This was the plight of Cassandra, who was the sister of Paris—he who stole Helen of Troy and thereby triggered the Trojan War. Cassandra was highly intuitive—she could foretell the future, but was cursed by Apollo so that no one ever believed her prophecy. She always knew what was coming but couldn't prevent it, which was a terrible kind of suffering.

The force of panarchy is realized through *transpersonal power*. That is, power and authority do not reside in any person, but in the whole itself. An individual may share in this energy to the extent that she embodies or attends to the whole. Transpersonal power moves through and transforms those who hold it. It changes the person, making one more available to the whole. Transpersonal power requires leaders who are stewards. It can annihilate the ego and any other obstacle that stands in the way.

Transpersonal power is not acquired through competition, but because the leader has learned to *surrender*. There is no other way to achieve confluence except by "getting out of your own way." One must become transparent so that the power can flow through the channels of the whole without becoming diverted to private aggrandizement. The religious person experiences this when he makes choices on the basis of the Islamic prayer *insha Allah* or the Spanish *si Dios quiere*—both meaning "if God wills it." The politician can learn to discern the commonweal before he plays to the media, the parent can consider the family before she accepts a transfer to a new town, the executive can reflect on the effect on real people of "cutting overhead."

On the other hand, because the experience of transpersonal power is so extraordinary, it can become *addictive*. One can become hooked on romantic love, which is the most common experience of transpersonal power, or on the ecstasy of group process or even on God. Father Leo Booth, in his book *When God Becomes a Drug*, describes religious addiction as

*using God, a religion, or a belief system as a means both to escape
and avoid painful feelings and to seek self-esteem. It involves
adopting a rigid belief system that specifies only one right way,
which you feel you must force onto others by means of guilt,
shame, fear, brain-washing, and elitism.*

We can become so "empowered" by our support group at church
or a training or a conversion experience or our corporate retreat that
we want to force it onto everyone and repeat it as often as possible.
This is again another form of resisting true openness, and soon it
hardens our conceptual arteries and reduces us to clichés and group-
speak. Panarchy must stay open, alive, ever-emerging.

INSTITUTIONS IN MOTION

In what ways are institutions established by hierarchical and panarchical systems different? After the Parliament of the World's
Religions ended, those who had been involved immediately confronted both hierarchical and panarchical models for continuing its
work.

The board of trustees of the organizing Council quickly began to
discuss how they might continue the interreligious dialogue that
started at the first Parliament in 1893 and was reflected again in
1993. The Council had been organized for the sole purpose of
sponsoring a one-time event, but the Parliament's great success and
the resulting international attention made it difficult to think about
folding up the tents.

Neither the Assembly of Religious and Spiritual Leaders nor the
Parliament of the People was asked to come to an agreement about
the Parliament's future role, but it was clear that most participants
wanted *something* to happen. There was too much momentum to
let things simply drop. In both sets of meetings, participants made it
apparent that they wanted the Parliament to provide the resources
that were created by the event—videotapes and transcripts of
speeches, manuals on interreligious dialogue, networks and

newsletters—to stay connected and carry the conversation around the world.

Many of the Assembly members and participants felt strongly that any organization created to carry on the work of the Parliament must be founded on a spiritual rather than on a political basis. That is, it must find a way to transcend the struggle for power and prominence that characterizes so many human endeavors— including, too often, religious organizations.

Over the past decades, a number of major international inter-religious organizations had become well established, including the World Conference on Religion and Peace, the International Association for Religious Freedom, the Temple of Understanding, and the World Council of Churches. But some Assembly members began to call for a new global legislative body, a "United Nations of Religions," and the hierarchical hook was set. Might there not be room for another player? Shouldn't there be some centralized organization that could speak with one strong voice?

The Council's board of trustees, consisting of local Chicagoans active in the city's many faith traditions, promptly grew from thirty-seven members before the Parliament to fifty-one members afterward. For over a year after the event, various committees struggled with the question of what role religion and spirituality should assume in the modern world. More particularly, what kind of organization might they establish to provide a unified religious response to the collapse of morality, the growth of violence, and the widening chasm between the rich and the poor?

Among some influential trustees, the idea of a "United Nations of Religions" had great appeal. But as discussions turned to hard questions of representation, funding, and the inevitable jockeying for control, it became increasingly apparent that any organization built around a hierarchical model would consume an enormous amount of talent and financial resources simply tending to its own complex needs, and might never get around to addressing the critical global issues facing the outside world. For too long, this precise dilemma had been the problem with institutional religion. It was in the struggle for power that religion and politics began to merge, and spirituality was lost altogether.

Shortly after the first anniversary of the Parliament event, the Council trustees realized that the notion of creating the ultimate interreligious bureaucracy, with a permanent policy-making body and an impressive headquarters, was futile. Even if it could be established, such an institution would create more problems than it could solve. Without a clear sense of purpose and mission, it would fall prey to the unavoidable human drive for personal and institutional power. As the excitement generated by the Parliament event began to recede, support for the hierarchical model slowly evaporated.

But while the Council struggled with its ambitions on the international plane, a very different model of organizational growth began to emerge right under its nose. At the local level, something was stirring. Around the world, grassroots organizations formed and found one another after the Parliament event. In Chicago, local members of the Council launched a "facilitative" interreligious organization called the Metropolitan Interreligious Initiative. On the Internet, a fluid collaboration called United Communities of Spirit emerged and sparked thousands of animated exchanges. By avoiding any pretense of being an official representative body, such groups could focus on the problems facing the community rather than becoming distracted by questions of their own structures. Anyone who wanted to help others address important interreligious issues could participate without having to fight the battles of a political hierarchy.

Finally, the Council recognized that the pursuit of power on the international front was pointless, and it turned to the model that was working so well on the local level—panarchy. Trustees started to remember that the Parliament itself was not created by powerful religious institutions but by volunteer "host committees" consisting of dedicated lay people at the grassroots. They did the work because they shared the dream, not because they wanted the power.

So the Council went back to its original and unambiguous mission—to convene a meeting of religious and spiritual seekers from throughout the world. Instead of once every hundred years, the Parliament now would be convened every five years, each time in a new part of the world. South Africa would be its next venue.

Without the burden of hierarchy, a renewed spirit of hope returned to the Council. It had nearly lost its soul in the struggle to lay claim to power and importance. From now on, the Council would simply serve as a good host. The next Parliament would be even better, more inclusive, more participatory. At the dawn of the new century, there was the possibility that the politics of power might now be finally discarded in favor of the politics of the whole.

NATURAL BOUNDARIES:
The Rock and the Hard Place

*For a long time it had seemed to me that life was about to
begin—real life. But there was always some obstacle in the
way, something to be got through first, some unfinished
business, time still to be served, a debt to be paid. Then,
life would begin. At last it dawned on me that these
obstacles were my life.*

D'Souza

It would be naive to claim that all differences can—or should—be
resolved. Sometimes, there is no agreement, no reconciliation, no
forgiveness, no peace. There are times when the conflict persists,
like a boulder in the stream, and the waters of life must divide and
find separate ways around it.

We encounter intractable differences wherever human will has
etched its beliefs and values deeply in our identity. Incompatible religious attitudes and clashing cultural norms are cited in support of
nearly 80 percent of all wars and organized violence. Notwithstanding
decades of cooperation (whether entirely voluntary or not) in unified
forms of government, ethnic groups throughout the world are now
reasserting their nationalistic hostilities with apocalyptic ferocity. In
this country, racial distinctions seem to multiply and intensify every
day as we "celebrate our diversity" and lose track of our unity.

War is the most salient symbol—and outcome—of intractable differences. As civilization marches forward, we continually improve our capacity to destroy ourselves. According to Michael Renner of Worldwatch Institute in its 1993 report, *State of the World*:

> *The frequency and intensity of war steadily increased from Roman times onward, and its destructive impact has escalated. Three quarters of all war deaths since the days of Julius Caesar have occurred in this century. The number of war-related deaths has risen from less than one million in the fifteenth century to some 110 million so far in this one, far outpacing the rate of population growth.*

Are there truly genuine cases of irreconcilable differences, or is it just a lack of imagination or perspective? If so, how can we know whether a particular conflict is irresolvable or just stubborn? What can we do, if anything, when such a conflict appears? Is it possible to live together when we are defined by fundamentally different ways of looking at the world?

IDENTITY AND CRISIS

Identity means "sameness." We identify with those who are the same as we, whose characteristics we share. We know who we are by looking at those with whom we identify. Identity is what we are willing to die for.

Psychologist Erik Erikson used the term "identity crisis" to refer to the experience of self-doubt and confusion about goals, character, and affinity that often occurs in times of great change and upheaval. We are familiar with this as a feature of adolescence. The crisis begins when we begin to lose our sense of connection with our family or culture. If we move successfully through this crisis, we will have differentiated from our roots so that we can claim our own uniqueness. Having established our own identity, we can then choose our path and our alliances more intentionally.

When we come home, it will be as more seasoned citizens of a larger world.

The crisis of identity affects not just adolescents but whole organizations and even cultures. There are many kinds of intractable differences, but virtually all of them can be reduced to threats against identity or to an identity crisis that arises in response to change.

When we breach that boundary between what is me and what is not, when my innermost chamber is threatened, the powerful instincts of the survivor are invoked. At all costs, we defend the "self"—not just the body, but the identity of which it is part. Because we humans derive our identity more from our consciousness (who we think we are or imagine ourselves to be) than from our physical form (which naturally changes and can be surgically altered without losing identity), we will fight harder for our ideas than for our actual corporeal survival. If we are willing to die for our identity, it assumes a kind of immortality that we otherwise cannot achieve.

Over lunch one afternoon I was discussing interreligious conflict with a Roman Catholic priest with expertise in comparative religion and who directed ecumenical matters for his diocese. In describing how conflicting parties can be moved past their identities to a sense of commonality, I related a story about meeting with representatives of fourteen major religions to plan a joint statement of principles, and repeated the comments of one participant: "When we started this morning, I didn't see how we could get along about anything. But now, I can't find anything in my heart that makes us different."

I then made the mistake of bringing the analogy closer to home. "Identity is a kind of stepping-stone to unity, don't you think? You, for example, Father, are a man, as well as a priest. You have much in common with other men, regardless of their beliefs."

The priest nearly exploded. "I am not a man first! I am a *priest!* You do not understand Catholicism if you don't understand that who I most fundamentally am is a Catholic, and everything else comes behind that!"

Because I was trained for eight years by Jesuits, I certainly could make no claim to understand Catholicism! But what was most significant was the sheer strength of the priest's identification with his religious views. Who he was, was Catholic. He did not wear his beliefs like a suit, to be taken off at night. He could not imagine coming to a point at which he could recognize himself yet not be aware of his religion.

To address those aspects of his being outside his religion was to put his very self at risk. The passion of his identity defense mechanism illustrated to me the force with which we meet challenges to what we claim as "I." On what basis could such a man engage with those who held contrary, but equally strong, religious views? Is intractable conflict with "nonbelievers" resolvable only through conversion or marginalization of the other? Is genuine dialogue even possible when identity is derived through fundamental beliefs about reality?

ETHNICITY

A clear example of the way in which challenges to identity can lead to seemingly irresolvable conflict is in the arena of ethnicity. In a world that now seems caught in an ever-accelerating cycle of rapid change, the proliferation of the ethnic identity crisis has escalated to the point where it now seems universal. The system as a whole is heating up and heading toward chaos.

An ethnic group is *family*. It is the connection among those who believe themselves to be ancestrally related. A nation is an extended ethnic family that both feels the ancestral tie and has some form of territorial connection. When we suffer a personal or shared identity crisis, or are induced to believe that we're having one (as when demagogues use propaganda to create mass ethnic hysteria among people who have been co-existing peacefully for generations), we can lose track of our private selves and invest the ethnic group with our identity. *I* becomes *us*.

The magnetic attraction of the ethnic group can be strong, and can pull us, unthinking, into identification with the symbols—and biases—of those around us. We surrender our identity to our peers, or to those who seem more powerful or effective, or to those we wish to emulate. This gives us comfort in a hostile world. We band together for warmth against the blowing winds.

Group identification seems fundamental to the human condition. Erik Erikson describes identity as a process located in the core of an individual and yet also in the core of his communal culture. The group gives a sense of belongingness and enhances our self-esteem. But group identity, as we saw in our earlier discussion, often leads to the identification of some other group against which to press. We are *us*. They are *them*.

A young gang member in Chicago once described for me his frustration at not being free to continue his friendship with a high-school classmate who belonged to a rival group in the same gang:

> *We went on, like, a retreat this summer and I realized that this guy and I were really the same, like the same guy. We talked about the shit that happened to us and our problems with drugs and all that, and even ended up crying in each other's arms. But when we came back to school, no way I could talk to him. Couldn't even say, "Wha's up?" Had to be enemies. Why? Because he's with them, and they're our enemies. Don't know why. Just that way.*

When there is no superior authority, principle, or common purpose to hold disparate ethnic groups together, the threat that "they" pose to "our" identity can bring both groups barreling toward the edge of chaos. There are two directions in which the process may go. To take an increasingly obvious case, having loosed the fetters of Soviet totalitarianism, we may find that ethnic chaos will continue indefinitely in its former republics until new forms of totalitarianism are put in place by victorious subgroups or until the process of genocide and forced migration is virtually complete.

Or, alternatively, the world might discover that traditional ethnic identification is simply unsupportable as a premise for civic organization. As Senator Daniel Patrick Moynihan contends in *Pandaemonium*, ethnic identity is important for culture, but it can be fatal in the realm of politics.

When tribal, racial, or ethnic affiliation is taken as the central organizing principle of a polity, usually under the rubric of "self-determination," the consequences can be disastrous. When Woodrow Wilson in 1917 announced the doctrine of "national self-determination" in support of his decision to enter World War I, he precipitously lifted the hopes of many:

> *National aspirations must be respected; peoples may now be dominated and governed only by their own consent. "Self-determination" is not a mere phrase. It is an imperative principle of action, which statesmen henceforth will ignore at their peril.*

But what is a "people"? Wilson realized too late that he had let the genie out of the bottle. Without any practical definition of the irreducible unit that was entitled to determine itself, anyone could make the claim. And anyone did. Twenty years later, Adolf Hitler explicitly relied on Wilson's rhetoric to support his invasion of Czechoslovakia. Minorities the world over seek self-determination in order to deny it to others. The rhetoric, which has raised the hopes of so many, in fact has been used to nourish the fast-spreading virus of civil deconstruction that Moynihan describes as "restless and mutating all the time."

Borrowing from socio-psychologist Harold Isaacs, Moynihan traces the repercussions of the collapse of great empires and systems of social coherence:

> *What we are experiencing . . . is not the shaping of new coherences but the world breaking into its bits and pieces, bursting like big and little stars from exploding galaxies . . . each one straining to hold its own small separate pieces from spinning off in their turn.*

CLOSED AND OPEN IDENTITY

Although it is a matter of degree, there are two basic ways in which individuals and groups hold their identity. The first is a static, or closed, identity; the second is dynamic, or open. When one suffers from an imbalance in the direction of one or the other, conflict becomes the vehicle through which the feeling of equilibrium is restored. This is especially so in the case of static identity.

For many of us, the working assumption in life seems to be—to borrow a line from Popeye—"I yam what I yam." We operate as if the structure of the self is as fixed as a mathematical formula or the frame of a house. The metaphor we adopt—and the self is nothing if not a metaphor—is inflexible, fortress-like, airtight. When we are able to repel the invasion of the "outside," our pride in the edifice is strengthened.

A closed identity defines itself through fixed symbols or boundaries received from outside itself. The security of static identity depends on one's *orthodoxy*—that is, the degree of a person's conformity with or loyalty to those symbols or beliefs. Thus, one is a "good Catholic," a "good Marine," or an "authentic Marxist." Intimacy with others is limited by the fear of being diluted by the encounter.

On the other hand, who are we without something that is firm, unshakable, and irreducible at the core? Without some unquestionable principle or belief, what will govern the morality of our conduct? To take an extreme example, without a clear and unalterable sense of self, how can the prisoner of war or the prisoner of conscience survive the cell and the thousand forms of torture our enemies have devised for us? On what basis do we take a stand against evil?

As in all systems, there is an essential part for the static personality—or better, the static part of the personality—to play. It keeps us anchored while we chart the next leg of our journey. But is there truly a single, constant idea of self against which all external influences and opinions must be measured? Writer Michael Ventura sees a whole tribe inhabiting his psyche:

> *This fiction* [of monopersonality] *is the notion that each person has a central and unified "I" which determines his or her acts. "I" have been writing this to say that I don't think people experience life that way. I do think they experience* language *that way, and hence are doomed to speak about life in structures contrary to their experience. This contributes to the pervasive and impotent sense of bafflement that very quickly can turn to violence. . . . The central "I" is not a fact, it's a longing—the longing of all the selves within the psyche that are starving because they are not recognized. . . . Our institutions don't match our experience, and that is causing chaos on a world scale.*

It might be said, then, that a person or group with a fundamentally static sense of self will encounter conflict every time its rigid identity, like an old tree, encounters the elements. In strong winds, its branches will break because they cannot bend. If the person or group cannot access other "selves" to relate compatibly with strangers from the outer world, resistance becomes its only strategy. The basic response of a static identity is to close itself off, to exclude, to repel. When frustrated, it turns to violence.

A dynamic personality, on the other hand, is open to influence from others, even to being changed by them. Identity is a permeable membrane through which the world may pass, and not only is the essence not endangered, but it is expanded and strengthened. The dynamic personality is committed to change and growth, and is willing to experience the death of its outer layers again and again so that the flow of life will not be blocked. It does not see the true self as anything that can be described, delineated, or defended. The true self is that which reveals its being in the process of *becoming.* The dynamic self does not fear conflict because it has nothing to lose.

In *The Way of Transformation,* Karlfried Graf von Durckheim

advises us to avoid the easy way, the call of comfort and the temptation to preserve the old self that we have outgrown:

> *Only to the extent that man exposes himself over and over*
> *again to annihilation can that which is indestructible arise*
> *within him. . . .* [Rather than seek peace, his practice] *should*
> *teach him to let himself be assaulted, perturbed, moved, insulted,*
> *broken, and battered—that is to say, it should enable him to dare*
> *to let go his futile hankering after harmony, surcease from pain,*
> *and a comfortable life in order that he may discover, in doing*
> *battle with the forces that oppose him, that which awaits him*
> *beyond the world of opposites.*

Not an easy way to live, perhaps. And there are dangers. There
are many who go so far as to abandon all beliefs and connections
with tradition but never go deep enough into raw experience to
encounter that which is "indestructible." Intending to live as trav-
elers, we merely become homeless drifters on the psychological
landscape. Canadian poet Robert W. Service (best remembered for
"The Cremation of Sam McGee") witnessed this sense of lostness at
the turn of the century in the hardy souls who ventured to the
Yukon to make their fortunes in the gold rush:

> *There's a race of men that don't fit in,*
> *A race that can't stay still;*
> *So they break the hearts of kith and kin,*
> *And they roam the world at will.*
> *They range the field and they rove the flood,*
> *And they climb the mountain's crest;*
> *Theirs is the curse of the gipsy blood,*
> *And they don't know how to rest.*
>
> *If they just went straight they might go far;*
> *They are strong and brave and true;*
> *But they're always tired of the things that are,*

And they want the strange and new.
They say: "Could I find my proper groove,
What a deep mark I would make!"
So they chop and change, and each fresh move
Is only a fresh mistake.

When people with closed identities confront one another, or confront those with open identities, the conflict often seems intractable. A closed system resists change, so collaboration, and probably even cooperation, is out of the question. A static identity is capable only of the finite game of domination. One man's loss is another man's gain.

The conflict doesn't stay intractable if either party has the power to overcome the other and is willing to use that power. But if there is an impasse, either between two static identities or between a static and a dynamic agent, it can be tremendously frustrating and destructive.

ZEUS AND PROMETHEUS

Perhaps the ultimate legend of intractable conflict—where the "immovable object" meets the "irresistible force"—is, again, the story of Prometheus. To punish Prometheus's theft of fire, Zeus had the rebellious Titan chained to a rocky crag in the desolate Caucasus Mountains and, because proud Prometheus would not submit to Zeus, an eagle was sent by Zeus daily to eat out the Titan's liver. Prometheus was immortal, and his flesh restored itself each night, so again the next day he suffered the same torment.

Prometheus knew a dark secret, however. He alone knew the name of the female who, if bedded by Zeus, would produce a son strong enough to depose his divine father. Even when Zeus sends Hermes to warn Prometheus that worse things yet are in store for him if he does not reveal the woman's name, Prometheus refuses to yield: "There is no wrong, however shameful, nor shift in malice whereby Zeus shall persuade me to unlock my lips until these shackles shall be cast loose."

Even though Prometheus saw the suffering ahead for him, he called on Zeus to "let curled lightnings clasp and clash and close upon my limbs," for "his sentence shall not doom this deathless self to die!"

Although Aeschylus's play ends with Prometheus sinking into the abyss, we learn from other sources that, in time, something shifted between them. The gods are not unalterable, after all. Thirteen generations later, Hercules, a son of Zeus, slew the ravenous eagle and released Prometheus. Prometheus then warned Zeus to avoid the considerable charms of Thetis, the sea nymph, if he was to stay in power. Classicist Rex Warner tells us that "each had, in a manner, submitted to the other," thus ending the quarrel that had divided heaven itself.

THE ROCK IN THE STREAM

When two boulders crash against each other, the impact may destroy one or both of them. When flowing water encounters what seems to be an unmovable obstacle, however, it has a few more options. It can go around it, gradually wear it down, or roll it down the river bed intact. These are the strategies that a dynamic, fluid person can employ when she encounters an implacable and closed adversary.

1. GO AROUND IT. Sometimes the best thing in life to do is to move on. Shake the dust off your sandals and head for the next town. Close this chapter of the story. Grow out of it. Get a life. Focus your attention on rebuilding your practice, your business, or your city. Any attempt to reach an accommodation with the boulder will only make waves without making progress.

Even in the midst of the worst parts of Chicago, with blocks of abandoned buildings and gangs and drugs and a pervasive sense of hopelessness, you can always find a house that's painted and well-tended and clean. Green grass in the front and a little garden in the back.

An oasis in the urban desert is a place where the water continues to bubble up, where the life force isn't consumed by the struggle against but creates the flow toward. Any of us can create an oasis, wherever we are, whatever we face. We can make a life. We can keep flowing, right around the rocks and the fallen buildings.

2. WEAR IT DOWN. It took thirteen generations, but eventually Zeus and Prometheus found a way to come to terms. In time, most adversaries reach the same point. Persistence and constancy, as the tortoise showed the hare, usually win out. What is required is the willingness to induce changes that may be so slight that they aren't apparent to the other person. There is little awareness that anything has loosened, so little resistance.

At my parents' fortieth wedding anniversary, an uncle remarked that my mother was like a dripping spring. One drop at a time, she gradually wore my father smooth, almost without his noticing. He was a boulder, and wouldn't have tolerated a more obvious reshaping.

3. ROLL IT DOWN THE RIVER. As long as a static personality stays intact, she may not realize that she has been quietly carried away by the strong currents of circumstance. Most people with closed identities like to think of themselves as more resistant to change than they in fact are. They find themselves moving along even as they insist that everything has remained perfectly still.

In politics, for example, whenever it suits them to do so, Democrats and Republicans frequently change position to adopt one another's policies even as they insist "this has always been our view." I remember attending a meeting once with some prominent liberals and conservatives. Each was asked to identify the values that were most important to the welfare of the nation. To our amazement, the entire group agreed to seven fundamental principles. "It's good to see that you liberals have finally come around," one conservative said, half laughing.

"It's *you guys* who have finally gotten it," rejoined a liberal.

Apparently, without wanting to admit they'd changed, everyone had.

I worked once for a brilliant but very argumentative lawyer. We seemed to disagree about nearly everything, and I always walked out of his office feeling frustrated and ineffective. The only way I knew that I had gotten through was when my point of view began to show up in his memoranda—as *his* point of view! Never would he acknowledge, or even notice, that he had changed.

IRRECONCILABLE DIFFERENCES: AGREEING TO DISAGREE

Returning to the problem of two boulders on a collision course, how do we deal with intractable conflict when there's no water around? Jungian analyst Robert Johnson, in *Owning Your Own Shadow*, says that it is precisely "when the unstoppable bullet hits the impenetrable wall, we find the religious experience."

Normally, two closed systems collide at the point of their lowest common denominator. Even the brightest lawyers and the shrewdest statesmen can be reduced to employing simple brute force when they confront unyielding opposition. Conflicts over important questions among dignified people can devolve into shouting matches, name-calling, and physical force.

As a young lawyer of Irish ancestry, I once was invited over to a local politician's home so that I might be solicited for support on behalf of the cause of Irish independence. Present for after-dinner drinks were an elected state official, a member of the governor's staff, a prominent Washington lobbyist, and their wives. The governor's aide, the only one of us actually born on the old sod, said he couldn't ask for money without reviewing a bit of the historical background on the conflict with Great Britain.

My friend hadn't quite gotten through the seventeenth century before his account of the state of Irish education at the time was called into question by the lobbyist. Within minutes, things had accelerated.

"The hedge schools were terrible for the Irish. You don't know what you're saying. You weren't even born there."

"What does that have to do with it? You were born there and you're still ignorant. And I've always thought you a bit pompous, too, throwing your brogue around like a credential."

Now the wives got into it. "It's about time somebody straightened this fellow out. I've been listening to this for years, and nobody brings it to a real conclusion."

Everyone's face was deep red. I looked around for the whiskey just as one of the fellows whipped off his jacket and grabbed the other by the lapel. "It's about time we stepped outside, don't you think? Take care of this once and for all?"

The elected official laughed heartily and put his arm around my shoulders. "Now you understand why the English are still there. We're too busy fighting each other about what happened in the seventeenth century to worry about fighting the British in the twentieth!"

When closed systems reduce one another to the lowest common denominator, they devolve toward entropy, depression, and violence. But there is another choice: pursuing the *highest common denominator.* When intractable opponents confront one another at their highest level, there may be no resolution, as such, but the exchange will still be beneficial to both sides. It lifts them both up by elevating the playing field, even though the game's still afoot. The highest common denominator is always a process—a new and better game—rather than an outcome. It is open-ended, ongoing.

Pope John Paul II created a stir among Buddhists when, in his book *Crossing the Threshold of Hope,* he described their religion as having a "negative soteriology"—meaning, salvation is achieved through the negation of attachments to the world. The term, which is a technical theological phrase, was interpreted as suggesting that Buddhism is "negative" or valueless. The Sri Lankan Buddhists protested his arrival in their country, and challenged the Pope to a debate.

Perhaps, rather than smoothing things out through diplomatic channels, the Pope should have taken the Buddhists up on their offer. The world would benefit from witnessing the intellectual and spiritual contest between two compelling but vastly different belief systems. Both Christians and Buddhists accord a distinguished position to debate within their own systems, and each would be well-positioned to challenge some of the unresolved questions in the other's tradition.

In his article "Why We Need Interreligious Polemics," University of Chicago Divinity School professor Paul Griffiths observes that

> *the intellectual life is essentially and constitutively agonistic. It progresses almost entirely by struggle, by challenge and response, by thesis and antithesis, by getting it wrong and then moving, always asymptotically, toward getting it right.*

Griffiths advocates polemics, an adversarial intellectual struggle, as "the kind of engagement that does and should occur when those who take what they believe seriously encounter others equally serious about, and committed to, their beliefs." Engaging in dialogue that has as its purpose the obfuscation of real and meaningful differences in the interest of a manufactured mutuality may be a short-term necessity or acceptable convenience, but it often leaves both sides feeling patronized or manipulated. Blurring distinctions that matter is an erosion not only of the ideas but also of the identity of the adversaries.

One of the frequent criticisms of mediation is that it usually pays little attention to the objective merits of the parties' positions and attends principally to reaching an agreement—sometimes, *any* agreement. The press of "bottom line" negotiations often fails to distinguish between strongly held and legitimate principles (such as, "Over the years, my trusted employee systematically embezzled money from the company, and should be held accountable") and pressures that amount to plain extortion ("We know you have no liability in the case, but you must pay us money because defending yourself will cost you thousands of dollars in legal fees if you don't settle").

One solution to this is to provide a fuller opportunity for the parties to contest one another in a way that is not subject to the abuse that often accompanies litigation but recognizes that some things are true, others are not; that some positions are right, and others are mistaken.

What are the possible outcomes of such an engagement? One, clarification. When you push me hardest, I must study my own reasoning carefully, and perhaps will come to understand my own mind better. By questioning you, I may come to understand you better. Two, correction. Maybe I was mistaken. Or you were. Or both. Three, an agreement to disagree.

One of the great achievements in human thought is the recognition that people can "agree to disagree." We both remain convinced that we are right—perhaps, even more so than before—but the encounter took away the edge from our disagreement. I can still have my position without savaging your right to yours.

At the Parliament of the World's Religions, I asked the venerable Thai Buddhist monk Ajahn Phra Maha Surasak Jivanando how the differences among the religions, which seemingly had caused so much bloodshed, might be reconciled. "Simple," he replied through an interpreter. "Each religion must follow its own precepts, be true to itself. Then there will be peace. War comes not from following religion but by disobeying it."

Something remarkable can happen when two irreconcilable positions encounter one another fully. At a level that is almost too subtle to describe, *they get over themselves.* The polarity remains, but it becomes something else, as well. If they stay true to their own integrity, their identity shifts, expands, becomes more flexible. Each is led by the encounter to a deeper identity in which contradictions are sustainable.

Change happens by itself. It is not something that can be forced or imposed. When I feel secure enough in myself, I can open my mind to another. In the meanwhile, I must hold our differences, allow them to churn inside me without hope of reconciliation, until the system itself makes the next leap forward.

LOVE IS THE PROBLEM, LOVE IS THE SOLUTION

When people touch their most fundamental core, their incontestable values, the natural boundaries past which they will not go, then love, in a sense, becomes the problem. Love of country, family, God; love of principle, love of morality, race, or nationality. When we discover the thing we would die for, too often, that's what we do.

It is part of human nature to become attached to the objects of our love. Love and attachment are not the same, however. Our idea of the thing, however compelling, is not the thing itself. It is an interpretation, a point of view. Perhaps our image comes from a fond memory, a treasured experience, or a hope for the future. Attachment occurs when this idea or image of the beloved replaces the thing itself. Attachment is a form of sentimentalism, in which we come to care more about the feeling that is generated than the thing that provokes the feeling. In this way, we fill the thing, as we perceive it, with ourselves.

When we encounter an adversary, our attachments come under attack. Burning the American flag is no threat to the ideals of democracy, but it offends the patriotic attachments we have formed. We have no reason to suspect that God is threatened by the atheist, the infidel, or the sinner, but millions have died in His (or Her) defense. It is fair to say that the greatest passions are aroused not by fundamental and essential differences but by threats to the images and symbols we have created in our search to make sense of it all.

Combatants are motivated by symbols because we can pour ourselves—our memories, aspirations, and beliefs—into them. In this way, we become prey to leaders who manipulate us with our own sentimentality and to enemies who threaten it. We are easily inspired to "rally 'round the flag," and may not take the time to inquire whether the cause is worthy of our sons and daughters. In a custody dispute, we may rush to the defense of motherhood or fatherhood or the best interests of the children, only to drown in our own rhetoric. We fight too often over images, rather than essences.

The task of the adversary (whether, like Buckminster Fuller's honey bee, she knows it or not) is to strip us of our attachments. Conflict destroys pretense. It takes us on a journey through the lower world and wrenches from our hands the things we call most precious. In this way, conflict liberates us from our illusions and makes us real.

In the movie *Jacob's Ladder*, the protagonist tells his chiropractor that he has been having terrible waking dreams about being pursued by awful demons. He fears for his life, and believes these frightening beings may be real. The chiropractor, a wise and loving man, assures his terrified friend that they seem to be demons only as long as he holds on to things he no longer needs. "When you let go, they turn into angels."

There is no shortcut in this process. The encounter with the adversary is required for us both. If we walk away from the irresolvable conflict, or give in when a fight is required, or make peace too soon, the spell of our attachments will not be broken. We sell both sides short.

The story of Krishna and his charioteer Arjuna from the earlier discussion of confrontation again comes to mind. When we rise to the occasion, when we stand like Arjuna on a battlefield that we cannot leave without leaving ourselves behind, we paradoxically both define and transcend our boundaries. We find ourselves on the field of glory with gods and goddesses at our side. And there it is that we see the truth about the other—*her* courage, *her* brilliance, *her* pure heart.

And, perhaps for the first time, it becomes possible to "love your enemy." At this place, having stood our ground, we find ourselves standing on common ground. We see how opposites attract, and understand that this contradictory attraction is a remarkable kind of love. There is no sentiment here. This is "tough love." We do not see the other simply as a reflection of ourselves or as a demon. We are actually able to break through our own weakened defenses to behold the other person as he or she actually is, without our projections or interpretations getting in the way. Such an encounter, if achieved, can be shattering and change us both.

Love as experienced through an encounter with the adversary is not an emotion but the mystery through which that which is separate is also one, without losing its separate nature. Theology calls the reconciliation of two distinct natures "hypostatic union." It is as if there is a third person that contains them both—man and God, man and woman, self and other. Those who are in love know this feeling, this third person. Through the door of the one I love, I encounter a self that is the self-of-the-two.

The Greek philosopher Empedocles said that the two forces that move the universe are love and strife. In fact, they are merely two sides of the same coin. If love or friendship are nurtured long enough, the other person eventually discovers (and usually points out) our faults and weaknesses. If these issues are not resolved, and things fall apart, the close friend or lover can become a powerful and well-armed adversary.

It is true the other way, as well. When adversaries fight with honor, they may come to respect and then to admire one another, and admiration often leads to genuine affection. I have watched hundreds of men in weekend trainings face off against each other, their voices booming with fierce rage and pain, only to fall laughing on the ground with each other in the sheer joy of unbounded animal aggression.

There's a relief in finding the place where force meets force, and nothing moves. We become free of the burden of our attachment to ourselves and our own agenda. We lose ourselves in it. And this is the adversary's strange gift. By pushing us to the edge, to the limits of our endurance, beyond what we thought we could survive, we experience the awakening of something much deeper in ourselves than we had suspected.

It is at this moment that we discover the living heart of conflict.

FINDING THE HEART OF CONFLICT:
Paradox and Genius

> *Not too often in the story of mankind does a man arrive on the earth who is both steel and velvet, who is as hard as a rock and soft as drifting fog, who holds in his heart and mind the paradox of terrible storm and peace unspeakable and perfect.*
>
> **Carl Sandburg**

CONFLICT AND CHARACTER

The strategies we have discussed so far principally explore ways to deal with conflict as an external event involving other people. With the exception of truly intractable differences, we have looked at our ability to impact a situation as a measure of success.

But the encounter with conflict is a profoundly personal one. Whatever the outcome of a strategy, the experience leaves a deep and often lasting impression on our character. The way we deal with conflict is not just a matter of what we do; it also has much to do with *who we are*. Winning does not guarantee happiness; loss sometimes is a bittersweet breakthrough to new dimensions of joy.

One of the great heroes of failure was Abraham Lincoln. He lost elections. His policies were often rejected. Famous for his depression, he became a profound and inspirational leader, perhaps because he harbored so few illusions. Loss and grief and weariness carved themselves on his soul. There was no room for pretense, for sentimentality, for arrogance. When he determined to preserve the Union, nothing would deter him. When he forgave his enemies, he was hugely generous.

In Lincoln, the waters of life flowed deeply. The greatness of his heart allowed him to contain contradiction—to wage war fiercely, to advance the cause of equality with cunning and brilliance, to reshape the very notion of what America was about in the 272 elegiac words he spoke at Gettysburg, and yet to honor the courage of Southern adversaries once the battle had been won.

Conflict is not indifferent to character. In fact, character has no existence apart from opposition. It is as if conflict is programmed into our genes as the catalytic agent through which our highest, and deepest, nature is enticed to appear and enter the world. At first, this nature is wild and untamed and reacts violently to the limits and demands of human society like a storm raining down upon mountains it cannot pass. Broken at last by gravity and mountainous geometry, the storm waters are transformed from a thousand small rivulets into streams, from streams into a river, and from a river into the sea.

We were born into conflict. Conflict is at the heart and soul of the human saga.

THE SERPENT IN THE GARDEN

Like all great epics, the story of conflict has its origins in a time before time. It all started with an appetite and an apple:

> And when the woman saw that the tree was good for food, and that it was pleasant to the eyes, and a tree to be desired to make one wise, she took of the fruit thereof, and did eat, and gave also to her husband with her; and he did eat.

The Genesis account of our departure from the primeval garden of harmony is a fascinating allegory about the insidious way that conflict works its way into lives that are otherwise peaceful and contented. The serpent whispers a few words about becoming lords of our own domain. The woman finds the offer attractive and bites. The man follows suit. Punishment is swift and certain. Adam loses his life of leisure and becomes a farmer, Eve learns about the pains of childbirth, and the serpent is scorned and demonized.

The serpent is a powerful and paradoxical symbol of the forces of conflict. On the one hand, it appears on the physician's caduceus (the winged staff with two entwined snakes carried by Hermes as messenger of the gods) as a sign of healing. And the serpent with its tail in its mouth is the Oriental symbol of eternal life. In the Bible, the Tempter directs Eve to the tree of eternal life. Yet the serpent is also for us the embodiment of evil and the fall from grace. A snake is shifty, not to be trusted. It speaks with a forked tongue. The serpent is dangerous. It comes from a dark realm.

It is entirely appropriate that the serpent is described as "more subtle than any beast." Because we humans are so clever, only the most cunning tempter would know how to maneuver past our defenses and our denial. Through its deception we are led beyond what we know and believe. The serpentine course of conflict forces us into unexplored territory where we must stumble until we decide to construct our own path.

The serpent deceives us into giving up unearned comfort for a lifetime of struggle—and growth. It is not so much the taste of the apple that gives us the knowledge of good and evil as it is the long journey that comes afterward.

It is interesting that the serpent appeals to the woman—not just the gender, but to the inner feminine that each of us carries. This is the part of us that is curious, has a ravenous appetite for all forms of experience, and trusts the voice of intuition. This is the part of us that is willing to break the rules and risk the consequences. Eve is the mother, not only of our mortality but also of our courage.

Eve embodies the force of life itself—she is the Earth Mother, the Goddess. Eden is her realm, and she wants to taste every particle of paradise. Eve wants it all. She is not deterred by authority or the strictures of morality. Eve is immediately willing to disregard any law that stands in the way of her transformation. Even though she has been born into paradise, she refuses to take things at face value. She wants more, even at the cost of everything she has been given. Like her spiritual offspring, Dr. Faustus, she makes a bargain with the devil so that she can experience the highest realms of human existence. Eve is the force of desire.

Eve is tempted by the suggestion that her eyes will be opened and that she and her male counterpart will "be as gods." This thought causes Eve to forget that she is a creature, not an equal, of God. Her fantasies of divinity cause her to question the fullness of the creation that she and Adam have been given. Eve's gift, and the cause of her suffering, is her willingness to upset the cosmic apple cart in order to satisfy the hunger in her soul.

The price of her ambition is separation from God. What once was whole is divided. The seamless harmony of the universe is shattered. No more long walks in the Garden with the Creator. No more effortless communion with all of nature. And she won't even be able to take comfort from the serpent, who now has become her enemy as a result of divine decree. Like the serpent, there is something about conflict that holds the promise both of transcendence and of annihilation. Conflict often breaks the heart even as it heals it. It disappoints our expectations while bestowing the unexpected.

Eve is the aspect of our soul that yearns for a higher order, even if it takes a lifetime of chaos to get there. She not only tolerates conflict, but practically longs for it. Eve understands that, without revolution, there is no evolution.

Adam, the first romantic, also has an important role in the story. Eve has precipitated the crisis, but the break with the established order is not complete until Adam joins the mutiny. The serpent has tempted Eve, and now it is Eve who tempts Adam. If Eve embodies desire and intuition, Adam represents the active principles of will, judgment, and moral choice. The possible loss of his companion forces Adam to examine his priorities. Eve is moved by the prospect of transformation, but Adam makes his choice more to keep Eve happy than because he wants to acquire the knowledge of good and evil. Adam remembers those lonely days when God Himself wasn't enough.

God has provided a soul mate to Adam, formed from his very being, and so vital is the wholeness she has brought to him that Adam is willing to risk everything rather than lose her. Eve is Adam's salvation and his downfall.

In taking that bite, Adam accepts the challenge of consciousness. Once, paradise was given to him; now he must earn it back with the sweat of his brow. Adam has been humbled, which literally means to be brought to humus, or earth. His fate is to cultivate the ground of human experience from which he was made. Through thousands of years and countless heartaches, Adam and Eve will walk the long road known only to those who have tasted the fruits of good and evil. Their journey is a heroic struggle to find paradise not in a cloistered garden but in a teeming, suffering world.

Perhaps this is no fall from grace at all, but the divine trickster at work. Could it be that, knowing full well that humans always are drawn to what has been forbidden, God was setting up Eve and her husband for His own purposes? Could it be that He needed their help for the ongoing work of creation? If so, we might catch a glimpse of the sacred shadow of conflict.

In the beginning, God created a silent universe into which He spoke His Word, its divine vibration moving through all things. Of all that He created, only man was the mirror of God, and only through man could He know Himself. The Creator was a God of action, bringing forth from the void, from the unconscious harmony of absolute potential.

As it turned out, for all its beauty and tranquility, Adam encountered emptiness in the Garden. There was something missing from the ordained harmony—independent human conscious-ness. God could not create this consciousness, which had to come from the making of choices by Adam and Eve. Before the Fall,

Adam and Eve only saw with God's eyes and thought God's thoughts. If God was ever to know Himself, man would have to take the risk of separating from the Creator so that the human mirror and its Image might become distinct. Like the God after whom he was designed, man would have to bring forth from the emptiness of unconscious bliss.

So God, through his foil, the serpent, permitted the temptation of Adam and Eve. The paradox is that they were tempted by truth—the possibility of being as gods. Their innocent eyes now would be opened, as in birth. Even God could not protect them from the consequences of their courageous choice. He had to play His part—and uphold the law. They would have to leave the nest.

Triggered by shame, but soon actively engaged in their work, Adam and Eve set out to transform the preconscious world of naive harmony into a consenting, conscious unity. God sent them into the world not to punish them but so that His work might be completed by those He made in His image. Without this foundational conflict, all creation would have been stillborn.

Paradise has been lost, but perhaps it is for the best. The grand story of struggle and reconciliation is now launched. And so it is with all conflict. Conflict arises out of a desire to grow and expand—to know more, be more, have more. Conflict comes from our refusal to accept things as they are. This restlessness forces us onto the path of progress and growth. Conflict thus gives birth to art, science, and consciousness.

Even as it creates us, conflict humbles us. Conflict teaches that being "as gods" is not quite what we had imagined. Like Adam, we ultimately are driven to the dust from which we first emerged. Conflict both inspires us to greatness and forces us abruptly down to earth. Conflict is nature's unmistakable invitation to take a hand in the formation of our very being, of consciousness itself. Consciousness is not the heritage of Eden because it cannot just be given; it must be earned, through toil in the fields of life, and forged in the furnace of chaos.

THE FLOW OF CONSCIOUSNESS

Chaos is a psychological event as well as a molecular one. In his book *Flow*, psychologist Mihaly Csikzentmihalyi describes the subjective experience of chaos as psychic entropy—pain, fear, rage, anxiety, or jealousy—which obstructs our capacity to realize our goals. Conflict puts us into a state of extreme sensitivity to influences that at other times might be dismissed as mere irritations.

Under the influence of hot conflict, we ourselves become a chaotic system. The entire stream of our activity can be seriously diverted by a missed train, an unexpected call in the night, or an angry glance. The Butterfly Effect—sensitive dependence on small changes—can send us reeling.

Consciousness, on the other hand, is the internal ordering of the world around us. When I am conscious, I am aware of the distinction between "I" and what is outside that sacred, indivisible domain. This primary distinction allows me to set things in their rightful place, to make sense of it all. I know who I am because I am different from you. This awakening comes only from opposition—when I am hungry and you do not feed me, when I am angry and you do not appease me. I cry out, but then hear my own voice and remember myself. Opposition draws me out and traces the circumference of my being.

But when my consciousness is invaded or thrown into turbulent circumstances, the disequilibrium can be unbearable. Conflict has the capacity either to destroy consciousness or to expand it. As Nietzsche observed, "That which does not kill me makes me strong." Like a ship in high seas, consciousness must struggle against the elements to right itself. Drop the sails, adjust the course, jettison the surplus ballast.

Consciousness is always in forward motion. Increasingly complex human problems are met by a continually expanding consciousness. Difficult problems are never solved in the past or by old solutions. A new, fresh response is always required if we want the outcome to be different this time. Consciousness just won't go into "reverse." It constantly absorbs new information and is always developing an increased capacity to deal with it. Even as simple or elegant solutions are discovered, they encompass and respond to continually higher degrees of complexity. Consciousness is not static. It inherently yearns for and moves toward ever-higher levels of differentiation, which it then reorganizes into a more profound simplicity.

We are in a state of what Csikzentmihalyi calls flow when we are governed by consciousness, rather than by the turbulence of reactivity. Consciousness lifts us above our own reactions so that life becomes a game in which we are able to experience joy in the moment, forgetting everything but the task at hand.

Consciousness is formed in the crucible of human suffering. We *know* because we have been *through it*. As we learned in the Garden of Eden, consciousness emerges only when ideals encounter experience. To put it differently, wisdom is truth tempered by anomaly. The soul does not spring, fully formed, into the world. The soul, which is the seat of consciousness, is not a "thing," like the body. Rather, it is the experienced confluence of the individual and the other, the self and the world, the one and the many. It is the place where the inner and outer worlds meet, the mystery in which we encounter ourselves in the other.

Consciousness is not possible without chaos, as the Christian-Hindu mystic Dom Bede Griffiths observed shortly before his death in India:

> *Science today recognizes that all order comes out of chaos. When the old structures break down and the traditional forms begin to disintegrate, precisely then in the chaos, a new form, a new structure, a new order of being and consciousness emerges.*

Consciousness provides the basis for a fully integrated response to conflict. Rather than fighting it or surrendering to it or even transforming it, consciousness is the means by which we *outgrow* conflict. By becoming "bigger," we are able to create a fluid container in which conflict serves as the fuel for our own growth. This growth requires that consciousness *evolve.*

Evolution is systemic change. In the case of human consciousness, this process involves an intimate relationship between the evolving individual and the entire human ecosystem to which he— and his adversary—both equally belong. But evolution is not possible when we cling to the external version of the self we have put between us and the living, breathing world around us. The self that is tormented by conflict is just an identity. We must look deeper if consciousness is to take us beyond the limitation of circumstance.

IDENTITY AND GENIUS

Identity is who we say we are, or who we allow others to say we are. Identity is a role, something we wear. There is always something manufactured about it, something more or less than we actually are. Identity speaks only to the ways in which we are distinct from others, or certain others—"I am a Texan" implies ". . . and not from Oklahoma." Identity can never quite embrace the something I am, without contrasting it with the identities I am not.

Our tendency to create identity by identifying is itself the problem. The late Jesuit spiritual guide and author Anthony deMello says it outright: "All suffering is caused by my identifying myself with something, whether that something is within me or outside me."

Thomas Merton said that we are born into the world with a "false self," and that the problem of salvation is solved by discovering the true self:

> For me to be a saint means to be myself. Therefore the problem
> of sanctity and salvation is in fact the problem of finding out who
> I am and of discovering my true self.

"Genius" is a term that comes close to describing the fluid vitality that can never be reduced to mere identity. My genius, if I discover it, is what is uniquely me. It is the animating spirit within me, my guardian angel, the still, small voice, my essence. "I am the genius of myself," James Carse explains in *Finite and Infinite Games*. Genius is who we are in our originality, the who beyond the role. The genius in us, Carse says, "knows the past is definitely the past." It isn't affected by the desire for revenge or the burden of grief.

When I encounter my genius, the crisis of identity is over. Genius is both whole and holy. It encompasses all of me, for better or for worse. If identity is what we are willing to die for, genius is what we live for.

A genius has an inner certainty, but may be eccentric or disruptive or turbulent when he encounters a sleeping world. As my friend Hal Edwards says, "Sometimes I just get so turned on by life that I look for the lightning bolts. Wherever they are, that's where I want to be!" There will be plenty of conflict, because every genius "is a problem for everybody else," but the conflict won't have anything to do with identity. The genius may be suppressed, ostracized, imprisoned, or evicted, but he knows that he cannot help but be who he is.

The Oxford English Dictionary defines genius as "the tutelary god or attendant spirit allotted to every person at its birth, to govern his fortunes and determine his character, and finally, to conduct him out of the world." This has come to connote the very character, essence, and brilliance of an individual.

A similar term is used by Native Americans when they speak of a certain person's "medicine." One's medicine is the particular gift or influence embodied by that person—warm-heartedness, ability to speak movingly, leadership, woundedness, vision, aggression, and so on. Both dark and light qualities are included. The medicine can be good or bad.

The genius has moved past all external indicia of identity to an inalienable connection with his own essence. It is in this place, where he is truly himself and doesn't even think of himself, that he connects with the universe and the transcendent. Here he finds his muse, his god, his inspiration. We think of the artist as having an exaggerated ego, but often it is the genius in him that is simply unwilling not to be expressed, and the ego has little to do with it. The artist may be obsessed with his work, but he himself does not matter much—he willingly suffers for his art. As its guardian angel or genius, the artist strives to bring his work—his child—into being and to shepherd it into the world's awareness.

True genius is strangely humble. Having found wholeness within and without, the ego is set aside so that one can become a vessel for that which must come through. The genius knows how to listen for the inner whisper.

As a college student, I was invited to an awards presentation honoring the late William Lear, inventor of the automatic pilot, the eight-track stereo, and the jet that bears his name. We spoke over dinner, since I was fortunate enough to be seated next to him. I was in awe of his brilliant mind, and asked him to describe the creative process by which he had developed such a wide array of imaginative inventions.

"I can't do it myself," he laughed. "I simply don't have the education. I could never have figured those things on my own."

"Then how did it happen?"

"Well," he said, "I read a book when I was young called *Universal Mind*. I realized that there is an intelligence at work that is as vast as the universe. All we have to do is let it do the thinking for us. So I did. I just ask, 'How can I make this happen?' and I wait for the answer. Isn't it amazing?" And he laughed again.

Bill Lear had found a way to access his own genius. He knew that it was far greater than any sense of identity he could ever attain by following the prescribed course. The same is true for most of those who are our great artists, philosophers, and scientists. It is not that they have a huge brain or a spectacular IQ—it is that they have found and remained loyal to their own genius.

Intractable conflict can so challenge the grip of our own identity that genius comes bursting through. What is needed is to hold the conflict, to enter into the conflict, to go deeply into it, to go into the heart of conflict. There, at the heart of conflict, waits genius. Past the dragons and the obstacles and the contradictions and the frustration and the failure.

There are those in every society whose lives are dedicated to the investigation of this mystery, to the quest for the whole, the absolute, the ultimate. They put aside their ambition for fame, money, and status, and devote their substance to the realization and expression of this primal experience. Artists, monks, mystics, scientists, lovers, care-givers, scholars, thinkers. It is these who search out the pathways of consciousness, who contemplate the dance between silence and symbol, who trace the veil that separates the manifest from the unmanifest, the actual and the possible. They seek not identity, but genius.

AT ONE WITH THE WHOLE

There is something of the artist or monk in all of us, a wonder about ultimacy as well as a desire for intimacy. We sense it in our need for time alone, for solitude, for the opportunity to contemplate, to look within. And for what? To revel in ourselves? No, to master ourselves. Intuitively we know that there is a gateway to something that transcends our divisions and duality, and that it can only be found by descending into the depths of our own interiority.

Inevitably, the search for unity requires that we step back from the values and assumptions that govern the world outside us and keep it from its evolutionary destiny. We learn to be "in the world" but not "of the world."

Only by withdrawing from restrictive social conventions and expectations, from the breathless race to impress our image upon the world, and from the narrow definitions of meaning can we become radically open to the vast and infinite space of the boundless. It is here, at the very precipice of existence, where we have exhausted our explanations and our reason and our very selves, at the edge of chaos, that we become open to what is spacious and profound and, at last, whole.

SUCCESS

What is the mark of success in mastering conflict? We are accustomed to measuring our success in most departments of life exclusively by external, material measures. How much did the jury award? (Never mind that the legal fees and the lost production at work and the psychic cost exceed the value of the verdict.) How much did you squeeze out of the other guy in the salary negotiations? (Never mind that he wants to be traded to another team next year.) We know we are good negotiators if the other side is angry or exasperated or has to file for bankruptcy. We rush to buy books that tell us how to swim with sharks, without stopping to question the company we keep.

Relying strictly on external manifestations of success predictably leads to empty victories because it ignores our internal dimension. And human beings are nothing if not internal—just count the number of psychotherapists listed in the telephone directory.

Recently a study showed that a huge number of practicing lawyers are clinically depressed, and over 80 percent of the attorneys in Chicago asserted that they would never have entered the field if they had known in advance what it would be like. Lawyers are leaving the law in droves. Why? Because, I suspect, the law is a closed system that turns bright, compassionate young people into "zealous advocates" trained to fragment the truth and polarize those who must confront it. This is a function of the system itself, not of the lawyers who act within it. The nature of the system is that it largely compels lawyers and judges to leave their souls behind when they come to work, to dispense advice "objectively," to render judgment dispassionately, to do their dark business without remorse.

Ultimately, perhaps, the lawyer remembers the dreams that

carried her through law school. But, over the years, the clients have included the evil as well as the good, both the cruel and the just, the parasite and the productive citizen. In accordance with the needs of the marketplace, she has become the handservant of both victim and victimizer. Has this advanced the cause of justice or just paid the yearly bonuses? Measured by the externals, things are no better and possibly worse for all the late nights and clever strategies. Like the truth, the lawyer has become fragmented—and cynical.

For the most part, the clients are no happier than the lawyers. The law is equipped to address only the outer dimensions of human suffering. We become a case, a file, a cause of action, an annoyance to an overworked court, and an underpaid lawyer. "The law is no respecter of persons," says the law proudly. It repudiates the person and reduces him to "plaintiff" or "defendant." Decisions often are based on obscure rules that seem entirely alien to the real issues, depriving the victor even of the satisfaction of his conquest.

The term "litigation stress syndrome" is now being used to describe the consequences of the adversarial process. It includes psychological manifestations of depression, anxiety, hostility, and anger. When these symptoms go unrecognized and untreated, parties are prone to getting themselves involved in other legal disputes and interpersonal conflicts. It can become cyclical. And, if we press our advantage too far and win at all costs, does this lead to happiness? When the jury award has been spent, what remains?

The answer lies in understanding the inner dimension of life. The struggle to construct a reliable map of the inner dimension traditionally has fallen to religion and psychology. Religion tells us what behavior is "good" and what is not. Psychology tells us what is "healthy" and what is not. But neither of these concepts is quite on the mark when it comes to conflict. They both embody the basic duality that is itself the problem. By what measure, then, can we determine whether we are managing our conflicts well? How do we account for the inner dimension in assessing our progress?

INTERIORITY: GETTING INSIDE CONFLICT

Each of the strategies we have discussed in earlier chapters focuses on what we can do with respect to *others* to manage or resolve conflict. This reflects the "without" of conflict resolution. But each external strategy corresponds to an internal quality—the within—that must be mastered to achieve virtuosity in dealing with conflict.

There are four inner virtues that have special relevance to responding to conflict. They take us to the heart of conflict through an inner door, which is opened only through solitude and reflection.

DISCIPLINE

Containment, which is a strategy for bringing order to a chaotic situation, has its corollary in *discipline*. Although the word often has a punitive or puritan connotation, discipline actually comes from a Latin root meaning "to learn." A disciple is a learner; one who has discipline has the ability to learn. A discipline is a whole field of learning. Learning, of course, takes self-control and dedication. There's no point in planting the seeds unless we are willing to put in the time to harvest the crop.

The essence of discipline is not hardship, but *order.* Our natures are often so unruly that establishing order can, at first, be painful. But the purpose of organization is to make it possible for us to realize our dreams. Try telling that to a nine-year-old who would rather be bouncing on a Pogo stick than training his talented fingers to play classical guitar!

The problem is not much more complicated—nor less intractable—among adults. The loss of "civility" is a growing concern of nearly all professional and social organizations these days. When we lose the binds of discipline, it becomes acceptable to deceive, to harangue, to insult, and to belittle those who occasion our displeasure. As a result, we get caught in endless cycles of reactivity that make it impossible for us to learn anything. We spend our afternoons in court or arguing with the boss or fighting with the kids, rather than producing our best work or composing a letter to an old friend or reading the Great Books or studying Spanish.

Socrates ascribed the highest good to the virtue of self-discipline:

> *This appears to me the aim which a man ought to have, and toward which he ought to direct all the energies both of himself and of the state, acting so that he may have temperance and justice present with himself and be happy. [Unless he does so], such a one is the friend neither of God nor man, for he is incapable of communion, and he who is incapable of communion is also incapable of friendship. And philosophers tell us, Callicles, that communion and friendship bind together heaven and earth and gods and men, and that this universe is therefore called Cosmos, or order, not disorder or misrule, my friend.*

Peter Senge, author of *The Fifth Discipline*, is a leader in reconceptualizing how corporations might become more effective and dynamic. He believes that the true role of any organization is to enhance learning—to become a learning organization, the purpose of which is to create an environment

> *where people continually expand their capacity to create the results they truly desire, where new and expansive patterns of thinking are nurtured, where collective aspiration is set free, and where people are continually learning how to learn together.*

Chaos is fueled by reaction. When our opponent is able to trigger reactive feelings—anger, betrayal, disappointment, or disgust—we can free ourselves from the impending maelstrom only by the exercise of self-discipline. We learn to smile as we deny an outrageous demand. We walk away from the poisoned bait. We don't respond to the false accusation. We contain our reactions, rather than allow them to accelerate the process of entropy. The monk pulls his hood over his ego and returns to his cell. We bring order to ourselves.

CONFIDENCE

The internal corollary to confrontation is *confidence*. When we are confident, we have a positive assurance that things will work out. We are willing to rely on ourselves, on a belief, or on the process as it unfolds.

Confidence precedes or is independent of proof. We know that things will work out, somehow, even though the resolution is still in the future. Confidence gives us the strength to confront the unknown that lies ahead, without letting it defeat us in advance. It is the state of mind that lets us dedicate all our attention and resources to the matter so that we have the best chance to emerge victorious.

Confidence often includes an element of paradox. Bill Ury, one of the co-authors of the revolutionary book *Getting to Yes*, and a man who deeply appreciates the solitude of his New Mexican mountains, is often consulted by governments throughout the world in the use of nonviolent conflict resolution in managing the seemingly endless proliferation of dangerous international disputes. I once asked him how he maintained his cheerful confidence. Was there some spiritual tradition that enabled him to plunge into situations like Bosnia without becoming discouraged?

Bill smiled. "Well, I suppose if I get my confidence from anywhere, it might be the Vikings. They believed that it was written in the Book of Doom that Loki, the god of chaos, ultimately would win. Odin, the god of order, would lose. Since the situation was hopeless, there was only one thing to do."

"What's that?" I asked.

Bill laughed. "Fight like hell!"

One of the keys to maintaining confidence, then, is "don't believe what you read in the newspapers." If the experts (including the authors of the Book of Doom) were always right, then the Cold War would still be solidly in place and the Soviet Union would be intact.

Confidence upsets the established disorder by claiming a higher vision. It changes the frame by denying inertia the right to control our direction. Confidence awakens possibilities that would still be sleeping if the past dictated the future. It shakes us out of our fears and paralysis and gives us a reason to take a bold stand.

When we are confident, we are willing to confront what must be faced. Confidence doesn't mean that we are without fear, but that our fear does not determine what we do. Confidence keeps us from despair. Franklin Roosevelt's admonition that "the only thing we have to fear is fear itself" is a legendary expression of confidence. Leaders are those who, when the clouds are darkest, give us confidence. It often means the difference between victory and defeat.

Conflict is not a linear process. That means that success, as well as disruption, can come to us from an unexpected direction. Confidence protects us from fear until the reinforcements appear. It stands for the truth of an opportunity not yet manifest, a future not yet apparent. Confidence gives us something to say about the unknown.

ACCEPTANCE

One of the highest achievements of the human heart is the *acceptance* of things as they are, without trying to change them. In our Western haste to improve, expand, and enlarge, we leave very little room for the appreciation of reality *as it is*. We assume that, if we are clever or determined enough, we can persuade or dominate or manipulate someone into shifting their position to our advantage. If things are not going well for us, then we'll just do something about it. Call the manager. Sue the company. Vote him out of office. Get a divorce. Hire somebody younger.

But there are times when the best thing to do is *nothing*. Accept things as they are. Let go. Stop fighting. Acceptance is a highly underrated virtue. Yet, many times, it is the only thing that brings peace of mind. In Chapter Six, we met Karl, the German immigrant who lost his son in a drowning accident. Karl ultimately resolved his conflict because he was able to accept the hard truth about his son.

Keeping a lawsuit "alive" was Karl's way of hanging on. It allowed Karl to stay angry without having to suffer through the bittersweet agony of grief.

Acceptance frees us from our illusions. Often our illusions are prettier than the truth, but we can suffer enormously from the struggle to sustain false hopes. We imprison ourselves and punish those around us when we refuse to accept what cannot be changed. Acceptance is required if we are to live with ourselves or with others. It gives us the patience to recognize and survive intractable conflict. It keeps us from becoming prisoners of hope.

Acceptance requires discernment. There is a kind of acceptance that comes from weakness or resignation, but this obviously won't resolve anything—it just leads to self-defeat and resentment. True acceptance is based on *clarity*—we accept things as they are because we see things as they are. There is no defeat in that. It saves us from wasting energy in self-deception. We are free to attend to the business at hand.

What the Buddhists call "enlightenment" is simply this capacity to see things for what they are. Chögyam Trungpa, a Tibetan teacher and founder of the Naropa Institute in Boulder, Colorado, says that enlightenment allows us to see "the raw and rugged quality of things precisely as they are." Being a realist, in the most absolute sense of the word, we no longer try to give things a rosy philosophical significance as a way to convince ourselves that things are not as bad as we think: "Things *are* as bad as we think!" That's where we start.

Anthony deMello made much the same point in his book *Awareness*:

> The chances that you will wake up are in direct proportion to the amount of truth you can take without running away. . . . Suffering points out that there is a falsehood somewhere. Suffering occurs when you clash with reality. When your illusions clash with reality, when your falsehoods clash with truth, then you have suffering. Otherwise, there is no suffering.

Acceptance, then, is compassion—compassion for ourselves. If we truly want to stop suffering, then we have to wake up and smell the coffee. He's not coming back. The case won't settle for a million dollars. You won't get to be President. They're not interested in your plans for overhauling the division.

So what? Life goes on. Brush your teeth, put on your dress, go to work. And treasure the wisdom that is growing in your soul. It was bought not by what you acquired, but by what you released.

Cultivating a capacity for acceptance makes it much easier to relate with other people without having to defend ourselves or make them feel defensive. We learn to become open to others, to welcome information, to go with the flow. Even if the news is unpleasant, it may be essential to our survival. If we are too busy shoring up the walls of our fortress, we will miss the messenger who is shouting at us from the other side.

A willingness to accept is needed if we are to practice listening, which is the external form of compassion. It's hard to listen if we reject the truth in what we hear. Hard-heartedness is often just a defense to having to face a reality that we do not like. We think that blaming the other person will protect us from the truth. However, if we have the courage to accept reality, then we can truly listen to others.

The major impediment to listening is our resistance to the implications of the truth that another person expresses. We are attached to our own version of things, and often fear the implications of what we hear, as psychologist Carl Rogers observed:

> *If you really understand another person . . . if you are willing to enter his private world and see the way life appears to him, without any attempt to make evaluative judgments, you run the risk of being changed yourself. You might see it his way; you might find yourself influenced in your attitudes or your personality. This risk of being changed is one of the most frightening prospects many of us can face.*

Acceptance, then, is based on courage. It is not the weak who know how to accept but the strong. It takes strength to listen, to hear the bad news, to adjust, to see things for what they are. And, in that strength, there is wisdom.

INTEGRITY

The internal analog of collaboration is *integrity*, which comes from the word "integer," meaning "wholeness." When we speak of someone as having integrity, it means far more than "she sticks to her guns, no matter what." It means, this person is complete, solid, self-aware.

Integrity comes from being integrated. We become whole to the extent that we integrate all sides of ourselves—the attractive and pleasant as well as the dark and foul. The opposite of integrity is not immorality but pretense. Someone without integrity is fragmented. They accept the parts of themselves that make them look good to the world but deny what Carl Jung called the "shadow"—the parts of ourselves that we hide, pretend not to see, or repress, but which doggedly follow us around anyway.

We acquire integrity only by digging deeply into our own darkness and coming to terms with the demon—and the genius—who lives there. The shadow consists not only of what is ugly but, often, of what is most beautiful about us. But these aspects of our personality may appear threatening to the security of the manicured image we show the world. The shadow holds the energies of our passions. We may not know how to contain ourselves, so we hold tightly to our self-image.

One who is integrated has found the courage to walk into that dark chamber, not to destroy the pieces of the self that live there but to befriend them. This is what therapist Robert Johnson calls "owning the shadow":

> *Any repair of our fractured world must start with individuals who have the insight and courage to own their own shadow.*

Nothing "out there" will help if the interior projecting mechanism is operating strongly. The tendency to see one's shadow "out there" in one's neighbor or in another race or culture is the most dangerous aspect of the modern psyche. It has created two devastating wars in this century and threatens the destruction of all the fine achievements of our modern world. We all decry war, but collectively we move toward it.

None of us is immune from the shadow. Everything we do that creates light also generates shadow. The greater the saint, the greater the demons she faces.

When we incorporate the full reality of ourselves, we are less liable to divide the world into "us" and "them." We see ourselves in others, and recognize that even our adversaries have their good days. This makes it possible to collaborate with the adversary when the occasion warrants. We're not stuck with the illusion that nothing "they" want or do could have any validity. We are free to make choices that serve us, without worrying about whether it also helps the other side.

THE TWO AND THE ONE

The strategies we have discussed so far, both internal and external, have been designed to help us manage, resolve, or come to terms with conflict. Implied in these approaches is the assumption of *duality*: that conflict arises from inherent differences between various polarities—you and me, black and white, male and female, strong and weak, right and wrong, liberal and conservative. Given those differences, we asked, how might we deal with adversity?

But this duality is not present in all forms of thinking. In the *Tao Te Ching*, an ancient Chinese text attributed to Lao-tzu, opposites are regarded as present in one another. In the familiar symbol of yin and yang, a stark point of blackness sits quietly in the middle of a white circle, which embraces a black circle that includes a white dot at its heart. The symbol seems to say: The deeper you go into one, the closer you come to the gateway to the other. Each holds the key to its opposite.

We are so accustomed to our dualistic model of thinking that we must listen very closely to the subtle meaning of what Lao-tzu called the Tao, or Way of Power. The Way is found not on one side or the other, but at the *center*, where the opposites meet and dance with each other:

> *Intangible, formless!*
> *At its center appears the Image.*
> *Formless, intangible!*
> *At its center appears Natural Law.*
> *Obscure, mysterious!*
> *At its center appears the Life Force.*
> *The Life Force is very real;*
> *At its center appears truth.*

Taoism advises us to try neither to win nor lose, to seek neither resolution nor impasse, but to study the rising and falling of the Way as it moves through the field of our conflict. As long as we are able to discern and follow the Way, we will not be tricked by the distractions of right and wrong, good and evil. At all times, we search for the center, for the fulcrum that creates balance. We stay within the eye of the hurricane. We look for the center, for that is where truth is to be found.

The medieval philosopher Nicholas of Cusa described God as "a circle whose center is everywhere and whose circumference is nowhere." It is in this sense that we seek to find the heart of conflict: In the constantly moving dynamic between opposing forces there is always a center point.

It is this center, the Way, that charts the map of our relationship with conflict. Our attention is on the process, not its outcome. If we can stay in the center, we don't need to concern ourselves with the outer appearances. In the matter of conflict, the edge of chaos is found at the center, where the forces meet. In the center lies genius. It is in the center, at the very heart of conflict, that we can at last meet.

So rather than becoming hypnotized by the duality of conflict, or ending it by seeking to win or walk away from the game, we transform the two into one by pursuing the center *between* the two. Our attention is on finding a place to stand where, for a moment, things are in balance. It is in that place that the Way—and the force of life itself—will be found. Life flows from the center.

THE HEART OF CONFLICT

Professor Masao Abe is a seventy-year-old Zen Master from Kyoto, Japan. When he sat down at my table at the Parliament of the World's Religions, I saw only a small, gentle man with very large eyebrows. He smiled, tranquil in the sea of activity swirling around us as delegates from all around the world looked for their seats and loudly fraternized with old friends. At the next table over, Minister Louis Farrakhan of the Nation of Islam sat surrounded by large, imposing bodyguards. The voices hushed as His Holiness the Dalai Lama arrived and graciously found his place.

After the opening of the session and some general introductions, the ten of us at the table each told a short story about our "spiritual journey" as a way to break the ice. After two perfunctory accounts by other guests, Professor Abe spoke. "When I was young, my family practiced what is called 'Pure Land' Buddhism. This is similar to Christianity, because it emphasizes human sinfulness and holds that salvation can be achieved only through faith in the mercy of Amidha Buddha. But when I went to college, I studied Zen Buddhism with a very strong teacher. He was the embodiment of enlightenment. Zen is very different from Pure Land. It requires that each person awaken to one's true Self through the Great Death."

The college professor insisted that Pure Land was not authentic. "This produced in me a very great conflict."

Professor Abe spoke quietly, but his voice was clear and firm. "I would argue with the teacher, and each day it got worse. What was authentic? Pure Land or Zen? Each day I defended Pure Land, and each day he attacked my beliefs. I suffered much. I had great admiration for my teacher, and great loyalty to my family. The conflict became unbearable. And at that moment of great strife, my mind awakened."

I looked up from my yellow legal pad, on which I had been taking notes. Awakened? I looked around. The other delegates seemed not to notice. Awakened? As in, "Enlightened"? I had studied Buddhism at a Catholic college and had met lots of Buddhists, but thought of enlightenment only as an impossibly remote and faraway destination, like heaven.

Professor Abe smiled and turned to listen to the next speaker. My mind was racing. I knew the look in his eyes. Years before, on the Navajo reservation, I had seen a medicine man—a "shapeshifter"— with the same penetrating stare. There was no point trying to hide or pretend with such people. They saw too deeply. There was a tangible difference in the quality of their presence.

Professor Abe's insight, as I understood it, was that the natural human tendency to resolve conflict by choosing between two opposing positions may relieve internal turmoil, but it doesn't reveal the deeper truth. By holding on to the contradiction, by refusing to "vote" for Pure Land or Zen, something had burst in his conceptual framework of the world. The truth was not static, like an answer, but *dynamic*, like a relationship. It was not an outcome, but a process. Awakening was the realization that reality is neither *this* nor *that*, but the living interaction between them both.

Holding on to contradictions can demand enormous strength. It is as if we have caught hold of a divine power; if only we can hold tight, it will reveal its secret. In the Book of Genesis, when Jacob wrestled the angel, he was wounded in the hip, but still he demanded, "I will not let you go until you have blessed me." There was no chance that Jacob could win a wrestling match with an angel, but his determination to hang on at any cost produced a great prize. The angel renamed him and indeed blessed the heir of Isaac, "For you have contended with divine and human beings and have prevailed."

Holding paradox is wrestling with angels. In the midst of prolonged struggle, our logic fails us, our beliefs falter, our distinctions and categories fade. Nothing we know works. It is only then that the soul emerges. The soul, the genius that guides us through life and ushers us back out. The soul, mirror of the divine. In the darkest heart of conflict, the lotus blossoms. The soul is beyond the dualities that obscure our daily path. As the Hindu Upanishads describe it, the soul, called Atman, is "neti neti"—not this, not that.

The capacity to sustain contradiction is a sign of depth and maturity. Walter Ong, a Jesuit thinker in Teilhard's tradition, has observed:

> The truly profound and meaningful principles and conclusions concerning matters of deep philosophical or cultural import are ... invariably ... paradoxical.... [T]he ultimately profound statements are always duplex: they say, at least by implication, two things that are related to one another by asymmetric opposition.

"Paradox" means "beyond opinion." Paradox is conflict that cannot be resolved. If we attempt to resolve it, we lose the paradox. It must be held as it is, immune to categorization or linear comprehension. To hold paradox, we must move past opinion, past our judgments and positions, and rely on modes of thinking that are nondualistic—the kind of thinking that understands that light is *both* a particle and a wave, that recognizes that the good and the bad are part of the same package, that even the best solutions create whole new problems, that right and wrong are together created by a single act.

By its refusal to fit into existing patterns in our thinking, paradox expands and deepens our internal space. Such space exists only at the center of our being, where the Tao moves, where the universal encounters the personal. Paradox operates like a kind of gravitational force that pulls us into the very center of our deepest consciousness. If we can hold tight to paradox without slipping into the comfort of one position or the other, it will lead us into the depths of self-knowledge.

Conflict, then, is essential to the formation and growth of the mature ego. It is the very force of conflict, the experience of contending with another, that forms me. The more I am faced with what is not only "not me," but that which is even "against me," the more completely does my unique "I" emerge. The more profound the conflict, the more fully I am pushed into myself, into my interiority, into the "within." As I am forced to face the reflection of my uncharted character by this inward-driving pressure, I see more truly who I am. Once seen, I can hardly pretend to be otherwise. Opposition, then, both presses me inward and pushes me outward.

It is because I have gone into myself deeply that I am capable of truly relating to another. Conflict, Ong declares, paradoxically deepens our capacity to become intimate:

> *Only persons, deeply interiorized, secluded from one another, are truly able to share themselves reflectively—"I" with "you." Only beings isolated as human beings have anything to say. . . . It is precisely this isolated, closed human person, thrown back on himself or herself, who is also paradoxically the most open of beings. . . . A human being is an open closure.*

When we have journeyed to the heart of conflict, we discover not an answer but a contradiction. To live it fully is our real salvation. Robert Johnson counsels us that this involves a leap of evolutionary proportions:

> *To transform opposition into paradox is to allow both sides of an issue, both pairs of opposites, to exist in equal dignity and worth. . . . If I stay with my conflicting impulses long enough, the two opposing forces will teach each other something and produce an insight that serves them both. This is not a compromise but a depth of understanding that puts my life in perspective and allows me to know with certainty what I should do. That certainty is one of the most precious qualities known to humankind . . . to stay loyal to paradox is to earn the right to unity. . . .*

Conflict to paradox to revelation; that is the divine progression.
[Emphasis added.]

THE GIFT OF PROMETHEUS

Conflict is not something that *happens* to us. Rather, as the ancient Greeks tried to tell us, it is essential to our very nature. It is the gift of Prometheus: the fire he stole from the gods. With fire, mankind could transform the earth itself into metals and tools and weapons. With fire, humanity could stand on its own even as to the gods. Fire, the element of change, was the very essence of humanity.

Prometheus, in bringing fire to mortals, provided the flames in which we forge our souls. He shared the burning secret of divinity, as we are reminded by the flickering tongues of temple lamps and vigil lights and candle lights the world over. What is divine is ever-changing and changeless in its unending transformation. Prometheus understood: It is not in tranquility and rest that we find our perfection, but in the fiery crucible of change. Like Eve and Adam, Prometheus challenged divine order. In so doing, he birthed human consciousness.

Thomas Merton saw in Prometheus's rebellion a sacred act of homage:

> *If we look at this theft of fire, we see that it was in the end not so much a gesture of defiance as an act of adoration. It was almost as if Prometheus had stolen the fire in order to give it back to the gods; as if he were coming to them with the flames in his hands like vivid and sentient flowers, instead of flying from them with his life flickering between his fingers.*

THE PEARL OF WISDOM

It is not an easy thing to be human. We struggle against the wombs of our own mothers just to breathe fresh air, and it only gets harder from there. We arrive with a body but have to fight the world to find our souls.

Like the pearl, we are formed in adversity. But it is this contest of life against life that makes us both hard and beautiful. The pearl of humanity is called wisdom. It is in our individual and collective wisdom that consciousness is contained and that it becomes ever more profound. In wisdom, all differences are made even more distinct as they flow together as one river. In wisdom, we achieve confluence, the lights of the distant sun dancing on the waters that flow forth from the springs of life itself.

In the words of poet Wendell Berry: "The river's injury is its shape."

FULL CIRCLE

All things are contained within the Medicine Wheel, and all things are equal within it.

Hyemeyohsts Storm, Seven Arrows

THE WHEEL OF LIFE

When I was a small boy, my brothers and I virtually lived in the woods behind our house. In the summer, we built forts in the tall trees and fried slices of packaged baloney over little campfires. In the winter, we tracked deer and caught rabbits in box traps. More than anything in the world, we wanted to be Indians.

As a young lawyer, I drifted out to Arizona and finally had the chance I had always dreamed of. The firm assigned me to work on a major case for the Navajo Nation. At last, I could be with the original people of this country, with the tribe that proudly calls itself "the Lords of the Land." My Navajo friend Reed Tso brought me inside, to the sacred places, to the beauty of the ceremony, to the stories that grandfathers tell when the snow is on the ground and the family huddles together in the hogan at night.

I was invited to sit in the prayer circle, to pass the eagle feathers, to speak from the heart as Native peoples have done since man first walked the earth. Coming from a career-oriented world, with meetings and deadlines and an obsession with pushing the waters upstream, it took me a while to adjust to "Indian time" and the sense of being in sync more with the slow passage of seasons, rather than the flight of hours. But there was a feeling of connection, an intimacy with nature, and an appreciation for the big picture of life that I've seldom seen elsewhere.

One of the strongest images I have retained from my experiences with Native people is that of the Medicine Wheel. It is the symbol of dynamic wholeness. Often made with a simple circle of stones, the Medicine Wheel reminds us that there is a place for each of us in the world. As Sioux teacher Hyemeyohsts Storm tells us:

> *Each one of the tiny stones within the Medicine Wheel represents one of the many things of the Universe. One of them represents you, and another represents me. Others hold within them our mothers, fathers, sisters, brothers, and our friends. Still others symbolize hawks, buffalo, elks and wolves. There are also stones which represent religions, governments, philosophies, and even entire nations. All things are contained within the Medicine Wheel, and all things are equal within it. The Medicine Wheel is the Total Universe.*

Of all things in the Universe, only man is a "determiner" and has a say in how he lives his life. It is the nature of all other things always to reflect their perfection, but man alone may refuse. We have to learn how to say Yes, and it is only then that we can find our place on the Wheel. The teaching of the Medicine Wheel is that "our determining spirit can be made whole only through the learning of our harmony with all our brothers and sisters, and with all the other spirits of the Universe."

In the course of a lifetime, we change positions on the Medicine

Wheel. The exuberance and rebellion of youth yield to fear and insecurity, loss gives way to power, experience brings wisdom. In time, we notice that we are no longer who we once were. As old positions are outgrown or abandoned, we lose a little confidence in the capacity of any single viewpoint to hold the truth for more than a moment. We embrace more of the horizon when we look up from our work. There is less need of walls.

The Medicine Wheel, which has its counterpart in the mandala of the East and sacred circles everywhere, is a symbol of the eternal hope of humanity that we will, at last, learn to live as one. It encodes the vision of harmony, of an implicate order that beckons us from our struggles and our sorrow.

THE PATH OF MANY PATHS

As I have tried to illustrate, managing conflict requires a whole host of skills, insights, and strategies. No single tool will work for all circumstances, whether we are dealing with conflict or building a cabinet. All things have their place. When facing hot conflict, we must be as a wise monarch and secure the gates so that it may be contained. Like warriors at battle we confront conflict that hides from exposure to justice. The healer in us is called upon to transform hearts of stone through compassion. The inner monk teaches acceptance of what cannot be changed. In this way, we move from one place in the circle to the next.

Following the words of Ecclesiastes:

> *There is an appointed time for everything,*
> *and a time for every affair under the heavens.*
> *A time to be born, and a time to die;*
> *a time to plant, and a time to uproot the plant.*
> *A time to kill, and a time to heal;*
> *a time to tear down, and a time to build.*
> *A time to weep, and a time to laugh;*
> *a time to mourn, and a time to dance.*

Ultimately, there is no strategy for life. We do what we can, hope for the best, prepare for the worst.

But what we most need is reconciliation—the miracle of healing that allows us to forgive and be forgiven. There is no over-the-counter medicine for this. We find it only by walking the hard, human road of the Medicine Wheel. As we feel the unyielding stones beneath our bare feet, we begin to connect, to soften. As Jack Kornfield writes in *A Path with Heart*:

> *To stop the war and come into the present is to discover a greatness of our own heart that can include the happiness of all beings as inseparable from our own. . . . As we allow the world to touch us deeply, we recognize that just as there is pain in our own lives, so there is pain in everyone else's life. This is the birth of wise understanding. Wise understanding sees that suffering is inevitable, that all things that are born die. Wise understanding sees and accepts life as a whole. With wise understanding we allow ourselves to contain all things, both dark and light, and we come to a sense of peace. This is not the peace of denial or running away, but the peace we find in the heart that has rejected nothing, that touches all things with compassion.*

RECONCILIATION

We are not entirely in charge of the process of reconciling ourselves to our enemies or the world at large. It seems to have a sense of its own timing. We need only hold the door open, or at least keep it unlocked, until the opportunity to reconcile arises.

My father and I argued for twenty years, about everything from Richard Nixon to Marxism to Frank Sinatra. After two decades of impasse, we finally agreed to disagree, and talked about the kids and the Cowboys and business. We were both too stubborn to give in, and spent another decade in the cooler.

The call came one night, and I caught the next flight to Dallas. The doctors said he was going to go at any minute, but with his eight children at last by his side, the Old Man recharged his batteries. For a week, he hung on, sleeping, fitfully waking, smiling, or looking surprised to see us there.

For a week, each of us watched him struggle with his final demons—including, no doubt, us—and working his way through to a profound inner peace. We said what had been unsaid, or left unsaid what no longer needed saying. We carried him to the bathroom when he was too weak to walk, and the rest of the time, we took turns stroking the thin gray hair at his temples. Tough as he was, we now could freely show our love, our forgiveness, our respect. The old adversity was gone from his eyes. He just had the strength to take it in.

There was nothing we could point to that brought it on, but there clearly was a kind of grace that settled in. No more need for struggle, the old battles mostly forgotten. After years of separation, we were a family again, and it was very sweet. Reconciliation appeared on our doorstep like an angel, a friendly stranger with good news.

So it is that only time, in the end, heals all wounds.

Index

About the Author

BRIAN MULDOON co-founded one of the country's first private mediation firms in 1985 and has helped settle literally thousands of disputes since that time. He has designed and taught courses in mediation, negotiation, and alternative dispute resolution at ITT Chicago—Kent College of Law, where he was an adjunct professor of law from 1986 to 1988. In 1992 he became executive director of the Dearborn Institute, which provides facilitation, mediation, and training services. He is also a founder of the Healthy Divorce Network and the American, Chinese and Tibetan Friendship Society.

Muldoon was the lead facilitator for the Parliament of World's Religions in 1993 and for other international gatherings dealing with human rights and interracial relations.

A graduate of St. Louis University in philosophy, Muldoon received his Juris Doctor, with honors, in 1977 from the University of Texas School of Law and practiced law in Arizona before turning to mediation. He has lived throughout the United States and has three children. Muldoon can be reached through the Internet at

http://www.dearbrn.org/mediator